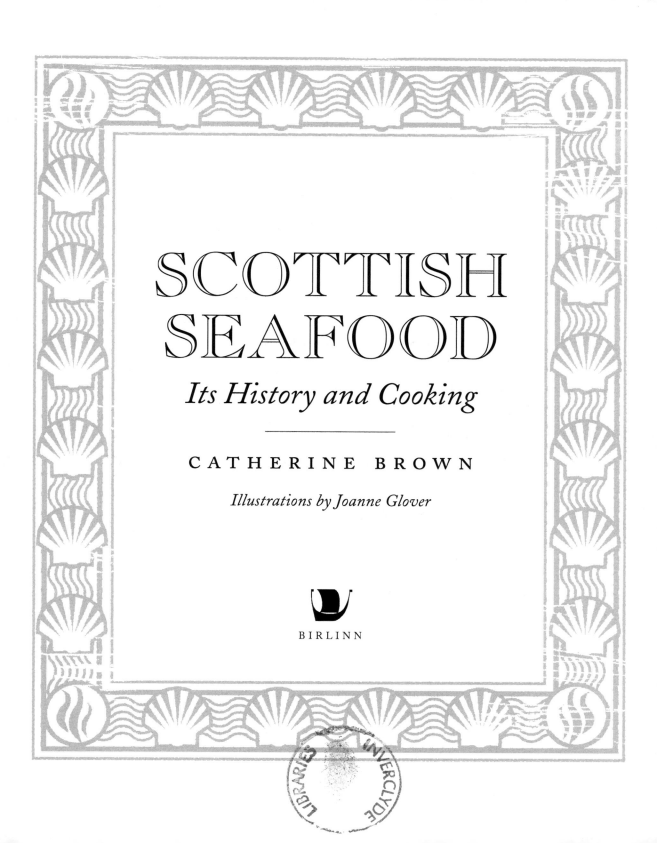

SCOTTISH SEAFOOD

Its History and Cooking

CATHERINE BROWN

Illustrations by Joanne Glover

BIRLINN

First published in 2011 by Birlinn Ltd
West Newington House
10 Newington Road
Edinburgh
EH9 1QS

www.birlinn.co.uk

© Catherine Brown, 2011

Illustrations © Joanne Glover, 2011

ISBN 978-1-84158-975-6
EBOOK ISBN 978-0-85790-182-8

British Library Cataloguing in Publication Data
A catalogue record for this book is available from the British Library

Set in Adobe Caslon Pro at Birlinn

Printed and bound by Gutenberg Press, Malta

Six Thoughts . . .

This is a very Scottish tale which draws together various threads of the nation's seafood assets into one grateful celebration of the ocean's bounty.

*

Local, regional, fresh and wild foods are not just unique to a time and place; they also give us a sense of identity with our country and our ancestors. They are the antidote to packaged, processed and mass-produced foods from the global marketplace.

*

Not being aware of what's going on in the world's oceans, while enjoying the seafood delights which they have to offer, would be to ignore the fact that some species of fish and shellfish may become extinct if we eat too much of them.

*

Fishmongers are our link from ocean to plate. The best will broadcast – verbally and visually – everything we need to know about the seafood they sell.

*

Photos of food, prepared by professionals, create an image in the mind of their food. But if the mind begins the cooking procedure with no pre-existing image, the cook can find more satisfaction in the creative art of making a real image of their own food.

*

Seafood cooking is an endless adventure.

CONTENTS

Plates

SEAFOOD
EARLY HISTORY

dulse

1 Seashore Food Search

First Settlers on Applecross Peninsula, near Sand Beach, around 7000 BC

She crawled quietly to the front of their cave shelter at first light. Standing up outside, she stretched for a few minutes beside the remains of last night's fire. There was an early morning chill in the air and she put on her sealskin coat to keep warm. Though the hearth stones had cooled, there was still heat in the large heap of grey powdery ash in the centre. It was perfect for her plan.

Looking through the dim, early morning light she could see that the tide was almost full out. She picked up a woven basket and ran barefoot towards the shore. This was her favourite shoreline foray, alone, without her children. She didn't have long, though. They would all be getting up soon, looking for food, and that heat in the dying fire would not last long.

For this first shoreline feed of the day she goes for easily collected and quick cooking shellfish. She knows exactly where to find big fat mussels clinging to the rocks and she fills her basket, also picking up some handfuls of smaller whelks and winkles. There is no time for knocking tightly-clamped limpets from their rocks, hunting cockles or razor clams in the sand, or rummaging under seaweed-covered rocks for bigger prizes such as crabs or small fish. And certainly no time for wading far out into the shallow bays to search for other seafood treasures like sea urchins. All that is maybe for later in the day when the children, and the older people in her family, will join her in a wander up and down the coastline in search of good-tasting shellfish and seaweed and anything else which might come in handy.

As she heads back, she grabs some stalks of red dulse which are the children's favourite and will keep them chewing happily if they get hungry. She has been away for less than half an hour, yet she has gathered enough food for this first meal of the day. All she has to do now is spread the hot ash out evenly and lay the shells on top, which she does quickly, as more early-morning risers begin appearing from the cave shelter.

They find a space to sit on the deer-skin rugs scattered round the hearth and, when the shellfish is ready, help themselves to a fresh taste of the sea.

Seafood was a valuable food source, caught or foraged by the first-settlers, who neither planted seed nor kept livestock, but survived very well, it seems, by adapting their hunter-gatherer lifestyle to the natural resources they found around them. At this particular area of the Scottish coastline, the sea surrounds many islands and penetrates deep inland among rugged mountains. It holds sway with its ebb and flow, providing a remarkable variety of good things to eat in plentiful quantity, which must have been greatly enjoyed by the first communities who fished and rummaged on the seashore here for their food supplies.

Though Mesolithic hunter-gatherers had been around in other parts of the world for much longer, radio-carbon dating shows the first evidence of them at sites in Scotland around 7000 BC, after the ice-cover from the last ice age had melted and while Britain was still joined to Europe.[1] They had either arrived on foot when there was still land joining Britain to Europe, or by following the coast in small canoe-like boats made out of thick tree trunks. The things they brought with them, and their survival skills, would have been handed down refined by trial and error through many generations. All this might seem like a distant irrelevance, yet the surprising fact which has recently emerged as a result of historical DNA testing is that their genes live on. Despite invaders and colonists who have integrated into the population during many millennia, there is a high percentage of the current population who are descendents of the first settlers.[2]

Sand Bay on the Applecross peninsula, where shellfish shells dating back to around 7000BC were found in a shell midden beside a rock shelter (Getty Images).

Prior to their arrival on Scotland's west coast they had managed to survive the previous ice age by sheltering in the caves of northern Spain, leaving evidence of their artistic talents on the walls. They were knowledgeable and inventive prospectors, well-equipped and expert fire-makers, though they had not yet seen the need to invent solid cooking pots. But they had designed other useful things, such as sharp stone implements to cut bones, meat and skin; needles made from fish bones to sew animal skin and fur to make themselves warm; fitted clothes and footwear; hooks for catching fish; traps and fish nets for fishing; deadly spears for killing game; woven baskets; and strong cords for tying things up. If they couldn't find a cave-shelter, they could erect a tipi-style tent of branches covered with animal skins. During this time of freedom to roam, the evidence of their prolific shellfish-eating has been found in rubbish heaps, known as *shell middens*. Many sites have been identified, scattered around the Scottish coast or beside rivers,[3] and excavation work continues to reveal more.

Oyster, mussel, cockle, whelk, limpet, spoot (razor clam), scallop and cowrie shells are just a few of the forty-odd varieties found in the shell debris. Some of the middens are huge, probably used by many people over hundreds of years.

The site on the Forth estuary at Polmonthill is 170 yards long and 25 yards wide, containing between six to seven million oyster shells.[4] On a multiple-midden site at Morton in Fife, mussels and limpets are the most prolific. One midden alone contains around ten million shells, weighing over five tons.[5]

In this self-sufficient culture, shellfish was not only plentiful, it was also easily collectable throughout the year. No special equipment was needed and it could be gathered by people of all ages. Catching free-swimming fish, on the other hand, required more complicated skills such as making tidal traps, practising the art of spearing fish in clear waters, fashioning effective nets to trawl for fish and learning how to cast a line with a bait and hook. These were some of the skills necessary for catching large fish as well as smaller fish like saithe, a common inshore fish round the Scottish coast, whose bone evidence has been found at the first-settlers' sites.

Those who ventured inland to make new campsites made their way in small boats up the larger rivers, where fish are likely to have been plentiful. Evidence of their sites inland have been found on the banks of the Tweed, Clyde, Forth and Dee, where they could have caught salmon and trout by spearing in clear waters or by damming streams with traps made of upright stakes laced with branches. The bow and arrow was another weapon which could be used for fishing. But possibly their most successful fishing idea was to use bait. They had discovered how to use it successfully to attract animal plunder, so why not for catching fish?[6] Attached to a line, the tough hook carved from bone or horn which held the bait turned out to be their most successful invention.

Better fishing meant surplus catches. Unlike shellfish which could be gathered to order and eaten immediately, a large catch of fish soon became rotten. To preserve and store the excess, it is likely the most common method was cleaning, washing and opening up the fish so it could be hung up and dried in the wind. And when it rained, or there were too many flies about, it could be brought inside to hang somewhere in the wafting heat and smoke from the fire.

Smoked fish was more common in cooler climates where there was more often a fire for drying and smoking. Sun-dried was more common in warmer climates. Another method of preserving fish was to tie the fish tightly in bundles, to keep out the air, then wrap them in dried-out skins to keep them dry when they could be stored in the dark, cool recesses of a dry cave or buried in a deep pit in the ground. Salting came later.

While the evidence of the hunter-gatherers' lifestyle around Scottish coasts remains scanty, there is no doubt that seafood was eaten in quantity. Independent and free-roaming, with all their skills and nature-knowledge, there are still a few of these communities left in remote places of the world today where this lifestyle continues. They may not survive much longer, yet they carry the same self-sufficient message as the first settlers who sheltered in caves around the Scottish coast so many thousands of years ago at a time when seafood played a much more important part of the diet than it does today.

It provided them with a valuable form of body-building protein, which nutritional science has now established also had a vital effect on human evolution. Leading the nutritional research in the 1960s and 70s, Professor Michael A. Crawford, of the Institute of Brain Chemistry and Human Nutrition at London Metropolitan University, established that the oils in seafood contained an essential fatty acid (Omega-3), without which human brains deteriorated. As he explained:

> A diet of fish containing Omega-3 is essential for the necessary cerebral expansion which transformed our predecessors into homo sapiens. Brain capacity expanded rapidly in our prehistoric ancestors living in east Africa near large freshwater lakes. Medical experts have long known of the benefits of oily fish in the fight against heart disease, but it is just as vital as brain food.[7]

So while hunter-gatherer men might go inland to kill animals, this was not the most vital food which pregnant women and the newborn child needed to supply the best nutrients for young brains to grow. A coastal habitat might lack the challenge of the hunt for the men and boys, but it was the perfect place for women and children to rummage for large quantities of shellfish and fish, which would help to create the astonishing power of the human brain.

2   Cooking in Pots
Farmer-Fishers on Orkney, around 3500 BC

The potter is on his knees, blowing for all he's worth. It's a warm summer's day and for once not a breath of wind. He's built the fire which he's trying to get going inside a cooking hearth of round stones laid in a circle on the beach.

What is exciting the onlookers is the unusual pot he's putting on the fire. Rough-textured, terracotta-red, it's quite large with a decorated rim, curved outwards for easy carrying. Its base nestles neatly into the fire.

He's got the fire going now. But will this pot cook their food? The potter hopes so. Will it crack? He hopes not. He sends them off to gather more shellfish.

For this first cook-up, he's lined the pot with some crinkly brown fronds of seaweed, then filled it with his assorted shellfish – a mix of blue-black mussels, white cockles and greyish-black whelks. Now it's on the fire, he adds a little sea water and a layer of seaweed, then a flat round stone he's found on the beach which makes the perfect lid.

Enticing shellfish aromas begin wafting across the beach and some of the onlookers come back to the fire to see what's happening. The pot has not cracked. The shellfish, the potter tells them, is almost ready, so they sit down round the fire to wait . . .

Finally, he decides to let them have a taste and slips the hot stone lid off the boiling pot. He uses a large earthenware spoon he's made to lift out the mussels and cockles, heaping them onto a flat stone. They wait for them to cool a little then dive in for a taste. Yes, it's worked. The potter is a genius.

He is delighted, and decides to have a go at cooking a couple of large crabs with the heat that's still left in the fire. When the water is almost boiling again, he puts the crabs into the water, covers them with seaweed and puts the stone lid on top. He reckons they will take quite a bit longer than the first potful, so he sends the onlookers off to find some more shellfish while he goes looking for more fuel.

When he thinks the crabs might be cooked, he takes one out and puts it on a stone to check. Using a length of animal bone with a ball joint on the end which he's carved into a hammer-like shape he smashes open a claw – it's cooked beautifully.

All gather round again for a share. Then, sitting on the beach, as the sun starts sinking in the sky, they suck the meat from the recesses of the shells, using long sharp-pointed fish-bone needles to pick out the rest, savouring every last morsel. The potter mixes up some brown meat from inside the crab shell with a little white meat from the body, lubricating it with a spoonful of the cooking liquid in the pot. He tastes the concoction and is amazed, and delighted, at the intensity of the rich crab flavours. He hands the shell round for others to taste.

The fire is out now and the pot has cooled down. Everyone has a taste of the liquid left in the pot. It is very strong fishy-salty, but they like it. They like everything about the potter's new cooking pot.

Moving from a hunter-gatherer, semi-nomadic lifestyle to a settled one in a house growing crops and rearing animals, was accompanied by the new skill of making pots. Until now, cooking methods had been limited to baking either in hot ash, or on heated stones, or roasting food spiked through wooden spits held over hot embers. Certainly, after a kill they would also have chopped up an animal's innards and stuffed them into the cleaned-out stomach bag with some water to moisten – and who knows what else in the way of flavouring – then hung this up over the fire to cook, making the original version of the stomach bag pudding and the precursor of the animal haggis.

Now that they have acquired this new skill, brought with the new farmers, of moulding pots with finger and thumb from soft clay dug from a suitable soil,

Seafood cooking experiments in replica Neolithic pots crafted by Orkney potter Andrew Appleby (© Andrew Appleby).

they have a new method of cooking. The prehistoric potters on Orkney made both round-bottomed and straight-sided pots which, after a slow firing at a low temperature, provided both convenient straight-sided pots as well as round-based pots for cooking.[8] With stomach-bag cooking they would have become familiar with the principles of wet cooking, which not only tenderised tough meat, but also created the new attraction of blending different flavours and textures. Now a more permanent container for their experiments opened up exciting opportunities. Among the newest ingredients in their diet were their home-grown grains which could now be cooked till soft in the pot without grinding. Even more interesting was what happened when they heated the grain which had been ground finely in water. It made the liquid thick.

The gradual coastal erosion of sand dunes on the Orkney Islands has provided remarkably clear evidence of the stone houses, built by the people of this period who began cooking in pots. On the island of Papa Westray, erosion in the 1920s revealed the remains of two prehistoric farm houses at the Knap of Howar (in use from 3600–3100 BC). Details of the farming set-up, and how the people might have lived here, have been investigated by radiocarbon analysis of what was found in their rubbish mounds (middens) and what remains of the houses.[9] The details provide evidence of their lifestyle, the significant features of which radically changed their means of survival, but also hinted back to a legacy from their self-sufficient hunter-gatherer ancestors.

Their permanent homestead faced seawards, its thick stone walls built to protect them from wild winter storms. The entrance to the house was through a very thick seaward wall which possibly had an inner and an outer door for protection from the ever-blowing wind. Shelves built into the walls gave storage space. Upright slabs of stone divided up the living areas into separate rooms, with either stone paved or clay floors. For heating and cooking there was one hearth with paving stones surrounded by a stone kerb, and another which was just an ash-filled hollow in the floor.

There are two houses on this site, connected by a passage. A room in the smaller house shows signs of being a workshop, with tools: hammer-stones from sandstone beach pebbles; whalebone and antler hammers; flint knives and scrapers; pointed tools for boring holes; blunt-ended embossing tools; and a heavy saddle-quern for grinding grain. This has a central indentation to hold the grain and an oval-shaped 'rubber' stone to grind it into flour – the rotary-quern did not arrive in Britain till 300–400 BC.

In the land round the houses there is evidence that they grew barley and wheat in fenced-in areas to protect them from livestock. They kept cattle, sheep and pigs which foraged on the surrounding grazing land and on the beach, probably eating the seaweed. Though the hunter-gatherer's skills with harpoons and bows and arrows still provided them with seals and deer, it's more likely that the whale bones in their middens came from a stranded carcass found on the beach. They also made a tool from whalebone, which is similar to Eskimo blubber knives. Blubber fat provided a rich source of energy, while whale meat was a useful supply of protein which could be dried and stored. They used whale ribs as rafters; trimmed the vertebrae to make dishes; and carved other bits into spatulas, fish-slices and mallet-heads.[10] As they were surrounded by the sea, seafood remained a vital part of their diet. Fish bones in middens from large fish caught some distance out to sea confirm that the techniques of boatbuilding had improved, as well as fishing expertise with hooks and lines.

Though settled farming might seem like a dramatic change of lifestyle from the semi-nomadic wanderings of their ancestors, it's likely that it was a gradual transition over hundreds of years. First the spoils from hunting would be used to barter for a cow, sheep or goat, or some barley or wheat seeds. With a few breeding animals, and enough cereal grains to plant a small patch, there might be offspring from the animals and some surplus seeds to grow on the next year. Their inventive resourcefulness would have found a challenge in learning the new techniques of livestock-rearing, crop-harvesting, threshing and grinding grains, adding to their already considerable talents. The evidence in their middens confirms that they still hunted, fished and foraged the land and the seashore, no doubt keeping alive their old food-searching traditions as seasonal occupations, fitting them in between the demands of farming. The new farming had, after all, its limitations. Success depended on fertile soils, favourable weather and good luck. All those who farmed on poorer soils, and in a harsh climate, were wise not to abandon other sources of food – especially seafood – which had sustained them so well in the past.

Around Scotland's long coastline there is archaeological evidence that seafood continued to be part of their diet. That more evidence has not been found is partly due to the high percentage of acidic, peaty soils which have destroyed prehistoric remains. But at a well-preserved, peat-free site on the island of Oronsay near Oban, a wide variety of fish bones show that the people were eating conger eel, haddock, sea bream, wrasse, thornback ray, skate and shark. Also crabs, which were possibly taken from the deep waters around the coast by trapping in plaited baskets.[11]

But by far the greatest evidence of seafood eating, during this period of transition to settled farming-fishing, has been found in Orkney, a location much investigated by archaeologists. Bream, wrasse, conger eel and oysters are among the seafood remains found at Midhowe, Knowes of Ramsay, on the island of Rousay, at Quanterness and at the well-preserved village settlement of Skara Brae on mainland Orkney.[12]

As in the past, the surplus was a problem. Meat and fish which was 'high' must have been eaten, but at some point the link between unexplained deaths and rotten food would have become clear. Fish, deteriorating so much faster than meat, posed a special problem. The old hunter-gatherer methods of drying in the wind would have continued to work well at windswept locations like Papa Westray. Now that the islanders lived in a roofed house, surplus wind-dried fish could be hung from the rafters, where it was well protected from flies in the smoke rising from the central hearth. Or it could have been hung on wooden contraptions attached to the stone walls of houses. Dried outside when the wind was blowing, then moved inside high up in the rafters in the cool smoke, the meat and fish would have developed an appealing flavour – and it would have remained edible.

Besides keeping off the flies, the cool smoke was slowly injecting the raw fish flesh with preservative compounds found in wood and peat smoke. It was an important discovery, for while hot smoke will cook the fish, cold smoke travels slowly through the entire flesh by the process of osmosis, flavouring and preserving the whole fish and removing almost all its moisture without coagulating the protein, thus giving it a longer shelf-life than cooked fish.

Smoking fish, in the days before salt became more widely available for curing, must have been widely practised. There is no evidence of sites of salmon smoking in Scotland as early as 2000 BC but it seems likely that there was an early salmon-curing industry in Ireland on the marshy flats beside the river Bann, a notable salmon river, around this time.[13] Evidence has been found at hearth sites revealing many layers of ash, but without any kitchen refuse, suggesting that they were used for smoking fish rather than for domestic cooking. Also, the hearth fires were only lit in summer when salmon fishing was at its peak.

Around the same time that the Irish appear to have been smoking salmon, another new method of dealing with a large amount of food was invented. Known as 'burnt mound' cooking, around two-hundred examples have been found in Orkney, including one at Backaskaill on Papa Westray.[14] Was this a celebration meal for a large gathering of people, or a preservation method for a large cull of meat or big catch of fish?

Whatever its purpose, the evidence of this large-scale cooking technique can be clearly seen in stone-lined pits, dug into the ground, situated near a source of fresh water and accompanied by piles of burnt stones. The pits were sealed, probably with clay, to make them watertight, and then filled with water. A large fire was built nearby and suitable-sized stones were heated up to a red-hot temperature and then dropped into the water till it began to boil. Then the food was added. The cook's task now was to keep adding enough heated stones to keep the water just simmering till the food was cooked.[15]

There is no evidence of the use of the salt in seaweed and seawater but, given their ingenuity, it's more than likely the more tasty results from using seaweed and seawater would have been discovered by now. Also it would have been found that fish soaked first in seawater dried out faster. In all parts of the prehistoric world which were unable to access salt mines or salt lakes, or evaporate sea water with solar power, the technique of boiling seawater in salt pans became the established method of obtaining crystallised salt. It was time-consuming and very fuel-expensive, but it was certainly produced in England around the coasts of Essex and Lincolnshire, by Celtic invaders of the early Iron Age around 600–400 BC.[16] At a much later date, the Scottish towns of Prestonpans and Saltcoats got their names from this activity.

It has been suggested that prehistoric practices of fishing, and fish curing, may have continued unchanged for hundreds or even thousands of years.[17] The discovery of bronze and iron certainly changed cooking equipment. But did the cooking methods change much when the first potter-crafted earthenware cooking pot was replaced by an iron cauldron hanging from a hook, suspended from an iron tripod? Perhaps not. The quantities would have been larger, but were it possible to take a peek into an Iron Age cauldron hanging over the permanently burning fire, there would probably have been a similar boil-up of small shellfish, giving a pot of left-over salty liquid which the first makers of earthenware pots would have cooked up.

More radical changes came with the Romans, who found themselves among 'the most distant dwellers on earth' when they invaded in 43 AD. Forty years later they had established Roman rule up to a line across the country marked by the rivers Forth and Clyde. All tribes living to the south of the line were in contact with Roman ways. Those above the line the Romans named the *Picti*, meaning 'the painted ones', because they painted their bodies and faces in warfare.

The Picts were a disparate people of different tribes, determinedly independent with a sophisticated pagan culture. They had built impressive *crannogs* (dwelling-houses) on stilts, out over the water of inland lochs, and were the architects of coastal forts and complicated circular, protected dwellings, known as *brochs*, which they also built at the coast. By the time the Romans arrived, their most powerful men had styled themselves kings. And though the Romans failed to conquer them, they may have influenced them in other ways.

An intriguing find was made by archaeologists of some pottery shards at Gurness on Orkney that came from a style of clay bottle used for transporting Roman wine and olive oil which had gone out of use by 60 AD.[18] The possibility that a powerful Pictish king in Orkney was importing fine Roman wine and/or olive oil suggests that others might have been importing it too. Perhaps the most distant dwellers were not so out of touch with the rest of the country. Perhaps they had even discovered how to cook with oil and wine. How would that have changed the contents of their cooking pots?

The other powerful flavouring ingredient which was common in Roman cooking pots at this time was a fish sauce known as *garum* or *liquamen*, which was so popular it was factory-produced in large quantities. Besides its use in the Roman kitchen, it was also in permanent use as a condiment on the table to flavour cooked food. It was made by fermenting in the sun for many months an unlikely mixture of salt and small fish, such as red mullet, sprats, anchovies and mackerel, which were stirred regularly with the discarded innards of other larger fish. Clearly it was a very practical and thrifty way of dealing with fiddly small fish with a lot of bones, as well as finding a use for fish entrails.

The resulting matured garum was stored in clay bottles, possibly the same type as used for oil and wine. The Romans' fermented fish sauce was the prototype for modern equivalents such as Thailand's *nam pla*, Vietnam's *nuoc man*, Cambodia's *tuk trey* and not forgetting Britain's Worcestershire Sauce, made from anchovies. What they all have in common is a naturally occurring flavouring compound (disodium inosinate) which has the ability to intensify savouriness, and which led to the savoury taste of *umami*[19] becoming the fifth taste to join sweet, salt, bitter and sour.

A version of garum, diluted with water, was given to the Roman legions which policed the land for the best part of four hundred years. The Romans also had some interesting cooking equipment, like metal gridirons for grilling. They also had tripods which supported their shallow round pans with long handles over a small charcoal fire. This was the way to control heat and thicken liquids without creating lumps.

In Apicius, the only surviving Roman cookery book of this period, the recipes are mostly for complicated banquet dishes, only suitable for cooking in well-equipped Roman villas or their Britannia equivalents. According to the recipes, their sauces were thickened with flour or egg yolks. They indulged in elaborate flavouring and spicing. An oyster got the full treatment: it was drowned in a mix of pepper, lovage, egg yolk, vinegar, garum, oil and wine – honey was optional. The Romans loved fish and imported large quantities of their salt-pickled Mediterranean fish such as sturgeon, tuna and swordfish.

Of more importance, long term, was that the Romans developed salt production. They valued it so highly that Roman soldiers were given an allowance for buying salt, known as their *salarium* from Latin *salis*, salt, which provided the English language with the word 'salary'. Despite their lengthy occupation, their cooking style appears to have left with them in 400 AD. Their other useful legacy besides salt-making was the plants which they introduced: Mediterranean herbs such as rosemary, thyme, bay leaf, basil and mint; and vegetables such as garlic, onions, leeks, cabbages, peas, celery, turnips, radishes and asparagus. These new tastes and flavours livened up the contents of many a peasant cooking pot long after the Roman legions and their fishy garum had left.

Unlike the Romans, the priests of the early Christian church, who arrived about the time they were leaving, were not so keen on fish. It had, the priests thought, an unhealthy connection with Venus, the pagan goddess of love and fertility, to whom fish was sacred. But when the Roman church arrived, about a century later, this attitude to fish-eating was overturned. Unlike the early church, the Roman church replaced the pagan rite with a Christian one, and fish continued to be eaten by those who had converted from paganism. From now on, fish became an important item of meatless religious fast days. Besides fish days during the week, there were also forty days of abstinence from sensuous flesh meats during Lent, when only fish was allowed.[20]

All of which stimulated the fishing industry and encouraged seafood-eating in areas, especially inland, where it had not previously been available. It would take an invasion, however, from an unwelcome band of pirates, sailing in from the North Sea, to show the native inhabitants the real value of the rich resource they had in the seas around their shores, and how to harvest it successfully.

3 Fishing and Preserving

Norse Settlers, Shetland, around 900 AD

As the crew pull on the oars, he navigates the elegantly curved wooden boat with its single sail out into the Atlantic waves towards the fishing grounds. Salty sea spray rises over the side of the boat every so often, hitting their faces. There is a clear sky out on the horizon, though a bitterly cold sea breeze is against them for the moment. But that could change.

Though he farms the land for most of the year, its produce is never quite enough to feed his family. So now that the barley is gathered and stored he is off in search of another source of food with a six-man crew, including two of his sons. He farms because he has to, but he goes to sea for the thrill of feeling again that fearless surge of excitement as the boat heads out into the open sea. Since he was a young boy, he has been as much at home in a boat as on the land – a legacy from his Viking grandfather who invaded these islands over a hundred years ago.

In a few hours they've reached the fishing grounds and pull in the oars. The carefully coiled long lines, baited by his wife and young children, are shot. Now he passes round some hard barley cake and slices of dried meat, they have a drink of water from an earthenware flagon and relax for a bit. The boat drifts.

Then it's back to work, hauling in lines, gutting fish, cutting up some of the small fish to re-bait the lines and send them out again into the deep waters. It's been a good haul so far. And so it goes on. There's a cheer when someone pulls in a huge cod with powerful shoulders and a fiercely thrashing tail. The boat is heavy with fish when he decides to head for home. The men put the oars into the sea, and with the wind behind them filling the sail, they move through the water quickly, despite the weight of the fish.

The people who lived on these remote islands, before his ancestors arrived, had always caught fish and foraged for shellfish. Unlike him, though, they stayed close to the coast, catching smaller fish. His grandfather's generation changed all that, for they were experienced seafaring navigators. Their boats were more skilfully crafted. Long and shallow for speed and ease of navigation, they were built to adventure across oceans, not potter round coastlines. This design was also part of his legacy.

His wife and children are on the shore, looking out for them, and he hears their welcoming shout across the waves. As they hit the beach, he jumps out with the crew and catches a side of the boat; they all pull it safely up over the pebbles and everyone gathers round to view the large catch.

It's late, and will soon be dark, but they begin to sort out the fish. They remove the small fish they will eat fresh. Cutting the large cod, ling and tusk at the back of their heads they pull out the guts. The livers, stomach bags and roes are put aside for later. Women take the gutted fish down to the sea to wash them. Young boys take the large fish heads and cut out the gills, rinsing them in the sea to get rid of all the blood. When all the fish are cleaned, they are piled in a heap and covered with skins and heavy stones to protect them.

The day's work is over and he heads for home. Already, the women have gone ahead with the small fish, innards and large heads, and a large pot of hot fish stew is simmering on the fire.

The next day he rises at dawn. There is a strong, icy wind blowing. Perfect for drying fish. He must get lines repaired, sort out the pile of fish, tie them up together in pairs by the tails, hang them up like washing on a line, over rows of wooden fish racks, supported by upright poles which are lined up beside the shore. Here they will get a good blast of salty sea breezes as they dry out.

Meantime, the women and children have a busy day ahead too. First they roast some of the small fish over the hot embers of the fire which has been kept burning through the night. This is the first meal of the day. Then they get to work chopping livers and roes and mixing them in an earthenware bowl, with some ground barley, to a thick paste with herbs to flavour. This is used to stuff the largest fish heads and the largest stomach bags. The small stomach bags are chopped up and put into the fish stew which will keep them going for several days.

Surplus livers are put into pots and heated gently to release their valuable oil which floats up to the surface. This pungent fishy oil is stored and used for lighting the oil lamps. Some good sharp-pointed fish bones are set aside to be carved into needles. Nothing is wasted.

Over the next few weeks he spends as much time as possible out in the boat fishing. The more he can catch, and cure, the more security they will have if there is a spell of bad luck with the crops or livestock. With a good spell of dry, freezing weather and a good strong wind blowing, today's catch could be freeze-dried in a couple of weeks. On the other hand it could turn wet and take up to six, or longer.

Whatever the weather, he must check and turn the fish regularly as it dries out, inspecting it for decay. Gradually, as it gets harder and harder, it matures in flavour till it is ready to be used as barter in the marketplace. When almost completely free of moisture and hard as a board, it will keep for years.

It is another legacy from his Viking ancestors.

A two-day sail in a light, fast Viking ship brought the first invaders to the nearest land to the west of Norway which they named *Hjaltland*, later to become Shetland (from Norse: *hjalt*, hilt of a sword). The island's Picts may have avoided a Roman invasion by land from the south centuries earlier, but they had no chance against this northern attack from the sea. The Viking raids which began in the 780s were followed by large numbers occupying the land. Both Shetland, and the political centre Orkney (from Norse: *orkneyjar*, seal islands), were subsequently ruled from Norway for the best part of six centuries. Most of the Highlands and Islands, as well as many other parts of the country, were also colonised by the Vikings, and only returned to the Scottish crown after the Battle of Largs in 1263. Orkney and Shetland were not returned till 1469.

How much of the old Pictish lifestyle survived after the Vikings invaded is not certain. There are differing theories. The Picts and Vikings might have become peaceable neighbours. Or the warrior Picts might have fled, or been ethnically-cleansed, by the more brutal Vikings.[21] Whatever happened, there is no doubt that Norse culture replaced the previous one, especially in Orkney and Shetland, and to varying degrees in other parts of the country where they settled. In both placenames, and genetic make-up, there is strong evidence of Viking dominance during this period.[22] What is also well-established is that Viking seafarers came with better boat-building skills and greater seafaring experience than the Picts.

Their adventures on other 'sea roads' had taken them to Iceland, the Faroe Islands and Greenland. They also appear to have reached the New World many centuries before Columbus. These expansionist Vikings, who had already established the economic importance of the northern seas, introduced their culture to the parts of Scotland where they settled, and opened up the possibility of harvesting the seas more productively.

Ruins of an early Viking farmhouse at Jarlshof, Shetland. An ideal base for Norse settlers with a beach to haul up fishing boats and beside prime agricultural land (Historic Scotland, licensor www.scran.ac.uk)

Central to this was the development of commercial fishing and fish preservation. The Vikings had more advanced methods of catching fish, particularly large white fish of the cod family. The middens of Iron and Viking Age Norway are dominated by large cod remains.[23] Their particular preservation expertise was a cure known as *torrfisk* (Norwegian for 'dried fish'), which was the earliest method of drying out large white fish without salt (stockfish). The hard, freeze-dried, dehydrated fish – with an almost indefinite shelf-life – provided a vital store-food for Viking adventurers during their plundering days. It was also one of the first protein foods to be traded by fish-surplus to fish-deficit countries around the world. According to the Norse *Egil's Saga*, the dried fish of western Norway was being imported to England to be traded for cloth and metal in the 800s.[24] Such was its subsequent commercial success that Henry VII set up the London Company of Stockfishmongers in 1509, which dealt in dried white fish: mainly cod, haddock, pollack and ling, mostly from Norway and Iceland.[25]

There can be little doubt that Viking invaders in Scotland established production of their traditional stockfish. Inevitably, there must have been subtle differences in the version of traditional Norse stockfish which was made in the colonised areas around the Scottish coast. The climate, though similar to Norway, is not identical. But the method is so in tune with the early Scots additive-free and natural way of life.

Evidence in Orkney's middens for this period indicates that the fisher-farmers, of Viking ancestry, were certainly catching large white fish of the cod family. Compared with previous Pictish middens, the amount of fish found is much larger. The variety of fish is also more extensive, since the bones in Pictish middens were mostly from small white fish such as saithe. At some point between 800 and 900, fishing for much larger fish became a major focus of Orcadian life.[26]

Later 'fish middens', dated around 1000, have been found in both Orkney and Caithness, which are thought to represent semi-specialised processing middens for the production of preserved fish. They contain mostly marine shells – probably some of the shellfish which was used for bait – and also the bones of large cod, saithe and ling. Domestic middens also show an increase in the quantity of fish bones compared with previous times.[27] Fish had become more important, both as a trading commodity and as a food for the native population. The seas were being exploited as never before.

So far, the evidence of increased fishing and seafood-eating can be related to the areas inhabited by the Viking settlers ruled by Norway. Hundreds of places with names derived from the Norse language are evidence of their permanent presence, also the discovery of many Viking graves and settlements. The area of their influence included all the Scottish islands and the land round most of the Scottish coastline, except for the coasts of the North East, Ayrshire, Dumfries and Galloway and Berwickshire, which were hostile Angle territory.[28]

But just as it looked like the entire country might be colonised by the seafaring invaders, their fortunes changed. The Picts and the Gaels, the most dominant tribes occupying the rest of the land, joined forces against them. It was a successful partnership which defeated the Vikings in 904 at Strathcarron, when Constantine, who had become the King of Alba (Pictish and Gaelic land), defeated the Viking, Ivar the Younger of Dublin. It halted the Viking advance, but did not remove their influence. Just forty years later, they made an alliance with the same Constantine in a major battle against the Angles and Saxons, whose expansionist ambitions were also set on conquering northern Britannia. Though the northern alliance did not win the battle, they did stop the north becoming Angle land (England).

Instead of colonising the north, by the early 1000s the Viking pirates had morphed into fully integrated Norse settlers. Most had also given up their pagan gods for Christianity. Whether by conviction or convenience, it has been suggested that the exclusion of non-Christians from trading in Europe might have had something to do with their conversion. Whatever the reason, it brought them into closer contact with the Christian community in the rest of the country, which had an established tradition of religious fish days, when fasting allowed seafood as an alternative to forbidden flesh meats. This would have been no penance for the seafood-loving Norse settlers.

What is also relevant to the future development of fishing and preserving is that, in the areas of Norse settlement, conditions for farming were not the most favourable. Seafood from foraging the shoreline, and fishing the seas, remained essential for survival as well as a valuable trading commodity. Supplies of preserved fish were needed for religious fast days; there were armies to victual and boats on long sea voyages to provision; not to mention fish-deficit countries eager to import. While they had established their expertise at catching large white fish to make into stockfish, they were also up to other fishing and processing ploys.

Certainly they were after the fast-swimming shoals of herring which migrated from one area of the seas to another throughout the year as they looked for food. The Viking search for herring is recorded in the Norse Sagas at the end of the 900s, and it has been suggested that their own migration might have been partly triggered by their pursuit of the migrating shoals of herring.[29] How much of their herring fishing and preserving expertise was passed on in the areas where they settled is not clear. Herring bones have not survived as archaeological evidence, but they were certainly an important catch in the early 1000s. A much more perishable fish than white fish, the solution was to mix them with salt soon after they were caught.

In an edict issued by the Scottish King David I in 1153, it is stated that all goods brought by sea should be landed prior to sale, with the exception of salt and herrings, which could be sold on board.[30] The salt, mixed with the herrings on board immediately after catching, would have increased both their shelf life and their value. There may also have been a method of drying herring, since Scottish Parliamentary Records for 1240 refer to both fresh and dried herring.[31]

Being high in fat, the drying process perfected by the Norse for white fish was less successful for herring, since its fat oxidised and went rancid when exposed to air. But this could be overcome by heavy salting, together with drying and smoking. It was a process already recorded in France in 1230 when trees were given to the poor for the purpose of smoking herring. More than a century later there is an English record of a 'black' house used for smoking 'black' (hard dried) herrings.[32]

While Norse-led fishing and preserving was developing on a commercial scale, the indigenous population in all coastal areas, unaffected by the Viking onslaught, continued their more modest harvesting of the sea, established over thousands of years. There were also freshwater fisheries inland which remained a valuable resource. Both herring and Atlantic salmon, returning to spawn, had been recognised for their value, and their fishing rights were claimed by the Scottish Crown, making them the first royal fish. Catching fish in traps and nets, with barbed harpoons and baited lines, were the native methods. Fishing and preserving skills may not have been as well developed as with the Norse settlers, but seafood continued to be a valuable food resource locally, especially when crops failed.

This resource included seabirds such as gannets, cormorants and shags, which also became more exploited for food at this time. Compared with Pictish remains on Orkney, there is more archaeological evidence of bones from these birds during the Viking age. With an increase in fishing, and general maritime activity, these birds would have made a welcome variety to the diet.[33] They could have been caught at sea while fishing. The alternative was to climb down the cliffs where the birds were nesting and catch them with a noose on the end of a long stick: a dangerous activity but often a vital food reservoir on remote islands with limited resources.

The unwelcome invaders' legacy of seafaring mastery, preservation expertise and boat-building skills did not immediately transform the emerging Scottish nation into a world trader in seafood. That would happen many centuries later. For the moment, it was enough that the country had been alerted to the potential around its shores. And had been influenced, too, by a northern country which was more advanced in its methods of handling seafood on a commercial scale. While previous generations had sound seafood knowledge and expertise in the potential of inner coastal waters, now they had been introduced to bigger fish from deeper offshore waters. And with these big fish came the culture of making use of every part of the fish – wasting nothing. It would become integrated into the people's attitude to fish, and other seafood, especially in those islands off the Scottish coast first plundered by the Vikings.

4 Salmon Fishing

Fish-Trappers at the Coast, near a Salmon River, around 1200

A heady aroma of burning peat and cooking salmon wafts across the hillside, whetting the appetites of those on their way – under cover of darkness – to join a secret salmon banquet in the hills. Soon they are sitting round the cooked fish laid on a bed of bracken as it's divided up into portions. It's their first taste this year of the delicately pink, succulent flesh of the royal fish which has no equal.

Though he is employed by the authorities to catch salmon in a trap on the beach, the daring organiser who has cooked this salmon for trusted neighbours belongs to a culture, inherited from previous generations, which believes the people have a right to this wild fish. He works with a mate during the salmon season, living in a bothy overlooking a crescent-shaped stone dyke on the beach between the high and low tide mark, round a deep pool, which is in the path of returning shoals of Atlantic salmon.

The unsuspecting fish, resting here on their way back to the river of their birth to spawn, only discover when the tide goes out that their intended route is blocked and they are 'caught' in the pool.

While he sits at the door of the bothy keeping an eye on the trap, his mate sleeps. They take turns at watching through the day and night at this time of year. The salmon belong to the Church. They were a gift from the Scottish king, Alexander I, who owns the rights to all salmon caught in Scottish waters. Such is the royal status of the salmon. It is a rich resource for Crown and Church, helping to keep their finances in good shape as they make excellent profits from curing and exporting much of the catch. He, and his mate, however, must wait till the end of the season before they are paid for their efforts.

A few days later, on a clear night, he sees a sudden flash of silver caught in the moonlight, and in no time, the whole pool is lit up with a thrashing mass of fish.

'They're back,' he shouts to his mate.

He runs down to the beach and begins to wade in. Catching each fish by its tail, he takes it back to the beach and gives it a vigorous whack on the head with a wooden club. His mate is not far behind him, and they work together until all the fish are lying in a large pile on the beach.

Next, they work together packing them carefully into wicker creels, layered with seaweed, putting almost all of their valuable catch safely into the bothy. While his mate stays at the bothy with the fish, he disappears into the darkness, heading for the hills with their 'share'.

As dawn breaks, he is back. Grabbing an oatcake and some cheese, he goes off to catch the ponies, grazing nearby. The creels of salmon are hitched over the pony's backs, and they set off to deliver the salmon. The monks are delighted. The first salmon of the season! What a treat. They will have a banquet tonight to celebrate. The catchers leave and make their way back to the bothy.

They discuss plans on the way back for their own illegal salmon banquet with others more in need of it than the well-fed monks. Best to wait a night or two, they agree.

He has hidden their 'share' in the deep recesses of a cool cave in the hills, safe from predators, well-hidden by undergrowth and with a secret entrance. A large black, cast-iron cauldron is also hidden, plus a supply of peat. On the first cloudy night, he alerts his close neighbours and slips off into the hills, leaving his mate at the bothy to watch the tide.

Once the fire is lit and the water in the cauldron is heating up nicely, he gets the fish, already cleaned and washed in the sea, and slips them into the almost boiling liquid. All he need do now is bring the water back up to the boil and the fish will cook through in the remaining heat.

The sooner he puts the fire out the better.

Scotland's mountainous terrain, combined with a wet climate and many fast-flowing, unpolluted, gravelly rivers which suit breeding salmon, have provided it with more salmon rivers than any other part of the British Isles. Trapping salmon, as they return to their home-river to breed, is the country's oldest recorded commercial fishing enterprise. Traps, built in coastal waters, at estuaries and in rivers were known as *cruives* or *yairs*. Some were simple crescent-shaped stone dykes attached to a point of land on either side, and designed to appear, or *crown*, about two hours before low water mark. [34] Others were more complicated affairs, described as: 'a sort of scaffold projecting into the water; upon which they build little huts to protect them from the weather; from these scaffolds they let down, at certain times of the tide, their nets, and are often very successful in taking the smaller fish. . .'[35] Another method was stretching a seine (drag) net across river

A tidal fish trap at low tide between Arisaig and Loch Ailort, Ardnamurchan, Inverness-shire (National Museums Scotland, licensor www.scran.ac.uk).

estuaries. Either end of the net, full of fish, was then pulled into the shore and the fish dragged up, one by one, onto the beach to meet its fate.

At some time in the early 1200s, it did occur to both the Crown and Church that if this highly successful system of exploiting their salmon stocks continued, one day there might be no salmon left to come back to breed in the pools of their home river. It was such an alarming prospect that there was a succession of Acts, relating to how salmon could be fished, so stocks might be preserved.

The first salmon conservation act was during the reign of Alexander II (1214–1249) which related to the size of the gap which was to be built into the cruive dyke to allow a proportion of fish to pass freely. Also, it banned salmon fishing from Saturday evensong till Monday after sunrise. King Robert the Bruce, in 1318, produced another act to widen the gap at the mouth of the river, so that small, year-old salmon smolts could get downstream and out to sea to begin their journey across the Atlantic to the winter feeding grounds. The next act, in 1424, banned all traps in fresh water which destroyed very young fish. It also banned salmon fishing from 15 August to 30 November. By 1563, what with the season curtailed, and bans which made existing traps less successful, lots of new traps had been constructed which triggered yet another act, instructing all recently constructed traps to be destroyed. This excluded new traps which had been developed on the Tweed and the Solway Firth, since getting rid of them would be giving an advantage to English salmon fishers.[36]

The productivity of salmon rivers varied according to size, the widest and longest usually having the most fish. Around the Scottish coastline the most productive salmon rivers have been those which flow eastwards into the North Sea. They include the Tweed, Tay, North and South Esk, Dee, Don, Deveron, Spey, Ness and Helmsdale. Apart from the Solway and the Clyde, most of the salmon rivers on the west coast are smaller and, in this early period in the history of salmon fishing, also the least accessible for commercial exploitation.

When the first salmon conservation acts were passed in the 1200s, there were plentiful supplies of salmon, most of which had to be cured.[37] Little evidence exists of how they were cured except for the Irish on the river Bann.[38] Certainly they would have used salt, possibly in combination with smoking if they had enough fuel. Smoking techniques were already well-established by this time, with the heavily smoked herring, known as a red herring, now a very successful cure.[39] In the peat-rich areas of Scotland, pre-salted salmon, dried out over a peat fire, gave it a unique flavour. The first mention of a smoked cure for salmon appears in the records of a monastery in Fife in the late 1400s, when local salmon-fishers were asked to deliver three dozen salmon to the monastery – fresh or *kippered*. The *Household Book* of James V (1513-42) also mentions *kippered* salmon.

Though salmon eventually lost its kipper-tag to the smoked herring, the more common cure at this time was salting salmon in layers in a barrel. This was an easier and more reliable cure which worked well with the fatty salmon, since it prevented rancidity so long as the air was excluded. Kippered salmon had a shorter shelf-life.

The salting method which had been used from earliest times was improved in 1383, when Wilhem Van Beukels, a Dutch curer, demonstrated how gutting, and more efficient packing to exclude all air, made a much better end-product. Salted salmon in barrels was traded in the Middle Ages from the ports of Aberdeen, Perth, Glasgow, and Berwick (with salmon which had been caught in the Dee, Don, Tay, Clyde and Tweed). It was exchanged for French, German and Italian cloth, silk, velvet, spices and wine. When not at war with them, it was also traded with the English for similar luxuries.[40]

Although the salmon fisheries were not a large national resource, they were a very lucrative source of local income for those who had the rights. Before the Reformation in the 1500s, the Catholic Church had been much favoured with gifts of salmon rights from the Crown. Salmon rights were also given by the Crown to some of the first royal burghs, when they were being set up in the early 1100s. Aberdeen was one of the first in 1124, and received a particularly rich source of income from the prolific salmon rivers of the Dee and the Don. Throughout the following centuries, Aberdeen merchants developed a thriving salmon trade, making it a major exporting port. Records for the 1600s show that in a good season the Dee and the Don could produce about 170 tons of cured salmon.[41] What was consumed fresh can only be imagined.

The magistrates of Aberdeen supervised the salting and packing of the fish to ensure that quality control was maintained, branding the barrels with the abbreviated ABD (Aberdeen) to denote its origin and that the curing had reached the necessary standard. In 1584 an act was passed to control the quality of salted salmon, requiring all other burghs, also exporting salmon, to set up controls. Officers had to brand every barrel with the town's mark, so poor quality barrels could be traced back to source. In 1712–13, 1,270 barrels were exported from Aberdeen, mainly to Germany, Holland, Spain and Portugal and Venice.[42]

During his tour of Scotland around this time, Daniel Defoe, the English writer, gives an account of the salmon industry and its importance.[43] Firstly, he was impressed by the 'prodigious quantity' of salmon from the Tay, which he thought were 'extraordinarily good'.

'They carry it,' he says, 'to Edinburgh and to all the towns where they have no salmon and they barrel up a great quantity for exportation.'

He found more 'prodigious quantity' in Aberdeen, in Caithness and the north of Scotland, generally. There were, he says: 'Salmon in such plenty as is scarce credible and so cheap that, to those who have any substance to buy with, it is not worth their while to catch it themselves. This they eat fresh in the season and for other times they cure it by drying in the sun, by which they preserve it all the year.' [44]

Forty-odd years later, John Richardson, a major salmon exporter in Perth in the 1760s, made more revealing comments on the salmon industry in his letters and records. They make clear that there was much variation in both the quality of the fish and the curing methods, which affected the price.

He highlights the already established fact that Aberdeen-cured salmon was of the highest quality, noting that the notoriously fussy Parisian fishmongers liked the Aberdeen cure so much that: 'they give any price when scarce since they buy no other salmon'. On the other hand, he says that barrels of cured salmon, picked up from small curing stations on the Western Isles, were regarded as relatively poor quality.[45]

Another salmon cure – the Newcastle pickle – first appears in the early 1700s, though it seems they got their salmon from the Tweed. The method involved cooking the fish first, then putting it into a spiced vinegar pickle.[46] It was yet another move towards more perishable and more palatable cures. Aberdeen took up the recipe and their version was exported to London, where this new cure had a certain novelty value in the mid-1700s. Less than a century later, however, it had become one of the cheapest foods, and was eaten by the urban poor, as Dickens reveals in *The Pickwick Papers* (1836) when Mr Weller refers to pickled salmon and oysters as foods of the 'mean streets and poverty'.

By this time a revolutionary new preservation idea had been discovered by Alexander Dalrymple, a Scottish ship's captain in the service of the East India Company. He was on a trip to Canton when he came across the Chinese storing snow in underground snow houses. The fishermen, he discovered, used this hard-packed snow on their boats to keep the fish cool and fresh in the summer heat. The heavily-insulated snow-packed fish could then be transported to the interior regions of China and stay fresh. He passed this information on to a fish merchant in 1786, and the icing of fresh fish to prevent it deteriorating was developed in Scotland.

Underground ice houses were built at all the chief salmon rivers. During the winter, cart-loads of ice from rivers, lochs and ponds were stored in the ice houses. When there was not enough ice to fill the ice houses, companies ordered ship-loads of Norwegian lake ice. By 1814, icing was the established method of preserving salmon from all the east coast Scottish salmon rivers. The fish was then sent by fast sailboats to the London market. By 1849, even fresher Scottish salmon was reaching London's dining tables, when faster steamboats rushed their iced salmon cargo down the east coast to Billingsgate. It was reckoned that salmon, properly packed and insulated, stayed fresh for eight to ten days in winter and six to eight in summer.[47]

Lavishing this sort of attention on salmon was entirely due to its status, along with herring, as the most highly valued fish from Scottish waters, especially when fresh and in its prime. By the time it reached London, needless to say, it had become much more expensive than it was back in Scotland. Unsuspecting Scots in London could easily get caught out, like the laird dining at a London inn who was shocked to discover that the salmon he'd ordered for his servant was many times more expensive than his own piece of roast beef.

Back in Scotland, salmon seems to have been a common item of the farm servant's daily fare. So much so that some claimed to be suffering from such an excess of salmon that their farm contracts contained a clause promising that they would not be given a salmon meal more than three times a week.[48] The salmon meals on offer, however, were most likely not the tastiest first salmon of the season, but some hard-salted kippered salmon or maybe the vinegar-pickled version which Dickens equated with poverty.

Various other salmon cures were developed. A cure is mentioned in 1882 for a salmon, split open and salted, with the addition of saltpetre, rum or sugar. This was not smoked, but put out in a cold dry wind, like a Norse stockfish, until hard as a board.[49] Curers were, by the late 1800s, moving away from heavily preserved techniques, developing lighter preservation methods aimed at improving the flavour and shortening the shelf life, now that improved transport had shortened the time in transit.

In 1921 smoked salmon curing on the family's Gairloch estate is described by Osgood Mackenzie (founder of Inverewe Gardens). It reflects the move to a milder, more balanced cure which has both sugar and salt in the initial salting. The old term 'kippered' has mostly been transferred to the herring by now, but it remains here in its old sense. Kate Archy's kippered salmon, as he describes it, had two versions. One is a strong cure for long keeping, the other a milder cure for more immediate consumption, and she adjusts the quantity of salt and sugar accordingly.

'As for her kippers,' he says, 'who nowadays could settle like her the exact quantities of salt, sugar and smoke each dried salmon and grilse required, to suit the date of their consumption, whether immediate or deferred . . Until salmon close time [out of season] ended the family was never disgraced through being out of salmon or wonderful kipper.'[50]

The Gairloch estate, in the north-west Highlands, included the salmon fishing rights at the mouth of the River Ewe, which were extensively exploited for estate use. Mackenzie gives an account written by his uncle (between 1803 and 1860) of setting the seine net at the mouth of the river in a semicircle, with one end of the net close to the shore and the other end about a hundred yards out at sea, with everyone on the shore holding onto the rope attached to the far out end of the net. As soon as the shoal of salmon had gone into the net, those on the shore started hauling 'like demons' to get the fish in.

'At one such haul,' his uncle recalls, 'I once saw over three hundred salmon, grilse, and trout, from 2 or 3 pounds up to 25 pounds, brought ashore.'[51]

Besides the seine net, the estate also had a cruive fish trap at the mouth of the river. During the season the seine net was hauled in twice a day, except Sunday, when the salmon were caught in the 'cruive boxes'. It is hardly surprising that commercial fishermen were frequently in dispute with estates about their methods of 'catching' salmon. From the salmon-trappers of the 1200s to the Mackenzies of Gairloch in the 1800s, despite laws to ensure the Atlantic salmon's survival, an excessive amount continued to be caught, by whatever means, from Scottish seas and rivers. Yet such were the salmon's powers of survival that it continued to return to the favourable breeding conditions in its Scottish home waters, though not for much longer.

5   Rich Fishing Grounds
Dutch Fishermen in the North Sea around 1600

As the huge piles of silver herring are shaken out of the drift nets, the *pekelharing* (pickled herring) curer gets to work. First he cuts out the gills and some of the long gut. Then he coats them with salt and turns them over and over in it. Next, sorting the fish by size.

Working in pairs now, one curer bends into the barrel while his mate supplies him with fish as he makes the first layer in the base. He works quickly, but the fish must be very tightly packed, head to tail, no spaces. He is being watched closely by the curing inspector who patrols the ship's deck, peering into the barrel to check on his packing as he straightens up for a moment. The inspector nods to his mate to sprinkle over the first layer of salt. Then the curer is onto the next layer of fish which must lie, alternately, across the previous one.

Once he's done about half the barrel, and his back feels as if it's about to break, he straightens up and changes places with his mate. At least the swell is not too bad tonight.

It's three months since he sailed out of Amsterdam on this Dutch *Haring Buis* (herring buss: a slow-sailing factory ship) and they are now in the seas off Shetland: just one of a fleet of hundreds of busses surrounded by an armada of smaller, faster boats which do most of the herring fishing. Their long drift nets, hanging in the sea like curtains, catch the herring in their mesh as they swim into them. As soon as the fish are pulled in they are taken to the buss for processing.

Most of the fifteen-man crew on his buss are, like him, working on the pekelharing. The rest are fisher-seamen who also put out nets from the buss. Such is the danger of their activities from attack by the Scottish authorities – who regard this fishing as illegal – that a fleet of Dutch men-of-war is on hand to protect them from any trouble.

A Dutch herring buss used in the North Sea for herring fishing c. *1480 (Science and Society Picture Library).*

So far, there's no sign of the Scottish authorities. The nearby Shetlanders are certainly not any trouble. Sometimes the Dutchman gets to join a boat going ashore for supplies of dairy produce, eggs, vegetables, mutton, pork and beef. He will spend a night or two on the island, be welcomed in the local hostelry, perhaps have a jolly drinking session with the islanders. Only those trusted to behave are allowed ashore. If news of drunken brawls, or other dubious activities, gets back to the captain he will not get ashore again.

With the prospect of many months exposed to the elements in these cold northern waters, he also goes in search of the expertly-knitted and richly-patterned, warm woolly jumpers and socks which the Shetland women make. Visiting them in their houses, he sees what little comfort they have compared to his living conditions at home.

The excellent Scottish herring have made his country rich. He can see that. But he pays a price for this prosperity too. It is not an easy life on the busses, away from his wife and family all summer. And there are times when the seas get so rough that they can hardly stand, yet the curing must continue. Curing the freshest herring immediately it's caught, and before its 'bloom' fades in less than twenty-four hours, is just the beginning of a long and meticulous process which has made their cure the best in the world.

When his work is passed by the inspector on the buss, the barrel is branded with the date and moved to make room on the deck. It's stored now, and left for a few days as the salt begins to extract the moisture from the fish and create the brine which will exclude all air and lengthen the herring's shelf-life.

Once the brine forms, the fish shrinks. So the curer's next job is topping up the barrel with herring from another barrel of the same date. They top up the now full barrel with brine, get the inspector to pass it and put on the lid to make an airtight seal. Now it's hung over the side of the boat to be picked up by a *jaeger* (fast transit boat) which will take it back to Amsterdam.

It's the end of his careful packing, but not the end of the Dutch curing process. Unloaded onto the quay at Amsterdam, two pier-side curers now open the barrel and unpack it into a new barrel, rejecting inferior or damaged fish, ensuring the final airtight seal. Only now does the barrel get its final, superior quality branding, which secures for the Dutch their reputation as the world's best curers of the excellent Scottish herring.

Viking invaders may have plundered the land some centuries earlier, but it was the seas round Scottish coasts which were plundered by the Dutch – and the Flemish and Germans to a lesser extent – from the 1350s onwards. Scotland lacked both a herring-curing technique to rival the Dutch and the capital to rival the richer, better-organised, European countries. By the early 1600s, the Dutch had become dominant, not only perfecting the method of preserving the highly perishable herring, but also investing heavily in boats, gear, seamen and fishermen. In Scotland there was a saying that 'Amsterdam was built on Scottish herring bones'.[52] At their peak production, there were upwards of 1,500 busses plus a large protection fleet of men-of-war.[53] Their enterprise lasted until the early 1800s, when their fleet needed renewing and the Dutch government decided to invest elsewhere.

Though well-positioned on the edge of the north-west European continental shelf, surrounded on all sides by extensive areas of valuable fishing grounds, by the early 1600s Scotland's fishing potential in these waters was undeveloped, despite the seafaring skills of its people and the influence of the Norse settlers. Round much of the coast, fishing activity was limited to inshore catches by self-sufficient coastal dwellers who salted enough excess fish to see them through the winter and Lent. There were few piers and harbours, and those who line-fished in open boats had to pull their small, light fishing boats up onto flat pebble beaches. Coastal burgh towns had the powers to build harbours and boats; secure wood for barrels; salt for curing; and to pass regulations about the sale and price of fish. But this development depended on the wealth of each burgh and the management skills of the burgesses. Early burgh towns were mostly on the east coast, at Inverness, Aberdeen, Dundee, Perth and Edinburgh, which were all made royal burghs in the 1100s.

In an attempt to increase their fishing potential, James IV, an enthusiastic builder of expensive royal battleships, passed an Act in 1493: 'Regarding the great and innumerable riches that are lost through the lack of using ships for fishing, just as is done in other realms . . .'[54] His solution was to instruct all coastal burghs throughout the country to build larger ships – nothing smaller than 20 tons – and to equip the ships with sailors: strong, idle men who were to be paid a wage and to be banned from the burgh if they refused to work. The burgesses were also to purchase nets and other necessary items for catching large and small fish. This was all to be done by February the following year, on penalty of a fine of £20.

Meanwhile, James himself indulged in an ambitious programme of building ships for the Scottish navy, while most of the country's burgesses lacked the funds to create the fishing fleet he wanted to 'ding the Dutch'.[55]

Unlike other coastal areas, in the seas surrounding the Argyll lochs, the Firth of Clyde, Ayrshire and the Solway Firth, there were successful herring fisheries. The Crown had given the herring fishing rights in the River Clyde to the Abbey of Holyrood in 1138.[56] There is more evidence of herring fishing in this area in 1555 when it was reported to the Scottish parliament that the fishermen of Glasgow, Dumbarton and Ayr had successful herring fisheries in Loch Fyne.[57]

In 1674 there is even more revealing information that the Clyde fisheries consisted of 600–900 small boats, and that there were 4,000 men, fishing for herring between July and Christmas. Some of the fish were sold fresh locally and some converted into 'reds'[58] (heavily smoked), but most were salt-pickled and exported. An annual export of 3,750 tons seems to have been an average amount.[59] By the 1730s and 40s a valuable herring fishery had also developed at Campbeltown, with a large fleet of boats operating in the Western Isles. The small boats were owned by the fishermen: each man had a share in the boat and took a corresponding share in the profits.[60]

Though a very small player, compared with the Dutch, this area had a number of positive factors which made it significant in the development of the herring fishery, and by the 1700s it had established a lucrative trade in barrels of salt-pickled herrings. The Clyde was becoming a major world trading seaport, making it a good place from which to find new markets for the Scottish barrels of herring which did not compete with the better quality Dutch cures sold into Europe.

Making use of trading links with the West Indies, the herring curers developed a large market for their – inferior to the Dutch – Scots cure as cheap food for plantation-working slaves. Strong trade links with Ireland, too, ensured a ready market for barrels of cheap pickled herring among the Irish peasants. Fishing prospered in the area, not only from the overseas sale of the pickled herring, but also from the sale of fresh herring and other fish in the local markets of this well-populated urban area. The Glasgow fish market dates from the 1500s.

This successful fishery did not, however, solve the problem of the Dutch and other foreigners fishing in Scottish waters. During the 1500s, the country was greatly taken up with the turmoil of religious upheaval and civil war caused by the Reformation, but in the late 1590s, shortly before the Union of the Crowns, James

VI was in such trouble financially that he encouraged a group of wealthy Scottish prospectors to develop a fishing industry in the Western Isles. They were known as the 'Fife Adventurers', and James supplied them with a small army with the aim of colonising this unruly part of his kingdom where warring clans prevailed. The plan was that their fishing enterprise would copy the Dutch style, and would bring him much needed revenue in the form of taxes.

Even with the help of an army, the Fife Adventurers were no match for clan chiefs, and after several efforts, and much bloodshed and financial loss, they abandoned the King's fishing project. This area had been independently ruled by the powerful Norse-Gaelic Lord of the Isles until the title was removed in 1493 by James IV, and the chiefs were still not willing to toe the line according to the wishes of a Scottish king.

Efforts at solving the fishing problem were not reconsidered by parliament until after the Union of the Crowns (1603), when an act was passed in 1609 making it illegal for foreigners to fish off Scottish coasts. A licence had to be bought and a payment of tax on the herring caught. But despite lengthy diplomatic negotiations to get the Dutch to pay taxes, they failed to comply. The tax was increased in 1617, and still the Dutch refused to pay, increasing their armed convoys and continuing to plunder the British seas. James's son, Charles I, made another attempt to solve the problem when he set up the first of the Royal Fishing Companies, known as The Association for the Fishing, in 1632. His aim was to build and operate boats similar to the Dutch busses. This, too, was unsuccessful, and six years later the enterprise had collapsed. [61]

In the long saga of Scotland's failure to make more profit from her seas, there is not much progress until the 1750s, when it became clear that Britain must rebuild its navy. Since the fishing industry has always been an important training ground for the navy, the London parliament now turned its mind to the problem, deciding that it was time to promote and develop a new fishing enterprise. They had noticed a reduction in Dutch busses in recent years. So if they were to capture the market, something must be done quickly.

The plan was, again, to copy the Dutch busses, and to do this The Society of Free British Fishery was set up in 1750. There was investment and some successes. The government's method of developing larger boats was to pay an incentive 'bounty' to them. So fleets of larger decked boats were built by speculators, mainly merchants, but some wealthy ship's masters also invested. While previously the crews owned their small boats and all had a share in the profits, now the crew held no shares and were hired on agreed wages.

The largest numbers of Scottish busses at this time operated out of Greenock, Rothesay and Campbeltown, all positioned well out of reach of the Dutch busses. The flaw in the system, however, was that profits were dependent on the bounty, which was reduced, after protest by those with boats too small to claim it. In the 1785 Fisheries Act, a bounty was also given to small boats on each individual cured barrel. By 1800, however, the investors began to withdraw their capital and yet another attempt to develop a successful fishing industry failed.

The latter half of the 1700s was not the best time, politically, for this project to succeed. There was the disruption of the Seven Years war (1756–1763) followed by the war in the American colonies (1776–1783). Only when there was a more settled period, and a better knowledge of the seas and the needs of the people, did something more effective and lasting begin to develop. This came, not from a royal decree or an enlightened government, but from the powerful arguments and revealing evidence marshalled by some dedicated individuals.

The first of these was James Anderson, a Glasgow University professor who wrote on the need to develop the Northern fisheries in 1777 and 1783.[62] He was followed by John Knox, a retired bookseller who made sixteen tours of Scotland, and wrote a series of books on developing the fisheries in 1795.[63]

Knox argued that the British should be investing in the Highlands and Islands, and not in the American colonies. The fish in the seas were plentiful. The people were industrious. But poverty and distress was everywhere and emigration was inevitable if nothing was done. Knox suggested that fishing villages and boats should be built at strategic locations with all the necessary fishing infrastructure, including curing facilities. A government committee was set up, and Anderson was sent on an official tour to report back to the committee.[64]

The outcome, in 1786, on the recommendation of a government committee, was *The British Society for extending the Fisheries and improving the Sea Coasts of this Kingdom* (later known as The British Fisheries Society). Also influential was The Highland Society of London, which had been set up in 1778 by twenty-five 'gentlemen of Scotland', who had formed the society at a meeting in the Spring Garden Coffee House in London, to consider what 'might prove beneficial to the Highlands'.[65] Among their concerns was relief for distressed Highlanders, and in particular a concern to develop fishing. In the course of eight years they had attracted many members who had subscribed a considerable amount of money.

Now things started happening: there was much deliberation, of course, on how and where to develop. There was much interest, too, in the Society's ideas, particularly among the existing landowners and other merchants and traders, some of whom had already started setting up their own small fishing companies. They had built curing and storehouses, and even built new villages. Plockton, Dornie and Kyleakin were created by landowners at this time, with the crofter-residents given land provided they also fished.

So far The British Fisheries Society was a positive force in an increasingly desperate situation. Its initial concern was the relief of distress in the North West, and in this area it attempted to build (between 1790 and 1798) new fishing communities with sheltered harbours, piers, boat-building facilities, curing and storehouses, croft houses with some land, schools and churches. Ullapool, the most successful, was set up so that the land the new settlers were given would provide them with some of their food supply, but not all, so they had to fish. At Lochbay on Skye, the land provided was much more fertile – so the crofters were less inclined to fish commercially. At Tobermory on Mull, wealthier men engaged in trade and commerce were attracted to the settlement. And though the aim was to develop fishing, in fact the town developed as a successful trading port with a limited amount of fishing.[66]

In the early years of the 1800s, the Society turned its attention east to Caithness, also a crofting county. Here, there were fewer problems with crofters who were reluctant to risk abandoning their crofts to become professional fishermen. Also, the herring shoals were becoming more plentiful here, and there were already some small fishing communities which had become largely dependent on fishing for their livelihood. Some had even organised their own curing houses. The Dutch by now had become less dominant in this area, and the most successful venture, initiated by the Society, was set up at Wick in 1803.

The Scots never did 'ding the Dutch', who left of their own accord, for their own reasons, in the 1700s. Swedish and Norwegian ships, however, began to appear in Scottish waters, also fishing for herring. But now the Scots were better organised to reap for themselves the benefits of the plentiful shoals of herring around their shores.

6 Herring Fishing
Crofter-Fishing, Loch Fyne, around 1840

Her husband and son are asleep in a wooden 'box' bed, with shutters to keep out the light, while she sits at the croft house door quietly working on a low stool. They've been out all night at the herring and came home with a creel-full of *sgadain taighe* (house herring). She separates out some extra-plump fish and puts them in a pail for their mid-day dinner.

Now she gets to work on the remainder. Picking up a herring in her left hand, belly-up, she slides her small sharp-pointed knife into its throat. With the knife still in her hand she howks out the long gut and the gills. In a flash she's on to the next one.

Speedy with practice. There's no saying how many millions of herring she's gutted in her day. Not sitting on a stool at her croft house doorway, but as one of the *clann nighean an sgadain* (herring lassies) standing from early morning till dusk, in all weathers, surrounded by fish and salt and splattered from head to toe with blood and guts.

Aye, it was a messy job, no doubt about that. But there were good times too... travelling . . . seeing new places . . . lots of fun with the other girls . . . When the work was done, of course, there was never much time for fun among the piles of herring. But they made up for it when they got off on a Saturday night. Always a dance to look forward to, once they'd done their best to get the smell of herring out of their hair and skin. But that was impossible.

'You a herring lassie?' the boy would say as he sniffed her hair. How could she deny it?

When she married, her days of *followin' the herrin'* were over. Now her eldest daughter is a herring lass. Up at dawn as the fleet comes in from the night's fishing, fingers bandaged with *clooties* (strips of cloth) to protect them from the sharp knife and the corrosive salt.

She'll be in Stornoway on the isle of Lewis by now. In the thick of it. Later, she'll follow the shoals when they move northwards on their journey round the top of the country and into east coast seas. She'll not likely be home till the autumn. Just three of them left at the croft now with her other two sons gone to crew on the herring fleet.

Now the house herring are gutted and *roused* (sprinkled with salt), she takes them over to the byre where the herring barrel sits in a corner, cleaned-out and ready. She bends over and begins layering them tightly, heads to tails, sprinkling over the salt which will preserve them as she finishes each layer.

Though she has a cow for milk and butter, and land to grow potatoes, turnips and kale, it's this barrel of *sgadan saillte* (salt herring), and the pile of potatoes from her potato patch which will, hopefully, see them through the winter. Today, they will have the tasty treat for their dinner of fresh herring and some early potatoes she's just dug up. She walks over to the burn, pail of potatoes in one hand and pail of fresh herring in the other, to wash them.

Back in the kitchen she fills her biggest black pot with hot water from the kettle which has been hanging over the peat fire all morning. Now she puts in the potatoes, covers them with the lid and hooks the pot on the chain over the fire.

When they're ready, she drains off the water, lays the herring carefully on top and sprinkles them with some salt. To keep in all the hot steam from the potatoes which will cook the herring, she ties a piece of cloth round the lid to make sure none escapes. Then the pot goes back over the fire, a few notches higher up the chain, so the potatoes will not burn yet stay just hot enough to continue steaming the fish. She hears the men moving.

'The herrin' are near done,' she shouts through to them.

They draw up low chairs and sit in a semicircle round the fire. She lifts the pot off the hook and puts it on a low stool so they can all reach. As she lifts off the lid a heady aroma of steamy potatoes and rich herring fills the kitchen. After a word of grace, they dip into the pot. Fishing out a warm, mealy potato with one hand and with the other taking a nip from the silvery flank of the nearest herring.

The turning point in the fortunes of the Scottish herring fishers and their families, in the deprived crofting communities of the Highlands and Islands, was in the early 1800s at Wick in Caithness, when the herring curers began giving fishermen a guaranteed price for their catch before the season began, setting up an 'engagement system'.[67] Herring fishermen flocked to Wick. Herring curers got organised. There was not enough local labour for curing, so they started hiring seasonal, migrant women for gutting and packing, offering them their transport costs and a small advance fee up-front.

Wick Harbour in 1865 with herring boats along the waterfront and herring barrels stacked on the quays (by kind permission of The Wick Society, Johnston Collection).

So far, so successful. But the industry still had to produce a higher quality cure if it was to compete in Europe, where the Dutch had set the standard with their meticulous attention to detail. What might be acceptable to a West Indian slave or an Irish peasant (up to this time the export destination of most barrels of Scottish salt-pickled herring) was not going to please the more discerning European palate which the Dutch had been satisfying for centuries and reaping the rich rewards.

Fortunately, the government were not unaware of the fishery's potential, and in 1809 set up a system of government aid in the form of a 'bounty' (monetary bonus) to aid its success. A government fishery board was created with government-appointed fishery officers given the task of raising the quality of the Scots herring cure. They imposed rules: the herring had to be put into salt within twenty-four hours of landing; different qualities and sizes had to be packed separately and the barrels had to be labelled accordingly; no damaged fish were to be hidden among the lower layers of the barrel; and there were other more technical details, all aimed at producing a top quality cure to match the Dutch. The fishery officer stamped those barrels which had passed his inspection with the Crown Brand which was the government's guarantee of quality.[68]

By 1820, there were around 1,000 herring sailing drifters at Wick, and the whole Scottish coast had been divided up into regions, each with its own fishery officers. The first herring ports to develop gutting and curing yards after Wick were Fraserburgh (1810), Helmsdale (1813), Macduff, Banff, Portsoy and Cullen (1815), Lossiemouth and Burghead (1819), Peterhead (1820), and Lybster (1830).[69] Between 1825 and 1830 the government started phasing out the bounties, since by this time the fishery was established, and the industry accepted that the government's help had served its purpose.

With this sustained expansion, there was a migration of barely surviving, crofter-fishermen from the Highlands and islands to the east coast herring fishing.[70] Some settled in the east and never returned to their uneconomic west coast crofting life. Efforts to help the west coast Highlanders succeed at commercial fishing from their own locations had only been partially successful, and the economic problems of the area remained. Most of the crofters in the Highlands and Islands remained self-sufficient, with seafood a vital food resource, especially their barrel of salt pickled herring in the byre and their tatties from their potato patch. They were often their only saviour from starvation.

Until the 1830s, east coast herring fishermen operated from mid-July to mid-September, when the shoals were on their clockwise, migratory trip round the Scottish coast which started in the seas around the Firth of Clyde and the Argyll lochs in late spring and early summer. Until now, no east coast fishermen had dared to take their small, open-decked sailing boats through the notoriously treacherous Pentland Firth with the idea of catching more herring earlier in the year. In the 1840s, however, some adventurous seamen from the Banff area set off to navigate the feared stretch of water, following their Viking ancestors to new lands and hopefully new treasures to be discovered by men of daring. The design of their boats was, after all, descended from the original Viking longboat. Of course they made it through the Firth and set up in Stornoway, on the isle of Lewis, and in Castlebay on the isle of Barra.

Where they went the others followed: curers, gutters, packers, coopers, and fishery officers. New fishing stations with curing and storage yards were built. Soon the bays were filled with the sails of hundreds of herring drifters heading out to sea. And the season was extended. By the 1840s, the strict controls of the fishery officers had produced a much improved Scottish cure. It was just as well, for the West Indian market had collapsed as the slaves had been given their freedom in 1833. Also, the Irish peasants were in the grip of a devastating potato famine, and in such extreme poverty that they could no longer even afford the cheapest barrel of salt herring.

Instead, the improved Scottish herring cure was beginning to make its mark in the markets of Europe. In Germany, Russia and Poland there were new buyers, very well pleased with the Scottish cure. From the mid-1800s to the start of World War I in 1914 – with a blip of about seven years in the mid-1880s – the herring industry, and the entire Scottish fishing industry, flourished.

The railway line to Aberdeen was opened in 1850, bringing fast transport for perishable fish. It increased home consumption of all fresh fish, including herring which had a much higher unit value fresh than cured. The introduction, in the 1860s, of cotton drift nets which were five times lighter than previous hemp nets, meant the herring drifters could carry larger nets and catch more fish. The herring drifters were still open boats with sails, but now fishermen were having bigger boats built which could travel farther offshore and carry more herring.

Around this time, some Fife fishermen in their open-decked sailing drifters decided to follow the herring shoals south, moving out of Scottish waters and ending up in East Anglia, thus catching even more herring and extending the herring fishing into October and November. By the 1870s, larger-decked boats were being built with cabins, bunks and cooking galleys, which were even more comfortable for the longer trip to East Anglia. In the 1880s there were several hundred Scottish boats at Yarmouth and Lowestoft, accompanied by their Scottish gutters and packers. In 1853 the annual Scottish herring catch had been a mere 20,000 tons; by 1889 it was 100,000 tons.[71]

The 1880s also saw expansion into the far northern isles of Shetland. The Scottish herring fleet had not yet exploited this area, though it was an extremely rich herring area and had been one of the major locations of the Dutch herring busses. Earlier, in the 1800s, Shetland fishermen had tried fishing herring, unsuccessfully. Now they were involved in *haaf* (deep-sea) fishing for large white fish, mainly cod and ling. It was a system biased against the fishermen, who were 'tied' to landlords and merchants who left the fishermen with little or no profit at the end of the season when they were paid.[72]

The arrival of the Scottish herring fleet began their liberation from this tyranny, and many of the younger men began fishing for Scottish curers. They also bought secondhand boats from Scottish fishermen who were upgrading to a larger size. Soon, the Shetland herring fleet had grown from virtually nothing to around 400 herring boats. During the last twenty years of the century, the combined efforts of the local Shetlanders, and the Scottish herring fishers based in Lerwick, made Shetland the largest herring fishery of any single district in Scotland.[73] The Dutch had finally been dinged.[74]

Meantime the era of steam had begun to affect the herring fisheries, and the fishing industry in general, when there was a gradual changeover from sailing drifter to steam drifter in the late 1800s. Though the new boats were three times more expensive than the sailing drifters, they were also faster and bigger, so there was more space and more time to increase the herring catch. They remained, however, like the previous sailing drifters, fishermen-owned. By the early 1900s, records show that Scotland had a total of 1,000 curing yards and 900 steam drifters, eighty-five per cent owned by fishermen belonging to the North East coastal communities from around Aberdeen to Nairn.[75] A large number of the boat crews, however, continued to be crofter-fishermen from the west coast and the Hebrides, who usually spoke mostly Gaelic and understood only a little English.

By now lucrative markets had been found for the huge increase in volume of the quality Scottish cure, and in the early years of the 1900s the herring fishery was at its peak. Thousands of barrels of Scottish-cured salt-pickled herring went to Libau in Latvia where they were put on trains which took them to all corners of the Russian Empire. Some went on the Trans-Siberian Railway to Vladivostok. Some went as far as Baku in Tashkent, a journey which took fourteen days. From the Polish port of Königsberg (now Kaliningrad) they were sent to Warsaw, central and eastern Poland, western Ukraine and Odessa. One curing firm at Portsoy, on the Moray Firth, sold its entire cure of 46,000 barrels to a dealer in Königsberg who sent them all to Kiev in Russia.[76]

The German port of Hamburg dominated the trade in the *matje* cure (Scots, mattie) a less salty cure made from the small, fatty, early-summer, immature Scottish west coast herring. While heavier-salted, mature summer and autumn herring were acceptable with potatoes, the German middle-classes liked the high-quality matje cure with their expensive spring vegetables.[77] Hamburg had built large cold-storage facilities especially for this cure, which was more perishable than the more heavily salted, less fatty midsummer herring. They sold on their matjes to buyers throughout Germany, Poland and western Russia. St Petersburg also bought 200,000 barrels of matjes from Castlebay, Stornoway and Ireland for consumption by its own population of around a million and for the nearby cities of Peterhof and Gatzina.[78]

In this final era of a food culture where preserved fish dominated the market, the herring was king of the seas. Other fish were preserved too, but none came near the huge volumes of cured herrings. Not all were salted in barrels. While Scotland cornered the market in salt pickled herring (known as *whites*) there was also the smoked cure for herring which involved a time-consuming process of heavy salting, combined with hard smoking, which produced the dried-out, reddish-brown herring (known as *reds*) which were also packed tightly into barrels.[79]

East Anglia, with plentiful supplies of wood for smoking, was a major supplier of reds where they had been smoked since the 1200s. The cure was also common in Scotland, first recorded in 1423 when James I imposed an export tax on reds being shipped to the Mediterranean for Lent. In 1777, at both Dunbar and Eyemouth, there were smokehouses which could cure large quantities of reds.[80] The East Anglian autumn herring, with less fat content, were more suitable for making reds, while Scottish-caught herring, early in the season, were far too fatty. The piquant flavour of red herring was enjoyed best when it was skinned and grilled, then eaten with lots of butter, mustard and mashed potatoes. In the early 1900s, the pungent red herring, dressed up in fancy paper like a doll, was considered a lucky first-foot present at Hogmanay. Though now obsolete, the red herring lives on as a metaphor for a distraction from the real issue, a relic of the days when its strong smell was used as a decoy when hunting with dogs.

It also lives on in the milder cures which developed from it. The ancient traditions of salting and smoking fish were not abandoned just because it became possible to supply everyone with fresh fish. Curers continued curing. Generations continued to hand on salted and smoked fish-eating traditions. Those whose childhoods involved large pots of *mealy tatties 'n' saut herrin* continued to eat them. Some even continue to salt their own herring today. For these are foods which bind people to a locality and to those who have gone before them. Eating such a dinner, especially when families and communities have been uprooted, becomes a symbolic reconnection with a place and the memory of their ancestors.

EARLY RECIPES

Burnt Mound Cooking; Salt Fish – Cod, Ling, Tusk, brine-salted then dried;
Pickled Salmon with Spices; Salt Pickled 'White' Herring; Smoked 'Red'
Herring

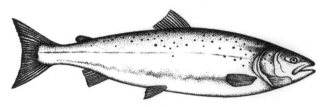

Salmon

Burnt Mound Cooking

Professor M. J. O'Kelly and his team experimented at a burnt-mound cooking site in County Cork, cooking a 10lb leg of mutton, wrapped in clean straw and tied with a twisted straw rope, in 3hrs and 40 mins (20 mins to the pound, plus 20 minutes). A large salmon of the same weight could be cooked in a fraction of this time.

10lb whole salmon, gutted
Foil to wrap it in
Large fire
Pile of medium sized stones (sandstone)
Deep pit lined with stones or wood and made watertight with clay (the size of the pit must be large enough to take all the stones necessary to heat the water plus the food to be cooked)

Light the fire. When hot add the stones.

Fill the pit with water.

When the stones are very hot, drop enough into the water to make it boil. If the stones are hot enough this should only take about half an hour.

Add the fish wrapped in foil.

Add two or three newly hot stones to keep the water simmering for about five minutes.

Leave the fish in the water till it cools. The latent heat in the pit will cook the fish through.

Salt Fish

salted in brine then dried: cod, ling and tusk

This method is a more heavily salted version of the naturally dried 'stockfish'. It was used by Shetlanders during the period of the *haaf fishery* which began in the early 1700s and lasted into the 1900s.

Large cod, ling or tusk
Salt

Cut across the neck, removing the head, to bleed fish immediately it is taken off the hook. Wash well in sea water as soon as landed and keep in sea water overnight.

Next day split from neck to tail with a very sharp knife. Wash carefully with a brush made of heather to remove all blood and slime, scrubbing from the neck towards the tail.

Strew the bottom of a large wooden vat with salt and put in a layer of fish, skin side underneath. Continue with layers of fish and salt. Cover with a layer of heavy stones to keep the fish weighted down under the brine which will develop.

Leave for three days and nights.

Take out the fish and rinse with a mixture of sea water and salt brine to prevent it developing a crust of crystallized salt when dried.

Leave to drip in a stack for three days.

Spread out, skin side underneath, on a flat, broad beach of small loose stones to allow some draught underneath. Prevent overheating in the sun.

At night, and when it rains, collect the fish into small heaps for the first two or three nights. When heaped in stacks, cover with nets and place pieces of wood and large stones on top to increase the pressure and remove more moisture.

Ling skin can be left in the sun, but cod skin may crack in the sun and should be laid out with flesh side uppermost. When properly dried, the thin, black peritoneal skin lining loosens and can be peeled off.

Keep in a dry store, lined with boards and covered with a double layer of nets.

Pickled Salmon

with spices

This early method became popular in London after the Union of 1707. Described as pickled the 'Newcastle Way', it was usually made with Scottish salmon. Though still common in the 1840s as quite a delicacy during Lent, when the railways arrived it became obsolete and died out.

Large salmon
Salt
For the pickle:
2ozs allspice
2ozs black pepper
1 gallon vinegar
Handful of salt

Scale salmon and split down the back, removing the backbone. Wash the fish and cut into 4-5 inch thick pieces.

Fill a pot with enough water to cover the salmon and bring to the boil.

Add some salt and put in the salmon. Cook for 23 minutes. Remove from the heat and leave to cool.

Make a pickle by mixing the allspice, pepper and vinegar and bring to the boil. When cold add a handful of salt and dissolve.

Put the salmon in a keg and pour over the pickle.

Leave to stand for one night, strain off the oil that may have risen to the top. Seal the keg.

Salt Pickled 'White' Herring
Dutch improved method – 1300s

Originally this was a rough and ready sprinkling of ungutted herrings with salt to keep for a few months, until the Dutch developed this gutted and washed method, packed into barrels to keep for years, which was widely traded throughout the world. Government regulations and inspections plus branding ensured the quality and supremacy of the Dutch cure.

Fresh herring
Salt

Make an incision in the throat to remove the gills and some of the viscera, including the long gut – the fish is now 'gipped'.

Sprinkle with salt. Turn over and over in the salt, making the fish 'roused'.

Sort according to size and quality.

Pack head to tail in barrel with salt sprinkled between the layers. The layers to be arranged alternately across each other.

Leave to stand ten days, when the herring will have sunk a little.

Fill up with herring from another barrel which was packed at the same time. Seal to make airtight. Brand with date of catch.

Smoked 'Red' Herring

Improved at Yarmouth in the early 1300s, they were made at other ports in England and Scotland. They figure in James I's stores at Berwick in 1299–1300 when he imposed an export duty on them. The Dutch also made 'red' herring, though in lesser quantity than 'white' herring.

6 tons – or 30 crans – of whole, ungutted, not too fatty herring
A lofty smoke house about 16ft square with a series of wooden frames reaching from the floor to the roof, with transverse beam 'loves', about 4ft apart, running from one side of the room to the other. The roof is covered with tiles which are not cemented and allow a good draught through the room
On the stone floor, about 16 fires are laid consisting of oak billets which give the best colour

At sea, immediately after catching, the herring is lightly layered with some salt.

When landed it is washed to get rid of the salt.

Then it is layered again with salt and left for 14 days.

After being washed again, 25 fish are hung on a spit – 'speated' or 'rived' through the gills and mouth.

To Smoke:

The spits are placed in rows one above another, with the ends of the spits resting on the beams.

Fires are lit and kept burning for 2 days, then allowed to go out and the fish allowed to drip and drain for a day. Then the fires are lit again and the same procedure is repeated: burning for two days, out for one day.

This continues for 14 days, when the fish are thoroughly cured or 'high dried'.

Then they are packed into barrels. When full, the lid is pressed down tightly with a screw press, then more are added.

Usually there are 650 full-sized fish to a barrel or more if the fish are smaller.

SOURCES

O'Kelly, M.J., 'Excavations and experiments in ancient Irish cooking places', *Journal of the Royal Society of Antiquities of Ireland* 95, 1954

Cutting, C.L., *Fish Saving*, 1955

Renfrew, Jane, *Food and Cooking in Prehistoric Britain, History and Recipes*, 1985

Wood, Jacqui, *Prehistoric Cooking*, 2001

SEAFOOD REGIONS
East and West Regional Heritage

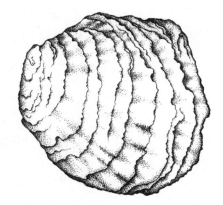

native oyster

The Regions

Despite migration from one area to another, it is possible to link fishing communities around the coast with some distinct regional variations in their seafood heritage. If we make an east west divide, the east coast, generally regarded as the coastline between the border with England and northernmost tip of Caithness, is notable for having developed the greatest number of successful fishing communities and some unique white fish cures. Since their land resources are more like those of the north east coasts of Caithness and Sutherland than the west coast, the Orkney Islands have been included in this area. Shetland, more usually associated with Orkney regionally, has been linked instead with the north west coast of the Highlands and Islands. These are all areas with similar limitations in land resources and therefore are more dependent on the sea for survival.

A distinctly different area on the east coast was around the Firth of Forth, whose fishing heritage was dominated by rich shellfish beds and a large urban market in nearby Edinburgh. Similarly, on the west coast there was a distinctly different area around the Firth of Clyde and on the Ayrshire coast, where there were more opportunities to develop a lucrative fishing industry linked to a large urban market in nearby Glasgow.

The fishing traditions which developed are richly varied: from the Shetlander far out in the Atlantic, deep sea fishing for large white fish for a worldwide market, to the Newhaven oyster-dredger trawling the prolific shellfish beds of the sheltered Firth of Forth to satisfy nearby Edinburgh's passion for oysters.

Crofter-fishers, 1800s

In the seven crofter counties of the north and west, for most of their history the descendents of Neolithic farmer-fishers eked a living from a mix of farming and fishing. It is a system demanded by the natural resources of the area, where the land fails to provide an adequate food supply and seafood is essential for the local population's survival. The word 'croft' was first used only to refer to arable and grazing land, but by 1800 it was applied to both the land and the dwelling house. It was the least productive system in the farming hierarchy at this time. Not only had people in the crofting counties poor natural resources, they usually had too small an area of land to increase their output and virtually no capital assets. Most had a cow for milk and cheese; sheep, goats and/or cattle on grazing land, and perhaps a horse for ploughing. All crofter-fishers at this point were tenants, paying a rent both in cash and in produce to a landlord, but with no security of tenure.

Exploitation of these communities took different forms. In some areas landlords kept reducing their amount of arable and grazing land. Others moved the crofters from fertile glens to the less fertile coastline. At other places they demanded a fishing tenure, tied to the croft, so the crofter-fishermen had to provide his fishing expertise during several months of the year, usually making significant profits for the landlord but very little for themselves, in some cases accumulating debt instead. In the case of the least fortunate, the landlords simply evicted their tenants to increase their estate's grazing, arable or sporting land.

The Crofters' Holding Act of 1886 was designed to give the crofting communities better protection from landlords and their agents. It did not, however, solve the problems of the community's struggle to survive, or change the fact that fishing remained vital to their subsistence economy. It did, however, give crofters security of tenure for their family and their heirs.

By this time Scotland's fishing industry was flourishing. In 1882 The Fisheries Board had been reconstituted and given expanded responsibilities for Scotland. The results for 1883 show that almost half the total of Scottish fishermen were crofter-fishers, mostly island-based. The Outer Hebrides, Shetland and Orkney had the greatest numbers, while there were also significant numbers based on Skye and at Lochcarron, Fort William and Campbeltown.

Though they were all practising the same crofting system of subsistence survival, each region had its own distinct variations. Some related to extreme remoteness, such as the isolated islands of Foula, Fair Isle and St Kilda, where survival depended on seafood, especially the gathering of seabirds' eggs and also catching seabirds from sea cliffs or at sea while they were fishing. Others arose from their proximity to certain fishing grounds, such as the northern areas of Shetland, which are a short distance from very rich white fishing grounds at the edge of the continental shelf.

Besides these regional differences, large numbers of crofter-fishers supplemented the meagre subsistence lifestyle on their croft by migrating to other parts of the country where they could get work as crew on a fishing boat. This was particularly evident with those who 'followed the herring', as the shoals travel clockwise round the country beginning in the south-west in spring.

Fisher-villages, 1800s

Like the crofter-fishers, all people living at the coast in other areas of the country also had Neolithic farmer-fishers ancestors. Many had similar smallholdings to the crofters, though usually benefitting from a more favourable climate and a better quality of arable and grazing land. As they had done in the past, so they continued to harvest the seas. What changed their fortunes compared with the crofter-fishers was easier transportation and easier access to markets and large centres of trade.

Even in areas some distance from the major centres of trade, small fisher-villages developed wherever small groups of families gathered together at a convenient shingle or pebble beach, where they could pull their boats safely out of the water. They traded independently in nearby markets, securing basic essentials often by bartering their fish for meal, butter and cheese etc. Otherwise they could sell to fish merchants, who provided them with much needed cash.

Gradually, coastal fisher-villages formed into distinct communities with a common purpose, setting them apart from other rural villages. The custom of young people marrying into other fisher families, who had the same values and the same demanding lifestyle, meant traditions were passed on, naturally from one generation to the next. Continuity was established. The proliferation of certain surnames in these early fisher-villages is evidence of this.

As trade developed, the need for fisher-villages to grow crops and tend animals decreased, and they became full-time fishing communities. In the latter part of the 1800s, harbour boards were set up and many small fisher-villages which had continued to push out, and pull up their boats onto the beach had piers and safe harbours built, which enabled them greatly to increase the size of their boats and their general efficiency.

Others moved to larger trading ports, yet despite living in large towns they still kept their distinct fisher-village community in a separate area of the town, usually somewhere near the harbour, known as the *fisher-toun*. Though there were seasonal fluctuations in the fishing industry, the men of the fisher-toun were always sure of work as crew on trading ships, or as pilots for ships going in and out of the port. They also migrated with the herring, taking their boats to Shetland or over to the west coast or the Outer Hebrides, as well as south to East Anglia. All of which created an entirely different fishing heritage to the crofter-fishers of the Highlands and Islands.

EAST

1   East Coast

The Auchmithie fishwife's luckens[81] – 1890

As soon as Nell was old enough to spend a whole Saturday walking with her mother round the neighbouring farms selling fish, she had begged to go with her. Every farm kitchen was different, but the welcome was always the same.

'Come awa in and tak that load aff your back. You'll be ready for a cup of tea.'

After the tea cups were laid out, the farmer's wife got out the biscuit tin.

'Let's see what's in here for Nell.'

While Nell went out to play in the yard – her biscuit safely tucked away to eat later on the road – the two women got on with the business. First the chat. Her mother, travelling round the country, was always a rich source of news and gossip, so it was not until this was shared over the cup of tea, that the fishy contents of her creel were investigated.

The farmer's wife picked out a cod, large enough for their dinner tonight, and a pile of whiting for a breakfast fry-up tomorrow. Then she turned to the basket of *luckens* (coppery-brown, smoked haddock). Nell's mother made a great job of the smoking and could never make enough for all her customers.

Happy memories of these carefree days came back to her as she worked, gutting and de-heading haddock on the same grassy stretch, half-way down the cliff face, where her mother had stood so many years before. Below her was the pebbly beach, the fishing boats pulled up after the men had landed the day's catch. Above was the row of *but an' ben* fisher houses, perched on the edge of the cliffs which surrounded the sheltered cove. She put her fish into a large basin with a wooden lid and climbed back up to the village. Her family were waiting for their supper.

It was the early hours of the next day when she joined the rest of the village wives and fishermen husbands, making their way down the cliff path in the dim light. The women carried the baited lines coiled in a creel, the men their keg of water and a canvas bag with a supply of oatcakes and cheese.

When they got to the beach, Nell, like the other wives, took off her boots and stockings and tucked up her skirts and petticoats to above her knees to help push the boat off the pebbles and into the sea. The men push too. But not into the water, since they can't get their feet wet. So her husband jumps onto her sturdy back and she picks her way carefully the few yards into the sea and he jumps into the boat. Stockings and boots back on, she climbs back up the cliff path with the other wives to have another few hours sleep before the children are up.

Then she's back to her haddock. Salting first to add flavour and firm up the skin. Then tying them in pairs by the tail and hanging them over wooden rods to harden the skin so they will 'take' the smoke. She has some ready for 'the barrel' – a half whisky barrel, partly sunk into the ground to keep it secure in high winds.

She lights the fire in its base, and when it's going nicely, she lays the rods of fish on top. Finally, she covers the fish with layers of smoke-blackened hessian sacking according to the weather: more layers if it's dry and windy, fewer if it's wet and windless. Today there's a har coming in from the sea and not much of a breeze, so she only puts a few layers over the fire.

Controlling the heat in the smoke, as her mother has taught her, is the secret of a good lucken. A few minutes too long over the hot smoke and the haddock will lose its moistness and flavour. A few minutes too short and it will be wet and flabby and will not keep.

A billowing haze of smoking fish rises through the hessian and wafts its way up the cliff, joining the smoke from other fishwives' barrels. The villagers up above are in no doubt about what's going on down below. As Nell sits by her barrel, she reaches into the pocket of her apron and gets out a sock she's knitting for her husband.

No other area of the Scottish coastline has sustained so many fishing communities as the east coast. From Wick to Eyemouth, they vary from large towns to small villages, from those still in the fishing business to obsolete fishing ports. They have all traded in every kind of seafood from around the coast and beyond. Their prosperity was built during the 1800s, largely due to prolific shoals of herring off their coasts, but also with some help from the haddock. What made the names of some villages live on, long after the fisherfolk had stopped fishing, is nothing to do with the herring but all about the special smoked haddock cures which can be credited to the first intrepid fishwives who perfected the methods, saw their commercial potential, and established the tradition which they handed on from one generation to the next.

In the mid-1800s, fishing communities along this coastline were involved in the successful herring industry which kept them busy for most of the summer and autumn. For the rest of the year, they got out the long lines and went in search of white fish and the plentiful haddock. A small fishing village might have a few hundred inhabitants and twenty or thirty boats pulled up on the beach. Piers and harbours were not built for them until the late 1800s. Until then, fisher-houses had to be near a good pebbly beach for pulling up the boats. It was a system which had not changed much since Neolithic times for those families who had made fishing their main source of income. They went out in the early hours of the morning to fish in small open boats with long lines, baited to catch haddock, whiting, cod, ling, skate, dogfish, mackerel and saithe, which could be found fairly close inshore. Then they returned in the late morning with the catch when their wives took over, going off to sell what they could, and preserving the remainder.

While a man fished, if it was fine, every day of the week except Sunday, the weekly routine for a woman was more varied. Two days of the week, usually Mondays and Thursdays, were smoking days when she preserved the surplus fish. Tuesdays, Wednesdays, Fridays and Saturdays – besides seeing to her domestic chores, baiting lines and carrying the men into the boats etc. – she went to 'the country'.

Auchmithie fishwife making smokies around 1900 (© The Fraser Collection).

Travelling on foot, usually round the nearby farms and inland villages, she was a couthy character, wearing a distinctive form of dress which differed from one area to another in style and colour. But on her head was usually a white starched mutch (bonnet) which tied under her chin and framed her browned, weatherbeaten face. Her long skirt, reaching almost to her ankles, was made from navy-blue woollen worsted cloth, thickly gathered at the waist. Underneath were her cotton petticoats. Tucked inside her skirt was a linen blouse, and on top a home-knitted cardigan and a heavy shawl for when it was cold. She wore an apron with pockets over her skirt. On her feet were stout black leather boots over black woollen stockings. When she went to the country, she made a pad to support the heavy creel of fish she carried on her back, usually just by tying a string round her thick skirts and hitching them up at the back.

While the men, who fished this coast in the century from 1850 to 1950, had their fishing boats and methods completely transformed, from three men fishing long lines in an open boat to steam trawling, many of the women carried on working as fishwives through this transition. They smoked surplus fish, wore the traditional fishwife's dress and carried creels of smoked and fresh-off-the-boats fish round the houses – often accompanied by some of their children – where they continued to find a seat and welcome cup of tea. Such was the strength of tradition among these hardy women who played such an important role in holding together the close-knit fishing communities of this coastline.

In every fishing community there was much intermarrying between families. Only those brought up in a fishing community knew how to survive the rigors of their precarious occupation. In the Auchmithie area, the prevailing fisher families were Swankies, Cargills and Spinks, all names with a Norse derivation, some of whom have been 'hot' smoking haddock for at least five generations. This area, like others, was invaded by the Vikings who later settled down as peaceful Norse immigrants. (A large metal disk of Viking design has been found by archaeologists in the Auchmithie area.)[82]

Though the Viking-named fisher families who continue to make the cure have no evidence of how or when it developed, their Viking ancestors were highly skilled fish preservers, widely travelled in Europe. Among those who settled on this east coast it's possible there were some who knew how to 'hot' smoke fish in holes in the ground. Archaeological evidence of this method was found in the 1960s at a site in northern Poland beside Lake Biskupin, by Zdzislaw Rajewski, a Polish archaeologist who dated his find to Viking times, around 900 AD.[83] Beside several hearths were 34 bag-shaped holes in the ground with fish debris and signs of a fire at the foot. On the basis of the information and the artefacts they had collected, Rajewski and a team of archaeologists worked with some fish-curing specialists to discover how the hearths, and the holes, would have been used for a 'hot' smoking process. Then they had a go themselves.[84] Rajewski concluded that some time later the holes were abandoned and the smoking equipment was moved to ground level when 'big barrels' were used for hot smoking fish. They found evidence of such smoking barrels being used in Poland in the 1400s as a minority cure (as at Auchmithie) to make a shorter-keeping but better-tasting cured fish compared with the universal, long shelf-life salted cure.

The Auchmithie lucken became known as an Arbroath smokie when the Auchmithie fishing community moved south to the better-equipped port of Arbroath in the early 1900s and took their cure with them. Though they no longer used barrels to make their 'smokies', they designed a square brick smoker, still calling it 'the barrel' and continuing to use the same smoking method. The original barrel method continues to be used by Iain Spink at markets and events.

Other white fish cures made by these remarkable east coast fishwives include the *spelding*, a split white fish from the Scots *spelder*, to split. The bone was removed, then the fish was washed in the sea and hung up to dry in the sun and wind. The earliest mention of them on this coast appears in the records of *Aberbrothock* (Arbroath) in 1489 as 'speldingis'.[85]

Though they were able to cure large numbers of speldings on pebbly beaches when it was dry, when it rained they had to take them inside, hanging some from the rafters or in the wide, open chimneys of their slow-burning peat fires. Enterprising fishwives on the coast between Stonehaven and Aberdeen, were the first to recognise that a salted and smoked spelding tasted a lot better than just a salted one. So they built *bothans*: wooden smoking sheds, about four feet square and seven feet high with *runners* (bars for supporting rods of fish). Often their bothan was conveniently situated on a strip of land between the house and the sea. There was no chimney, so that when the fire was lit in the middle of the earth floor, it smouldered and the shed filled with flavourful cool smoke.

Haddock was the preferred fish for this cure: beheaded, gutted, split-open, and washed to remove traces of blood. Next, layered in a tub, with a sprinkling of salt between, they were left for about half an hour. Then the fish were removed and hung onto *speets* (spits) to dry off a little. For how long depended on the weather, but the aim was to develop a shiny surface which would 'take' the smoke. Finally the speets were hung up on the runners to hold them in place and the smoking began. A bothan could hold several dozen fish. The fire had to be carefully regulated, damped down to keep the smoke 'cool' so the fish would not cook.

The first record of this distinctive cure is in 1707, when it is described by an English writer as: 'Findon-Haddocks, which abound at Aberdeen, being dry'd, eat with a marrow Taste, and are much admir'd by strangers'.[86] They were commonly known as *Finnans*, from the vernacular pronunciation of the small fishing community at Findon, just south of Aberdeen. It was here that the local fishwives are credited with pioneering the cure which was soon copied in all fishing villages between Aberdeen and Stonehaven. In its early days, a Finnan was smoked in the distinctive flavour of peat smoke. As in blending a whisky, the fishwives soon acquired the skills to judge just the right balance of astringent peat to create their memorable cure.

The word was spread further afield, the story goes, by a guard on the stage-coach which ran between Aberdeen and Edinburgh, who suggested to one of the fishwives that he might try selling some of her excellent Finnans to his fish-retailer brother in Edinburgh. The delicious new fish cure was soon in great demand in the capital, and by the 1820s a regular trade had developed.[87] Here was an opportunity for commercial fish curers, and with the popularity of the cure and the plentiful supplies of haddock, they began building large smoking sheds and had soon established the industrial curing of Finnans.[88]

The cures from different areas had subtle differences and were known according to their location: Moray Firths; Bervies; Buckies; or Eyemouth and Glasgow Pales. The factory-curers had their eye on the markets in the developing industrial towns of central Scotland as well as the London market which railways made possible. Meanwhile, the fishwives who had given the cure its original name continued to make it in their artisanal way, selling it to their loyal customers on their trips to the country. While the urban Central Belt bought factory-cured Finnans, the people on the east coast continued to buy their fishwife's bothan cure. They knew the difference.

Though factory-cured smoked haddock had taken on a number of local names, those made in and around Aberdeen kept the Finnan tag which eventually became the generic name, the fish often called a *finnan-haddie* or just a *finnan*. In 1856 the first finnan-smoking Grimsby smokehouse was built, and in the next twenty years a further forty were built to cure Grimsby finnans, causing much concern to factory-cured finnan producers in Aberdeen, though probably not to the bothan-curing fishwives.

The factory-cured finnan's representative was John Ross Jr., of Muchalls, near Stonehaven. He had just won first prize at the Edinburgh Fisheries Exhibition in 1882 for 'Real Peat-smoked' Aberdeen finnan-haddies.[89] And to set the record straight, he produced a pamphlet called *The Real Aberdeen Finnan Haddie: Where and How it is Made*.[90] In it he describes his own labour-intensive technique, in answer to why his cure was so much more expensive than other cures such as 'Eyemouths or English-cured'.

Were he to return today he would surely be even more upset to discover so many variations on the finnan theme, few matching his version of the real thing. Does this alteration of a food linked to a place, and with a history and commercial reputation, matter? The Spink family, still making real Arbroath smokies in the

2000s, thought that it did, and were upset to discover a different, and by their standards, an inferior version of the Arbroath smokie on the market. Made by inventive food industry technicians using computer-controlled smoking kilns, some were not – like the Grimsby finnans – even made in Scotland.

To the rescue of Spink, other Arbroath smokie producers, and anyone else wishing to protect the integrity of a commercial product with a regional or national history, came one of the advantages of Britain's union with Europe. It was sparked first by the French, who, fiercely protective of their national and regional food traditions, had made a suggestion to the European Parliament that it should set up a European Culinary Heritage project to codify all foods with a traditional or regional affiliation, so that they could be defended if their quality was under threat.

The idea was that traditional foods should be the property of a place and its community, rather than the trademarked possession of an individual or company.[91] The new weapon which the EU first introduced in 1993 was designed to give commercial producers of local, regional and traditional foods the legal opportunity to protect the integrity of their products, in the case of the Arbroath smokie, for example, with a PGI (Protected Geographical Indication).[92]

The successful outcome has secured the cure's future, bringing it several national awards. But the greatest reward is that those who buy it can feel confident they are eating a real Arbroath smokie with an ancient east coast fishing heritage, possibly of Viking origins.

2   Firth of Forth

An Edinburgh tavern oyster-ploy – September, late 1700s

As the night darkens, Stewart checks on those downstairs opening the oysters. He picks up an opened shell and lifts it to his lips. Opening his mouth he tilts his head back and in goes the cool oyster with its clean, refreshing sea juices. Enjoying its succulence in his mouth he squashes it slowly, savouring every drop of its special flavour. Finally he swallows, but its aftertaste lingers long after it is gone. It's good to have them back.

He picks up a couple of *brods o' eisters* (round wooden boards piled with several dozen opened oysters) and takes them up to his customers.

'Grand eisters tonight,' he says as he lays down the boards in the middle of the table.

Already there is a loaf of bread and a crock of butter on the table beside cruets of vinegar and pepper. The rooms are filling up as Stewart goes off for more oysters, and his eager customers get their first taste of the season too. Some add a drop of vinegar and a pinch of pepper, while others add nothing, preferring, like Stewart, the pure sea flavours without any distraction.

There are other oyster taverns down the Old Fishmarket Close, but Stewart's is a favourite. Those who settle for the night beside the glowing fire in the flickering yellow light of the tallow candles, are here to enjoy a good night's entertainment and to celebrate the oysters' return, now their summer spawning is over.

His oysters are delivered daily, tightly packed in wooden barrels, carried up the hill into the town from the pier at Newhaven on a horse-drawn cart. Such is the demand that he can sell a couple of thousand a night.

Auld Reekie (old smoky) as it's known, is the network of streets, wynds and closes between the Castle at the top of the hill and the royal palace at the bottom, once enclosed by a medieval wall. Such are the cramped conditions in its five to six storied tenement 'lands' (homes), that most citizens spend much of their days, and nights, in their cosy local tavern. They are at the heart of city life. Some have rooms large enough for a party, while others are small snuggeries for two, called 'coffins'. Furnished simply with tables and benches or chairs, there are shelves round the walls for spent bottles, rows of hooks for pewter drinking pots of different sizes – tappit hens, chopins and mutchkins.

Drams of gin and pots of porter are poured. Bread is buttered and eaten while pausing between the oysters. More brods o' eisters are ordered by the enthusiastic tavern crowd. Tonight, there is a jolly party in one of his largest rooms. Amongst them, a gathering of fashionable ladies who have abandoned the dainties of tea-and-cards for an oyster-ploy.

In Auld Reekie's relaxed manners of the day such a lady can be elegantly tipsy, without any loss of face. All classes mix socially in the tavern. Publishers, street-traders, cabbies, shopkeepers, printers, judges, barristers and dispossessed Highlanders – everyone is welcome as they celebrate the oyster's return. Heads back, mouths open, catching every drop of sea juices from the Forth oysters.

And as the night wears on, a Highlander with a fiddle strikes up a lively jig and a space is cleared for dancers. The fun continues with strathspeys and reels.

Then one of the ladies is persuaded to sing a lilting Lowland love song. The fiddler follows it with a melancholy Highland air as Stewart appears, carrying a large bowl of hot punch which he's flavoured with ale, brandy, sugar and lemons. There is a ladle and tray of small glasses.

'Nae lang t'll the drum,' he says.

And as they sip the warming drink, they can hear the familiar sound of the city officers marching round the town beating out the 'ten o' clock drum'. Time for all revellers to make their way home. Unless, of course, they have disappeared under a table and are already fast asleep, where the kindly Stewart will leave them undisturbed till the morning.

Not all Forth oysters are carried into Edinburgh by a horse and cart. Not all are consumed in an old-town tavern oyster-ploy.[93] Fishwives also do a roaring trade in the streets, carrying heavy creels of oysters, and other fish and shellfish, on their strong backs, trudging up the hill from Newhaven. They join other traders who have pushed their *hurlies* (barrows) from the outskirts of the city with their fruits and vegetables to the city market. The fishwives have no barrow to sell from, so they lay out their fish and shellfish round their creel.

'Caller ou! Caller ou!' (fresh oysters) they shout.

'There is no spot on earth where oysters were enjoyed in such perfection as the head of Old Fishmarket Close . . . swallowed alive with its own gravy the moment it was opened by the fishwife,' says Mistress Margaret (Meg) Dods (1829).[94] But earlier than this, it is the poet, Robert Fergusson, who immortalises Forth oysters in his poem *Auld Reekie* in 1773:

> September's merry month is near
> That brings in Neptune's caller cheer,
> New oysters fresh;
> The halesomest and nicest gear
> O' fish or flesh.

Later, another poet, James Hogg (the Ettrick Shepherd), also gets lyrical about Forth oysters, when he meets with his cronies in Ambrose's Tavern:

Hoo mony hunder eisters are there on the brod, Mr Awmrose? – Oh! Ho! Three brods! – One for each o' us – A month without an R has nae richt being in the year. Noo gentlemen, let naebody speak to me for the neist half-hour . . . Help Mr North to butter and bread, – and there sir, – there's the vinnekar cruet. Pepper awa, gents.[95]

Such a quantity of oysters at one sitting! Other sources suggest that three to four dozen was a more likely number for the most enthusiastic oyster-lover. They were a supper item, also much enjoyed by the eminent judge, Lord Cockburn (1779–1854) who would have had a barrel delivered to his kitchen. He liked to invite his friends to impromptu suppers, and on one occasion scribbles the following note to his friends – '14 Charlotte Square, Saturday. My Dear .....,' then he sketches the layout of the supper table with 'Oysters' in the centre flanked on either side by 'Cold Beef' and 'Two Hens'. The drink was punch. The final detail was the time: 'Tonight before 10'.[96]

Oysters were also used widely in cooked dishes. According to early cookery books, they were added – by the hundred – to sauces and stews. But it is the fresh oyster which remained the gourmet's delight, as Faujas de St Fond, a well-travelled French Commissioner of Wines with a discerning palate, recalls tasting Forth oysters *au naturel* at the fishing village of Prestonpans in the 1780s. Fresh out of the sea, 'plump' and with an 'exquisite' flavour, they were so fine, he says, that the fishermen were packing them in barrels and had no trouble finding a market in England and Wales.[97]

Though there were oyster beds at other locations around the Scottish coastline – in the Clyde and Solway, on Skye, Lewis, Orkney and Shetland – none were as extensive or as celebrated as those in the Firth of Forth. And in no other part of the country did the local population appear to consume them in such quantities.

There is prehistoric evidence of oysters and mussels in the mound at Polmonthill on the Forth, thought to contain between six and seven million oyster shells.[98] Though these were probably gathered by hand, the oyster dredge became the more usual method of gathering. In its earliest form it was a metal-framed trap, open at one end and covered with a net. It was attached by a rope to the stern of the boat and dragged along the bottom of the seabed, scooping the oysters off the rocks as the men rowed over the oyster beds. A five-manned boat could dredge several thousand oysters in a day.

Groups of fishing communities had formed into villages along the southern coastline of the Forth, at least by the 1400s, all within easy access of the Edinburgh market. Among them were, from east to west: Cockenzie, Port Seton, Musselburgh and Newhaven. There was also Edinburgh's port of Leith. All had interests in dredging oysters.

The best and most prolific oyster beds (thought to have measured around 129 square km)[99] were in the middle of the Forth and were claimed by the Newhaven fishermen. Not only James VI (1567-1625) but also Charles I (1625-1649) had, they claimed, granted them charters to the sole rights to this area. In addition, Newhaven claimed to have been given the sole rights to operate the oyster beds belonging to the city of Edinburgh under an even earlier charter of James IV (1488-1513). It was estimated that in peak years the beds yielded around thirty million oysters annually.[100] In effect, Newhaven's Society of Free Fishermen, as they were called, had established an oyster-fishing monopoly in the best areas.

Not all went according to plan, however, since the city of Edinburgh disputed the authenticity of the King's charter. In the late 1690s, the city fathers, it seems, also had conservation concerns on their minds and tried to control the size of the oysters which the fishermen were removing from the beds, introducing a legal minimum size. They also tried to enforce the close season (May to August) when the oysters were spawning. All of which seems to have been regarded, by Newhaven fishermen, as unwelcome interference. Meanwhile, there was also trouble with other fishermen from neighbouring villages, who also disputed Newhaven's rights to the best oyster-fishing. There were arguments over boundaries, and it seems this wrangling went on during most of the 1700s.

Meanwhile, as the fame of the Forth oyster began to spread beyond the streets and taverns of Edinburgh, the volume of oysters dredged increased. Such was the market potential that in the 1770s a Leith merchant commissioned ten different shipping companies to take Forth oysters to London. Throughout the season, twelve ships were each carrying cargoes of between 350,000 and 400,000 oysters.[101] Packed in barrels they would keep fresh for a week or two. They were also being taken by the better-constructed turnpike roads to other parts of Scotland, particularly Glasgow. More exploitation involved the export of small oysters which, rather than being thrown back into the Forth beds, were being sold to restock English, French and Dutch beds. Not surprisingly, by the early 1800s, there were signs of decline of the once prolific Forth oyster beds, but still conservation attempts were having little success.

In 1814, the city did act by restricting fishing on its oyster beds and began charging fishermen rent. Though the Newhaven fishermen continued to claim

Open-air fish sale at Cockenzie in 1900. Fishwives share a joke with a fisherman surrounded by the fish laid out on the beach (East Lothian Library Service, licensor www.scran.ac.uk).

their sole right to fish the city's oyster beds, they were obliged to pay the rent, but continued to flout the city's attempts to make conservation rules. They did try, themselves, to restrict the daily catches of individual fishermen, but this was eventually given up as unworkable.[102]

This situation, it seems, continued for the next couple of decades until 1834, when the Newhaven fishermen acquired the sole rights to export oysters to London. This seems to have been the last straw for Edinburgh's Town Council who refused to renew Newhaven's lease in 1839, raised the rent, and gave a ten-year lease to George Clark, an Englishman. Disputes in court ensued and the unfortunate Clark withdrew within a few months.[103] Unmistakable signs of collapse of the oyster stocks were beginning to show in the 1870s, and despite more attempts to enforce conservation measures, by 1883–84 the Forth oyster fishing was more or less at an end.

Yet such was the appetite for native oysters that other locations where there were oyster beds, were now investigated. At Garelochhead on the Clyde, in

Argyll at West Loch Tarbert, in Loch Ryan in Galloway, in the Solway bays, in the Moray Firth, on the coasts round Skye, Orkney and Shetland: all had native oyster beds. None, it turned out, were anything like the size of the Forth beds but, nevertheless, the oyster-dredging boats began to take oysters from these places to satisfy demand. At Garelochhead it was reported, in 1887, that big boats were dredging a haul of thirty to fifty tons of oysters, which, needless to say, resulted in the demise of these beds too.[104]

Only at Loch Ryan in Galloway, where the oyster-bed charter was held by the local landowner, Sir William Wallace, whose family had been given the rights by William III (1689–1702) were there attempts to conserve stocks. Wallace appears to have been a lone activist on the conservation front. As early as the 1860s, unlike the rest of the country, he was not only re-seeding the beds, but also trying to control the fishermen's destructive habit of refusing to throw back small oysters. Disputes arose here too. In 1875 Wallace stopped all oyster-dredging on his beds, and for the next ten years set about restocking them. His success, however, was short-lived, as elusive oyster poachers soon depleted the stocks and were never caught.[105] Despite this, the Wallace family did not give up, and the oyster beds in Loch Ryan survived.

Some attempts were made by the Fisheries Board, with the act of 1885, to establish, firstly, the ownership of oyster beds, and, secondly, the need for the owners to restock, as Wallace had tried to do. By now, with their scarcity, native oysters were no longer a cheap street food and staple item of the national diet, but had become an expensive luxury. Their high value became their final undoing, as over-exploitation, despite some best intentions, continued.

What was unknown then about their breeding habits, but became an established scientific fact, was that there were certain conditions necessary for oyster fertilisation. The number of young oysters joining the population each year depended on a warm enough temperature for eggs to be released; a good food supply; not too fierce a current; and the availability of a suitable habitat. None of this would help, though, if there were too few oysters in the oyster bed. The most vital condition for reproduction was a high population density of existing oysters. So long as the population density was high, lots of oysters spawned together and lots of eggs got fertilised. But if there were too few oysters, or small populations became isolated, the oysters might spawn at different times and very few eggs would get fertilised.

Wallace may not have understood this fact when he battled to save Loch Ryan's native oysters, but his actions were always with the aim of increasing the oyster population. Despite the poachers on Loch Ryan, the beds nurtured by him have survived and continue to support Scotland's only 'managed' native oyster fishery, leased to an English company which also farms Portuguese oysters (*Crassotrea gigas*) in Jersey. Today's method of dredging on Loch Ryan – as Wallace tried to enforce – ensures that the fishermen have a place on the boat where they must sort the oysters immediately they are landed, and throw back all the small oysters.[106]

While oysters became the most famous seafood to come from the Firth of Forth, there were other thriving fisheries on both south and north coasts, with many strong fishing communities on the Fife coast at the *East Neuk* (corner), well-established in the centuries before the mid-1800s, when it became statutory to record fish landings. There was certainly a thriving salmon and sea trout fishery, as well as for herring. There were mussel beds, used mostly for baiting lines for catching haddock, cod and ling. Post the mid-1800s, the most important fisheries in the Forth area were the 'Lammas Drave' for white fish, lasting through August and September, and the 'Winter Herring', which lasted from January to March and reached peak landings in 1936, but had practically disappeared by 1946.

What has survived here is a fleet of creel-fishing boats catching lobster and brown crab. Most of the other species of fish and shellfish, once found in plenty in these waters, have suffered a similar fate to the native Forth oyster, commercially over-exploited over many centuries, so that many of the once thriving fishing communities have had to reinvent themselves. Yet the fishing culture remains strong.

On the Fife coast, fish and shellfish, mostly langoustine, is landed at Pittenweem. There are no oysters, but creel fishermen land supplies of crabs and lobsters also at Crail and St Andrews. There are seafood restaurants making this a feature on their menus, and the local community have taken up the cause of celebrating a wider range of seafood.[107] This area is also home to a fisheries museum in a building overlooking the harbour in Anstruther, the leading fishing port in this area throughout the herring boom of the early twentieth century. A hundred years on, the herring may have gone, but the memory, and the evidence, of the fishing heritage on this coast lives on.

3 Orkney

Gaeing tae the cuithes, 1850

On cold winter nights, when the wind howled in the chimney and the windows rattled in their frames, the family gathered round for a meal of boiled tatties and *saut cuithes* (hard-salted, young saithe). Taking a mouthful of bland mealie tattie, and strong-tasting fish, lubricated with a little sweet home-made butter, Mary remembered the summer nights in the boat 'gaeing tae the cuithes'.

Work was hard in the summer. Her father and her brothers were out at dawn to scythe the *bere* (a variety of barley) while she went off with her mother to milk the cows. Then there was yesterday's milk – most of the cream already skimmed off – waiting to be heated gently till it curdled, then hung up in a muslin bag to drip before pressing into a soft curd cheese. The men would soon be back for their breakfast bowls of porridge, served with the newly-skimmed cream

As the day wore on, the sun rose in a cloudless blue sky. While the men worked in the field, she worked with her mother finishing the chores, then later in the day they packed a supply of bannocks, cheese and bottles of cool spring water, to take to the men. They sat together among the corn-yellow stubble, looking out across the flat treeless land to the sea, shimmering against the outline of distant islands.

It was early evening, yet the sun was still high in the sky when they finished gathering and stooking sheaves.

'We're gaeing tae the cuithes,' said one of her brothers, 'Want to come?'

This was the greatest end to the day. The thrill of getting out in the boat with her brothers. And to fish too! Sometimes she went out with her father to his lobster pots, but that was nothing like the fun of gaein tae the cuithes. They would likely stay out till past midnight.

Back at the house they collected the fishing gear and some food. Once they'd got the boat launched, one of the boys rowed out while she sat in the bow, trailing her hand in the cool water. So happy to be sitting down at last. Shoals of cuithes were plentiful at this time of year, and the boys spent as much time as they could, when the weather was fine, out fishing.

They had three rods and lines, with baited hooks, to attract the fish. As one rowed the boat, the others cast the lines and soon they were pulling in good-sized cuithes. Then the shoal moved on and they rowed off to another location. She did her share of the rowing. It was part of the deal. As she rowed, she watched the changing patterns on the water as the reds and golds of the dying sun hit the horizon and slowly disappeared.

Then it was her turn to *dite* (clean) the fish. The creels were fairly filling up. The sun had just gone, yet it was still light when they got back to the beach. Now they threw some seaweed on top of the fish and carried them home to the croft kitchen. She put some oatmeal from the *girnal* (wooden meal chest) on a plate and threw over a sprinkling of salt.

'I'll get the pan on for a fry.'

Cuithes, fresh out the water, was the greatest treat. The fish flesh was less perfectly white than a cod or haddock's, perhaps, but the taste far superior, so they thought. They ate them with dark-brown, earthy-tasting bere bannocks spread with their own butter.

The next day she got to work with her mother on their fishing haul, picking out enough fish for a couple of meals for the whole family. They rubbed salt along the bones where the guts had been removed and hung the fish up on the *hake* (wooden frame for drying fish) in a windy place out of the sun to dry them a little. Her father liked these *blawn* (wind-blown) cuithes better than the freshly caught fish.

They layered the rest in a barrel with coarse salt for a few days. Later, they tied them in pairs by the tail and hung them over a washing line till they were completely dry and hard. These were the *saut* (salt) cuithes to see them through the winter, kept dry in the byre . . . full of magical summer memories.

While young saithe are called *cuithes* in Orkney, they're *pilticks* in Shetland. It's often assumed that these separate clusters of islands off the north coast of Scotland have a lot in common. Certainly, they were both invaded by the Vikings and subsequently ruled by Norway. Both have a rich archaeological past. Both are areas within Scotland's crofting counties and both have outstanding supplies of seafood around their coasts. Yet their fishing traditions, their uses of seafood – and their fish names – are uniquely their own.

It's always been easier for Orcadians to survive from the produce of their land, since it is flatter, more fertile and – unlike Shetland – less interrupted by bogs, rocky outcrops and rough moorland. All this has made it more possible for Orkney's crofter-fisher communities to make more profit from working the land

Orkney lobster fisherman off to set his creels in the early 1900s (National Museums Scotland, licensor www.scran.ac.uk).

and exporting their surplus, mainly barley and oats, to Shetland and mainland UK. The need to harvest the seas has been less vital to Orkney's survival, but not by any means ignored.

Universal fishing for saithe (*Pollachius virens*) was part of a centuries' old tradition of Orkney's subsistence economy. Also known as coal fish, or coley, from the black as coal colour of its back, they were the most abundant, most accessible and the most reliable fish found in the seas round Orkney. Herring and mackerel were erratic in their movements, but saithe were always there. No other fish from Scottish waters has so many vernacular names for it at different stages in its development (*cuddies* are the west coast equivalent of cuithes).

Not all were caught with a line from a boat. At certain parts of the coastline, where the fish came very close inshore, a popular tradition was fishing with rod and line from rocks. At good fishing locations, seats were established by the fishers, usually in a comfortable cup-shaped hollow in the rock. These fishers were known as *craigars* from the Scots *craig*, or *crag*, meaning a rock.[108] Fish caught from the rocks were usually for home consumption. Other methods used nets to scoop up a load of *sillocks* (immature saithe about four inches long which were used for fertiliser and bait) which were caught for 'income'.[109]

The tradition of the independent Orkney crofter-fishers still working this old system was remarkably resistant to change and survived well into the twentieth century, as Stephen Bruce (b.1933) of Burray describes:

There was fishing with lines ... [we] set out off to the area where the church was, in the sandy area off the Bu Sands, which allowed you to catch flounder and numerous flat fish ... You would be out, I would say, about a quarter of a mile. Beyond that point, you are off the sand and so you were able to have a bit of income from that.

These fish were for selling ... you sold them the day they were caught locally, you went round and people could come and buy them from you and then, as the Barriers came in [roads linking the south islands with mainland Orkney] you were able to transport them to the fish merchant in Kirkwall. The fish that you did take for drying for the winter were cod which you caught off the Point of Rose Ness and Copinsay.

I remember my father saying, while we were in the turnips – 'look at that massive shoal of herring, I think we should look out one of the old nets' – nets that had lain a long time ... We went out that night about two o'clock and by five in the morning we were pulling it in ... I remember the herring glistening with the fluorescence of the salt sea ...

These were salted down into four or five barrels which did you over the winter along with the cod fish ... they were salted and dried behind the fire [with] some haddock and the cuithes ... They were a very welcome addition to a winter meal because they could be boiled and they could be made into fish cakes. They were strong but they were very, very good.[110]

While there were hundreds of Orcadian crofter-fishers who followed this part-time fishing, not so many made the break from the land and became full-time fishermen. Records of Orkney boats fishing full-time in the late 1700s show that there were a small group of six boats, fishing for cod and probably ling, with long lines, from Stromness, and twelve boats following a similar fishing method from Walls. There were said to be a total of sixty Orkney boats fishing for lobster and twenty-four fitted out for catching dog-fish, for the oil in their livers, as well as for curing and smoking.[111]

This increased throughout the 1800s. The Orkney crofter-fishers, unlike the Shetlanders who were tied to commercial haaf-fishing in the summer, could take a few months seasonal work as crew on the Scottish herring fleet's busses (large factory ships) which followed the shoals round Scotland from spring to autumn, or to work for short periods, when it suited, crewing on the Shetland cod smacks going to Iceland and the Faroe Isles.

Commercial fishing by Orcadian fishermen from both Kirkwall and Stromness increased throughout the 1800s. At the turn of the century there were 1,000 dried ling exported from Stromness, a trade which continued into the early 1900s, when large quantities of the fish were dried on the beach and stored in sheds. There was cod fishing too, reaching a peak in 1833, with forty Orkney cod boats. In 1816, there were four hundred Orkney boats herring fishing.[112] The herring boom lasted from the mid-1800s to the beginning of World War I, with most of the commercial herring curing controlled by merchants from mainland ports.

Lobster fishing was Orkney's other important fishery at this time. Well-suited to Orcadian resources and lifestyle, some of the richest lobster grounds in Scotland were off the Orkney coast. There was minimal capital investment required for gear, since they made the lobster creels themselves. In the early days (late 1700s) the method of catching was to sink a weighted and baited poke (pouch) net attached to an iron ring tied to a long rope, which was frequently lowered and hauled up as they fished.[113] A much better idea, a baited-creel trap which had a narrow net funnel allowing the lobster in, but not out, was invented in the early 1800s. This meant the lobster fishermen could work as many creels as they liked, leaving them for days if necessary.

The lobster grounds were quite close inshore, so small, one or two-man boats which they already had worked well. Going to the creels could also be slotted into their farming routine: they went to the creels when the weather was too wet for the land; to the land when the weather was too windy for the creels.

Fast sailing ships, owned by English merchants, had begun transporting Orkney lobsters to the London market in the late 1700s to satisfy the appetites of discerning gourmets in the capital. Since lobsters deteriorate once dead, they were kept alive in ships, known as *well-smacks*, with 'wells' (tanks) below the waterline with holes in the hull, so the lobsters could be kept alive in freshly-changing sea water. Orkney was the most intensive area of production, though supplies also came from the west coast, the Hebrides and the east coast. Lobsters were the first shellfish to become a major Scottish export, and the price tripled in the latter part of the 1800s, which was good news for lobster fishermen.[114] Few lobsters, though, found their way into Orkney cooking pots. Such a valuable source of income – like prime Scottish beef – was a capital asset, not an item for home consumption.

Stromness was the pick-up port for the lobster well-smacks from London. It is one of Scotland's oldest seatowns, where the harbour has a long history dating back to 1701.[115] Situated on the shores of Hamnavoe (Norse for 'haven's bay') it developed as an important trading port and stopping place for seafarers, whalers and Arctic explorers in transit. Though Kirkwall was the Royal Burgh, with trading links to North Sea ports, Stromness traded with the New World, Africa and the Far East. European wars, from the late 1600s to the early 1800s, frequently made the English Channel unsafe for trading vessels, and so they took the northern route instead, stopping at the safe haven of Stromness. Tied up at the harbour in 1792 were a total of 338 vessels of various descriptions, from whalers and Arctic explorers to trading ships owned by the Hudson Bay Company.

Stromness flourished, growing upwards on Brinkie's Brae. It also grew along the shore, creating a unique waterfront of houses, with walled gardens and their own stone-built slips and piers giving them direct access to the sea. The town was home to ship captains and merchants as well as fishermen and pilots. There was a fish market at the bottom of Church Road where fishermen sold their catch. There were smokehouses where some of the catch was salted and smoked. Besides the boats in the harbour, there were the floating *sea kists* – wooden boxes filled with seawater where the lobsters were kept alive till the well-smacks arrived to collect them. Blubber from whales (used for lighting) was rendered down at the *Oily Hoose* on the shore beyond Cromwell Road.

When Sir Walter Scott arrived by boat in the early 1800s, he wrote an account in his journal of his first impressions of Stromness. He comments on the lack of transport – not even a horse at the pier to take him into the town.[116] He had to make his way up and down steps on foot, then negotiate through the dirty streets, inhaling the fumes from smoking fish and rendering whale oil. The street, he appears slightly irritated to discover, was unsuitable for public transport. As it still is, set in stone like the many slips and piers of the waterfront, giving the town its special character.

'As youngsters we manoeuvred around the piers and slipways on boats and swam from slip to slip, totally unaware of the unique nature of our heritage,' says Captain Robbie Sutherland (b.1924), who set up the Nautical School in Stromness in 1967, recalls looking back on his childhood. 'During the last few years I have marvelled at how this sea frontage was created. I can only ponder on the effort involved; in obtaining the stone, using the ebb for the base, applying a technique that has withstood many decades of winter storms.'[117]

Not only a haven for generations of fishermen, traders, seamen and adventurers in the past, it preserved the continuity of its seafaring and fishing heritage for the generation who played around its slips and piers in the 1920s and 30s. Like previous generations, they would make their mark too on the islands' fishing heritage. In the late 1960s the lucrative herring industry had declined, though an Orcadian of Norwegian ancestry, Ken Sutherland, has kept the tradition alive with his marinated herring cure. The ancient trade in live lobsters remained, but this only employed small-scale creel fishermen. It was around this time that it began to dawn on shellfish eaters that lobster, at more than twice the price of crab, was not actually twice as good to eat. Sleekly elegant, scarlet lobster might have the looks; but dumpy, sideways walking crab had its charms too.

On the waterfront at Stromness, an enterprise began in a small crab processing unit adjoining the shed where live lobsters were being kept in tanks awaiting shipment. Local people were employed, removing crabmeat from shells, and Stromness Processors Ltd. began trading. There was a similar crab-processing development on the island of Westray, with a purpose-built factory which started production in 1968 with fourteen workers. The processors and the creel fishermen remained separate businesses until the early 1990s, when they joined forces to form a cooperative, the Orkney Fishermen's Society (OFS), chaired by Captain Robbie Sutherland and managed by Stewart Crichton, who had begun crab processing on the Stromness waterfront. It has been a hugely successful partnership with a modern processing factory built at Stromness in 1995.[118]

Caught in creels around the 500 miles of coastline which surrounds the cluster of 70-odd islands which makes up the Orkney archipelago, brown and velvet crabs and lobsters are brought never more than thirty miles to the factory. The OFS employs a shellfish sustainability officer to asses stocks of crabs and lobsters. Juvenile lobsters from a hatchery on the islands are also being released and monitored to protect stocks. Hardy and resourceful, the Orkney community have worked together for the common good, protecting their seafood heritage and creating a new source of fishing prosperity for the islands.

WEST

1 Shetland

Haaf-fishermen, Fethaland, 1800

When Magnie and his crew arrive at the fishing station, they head for their 'summer lodge', four dry stone walls with a thatched roof which has been empty since they left last autumn. It's windowless and damp inside with the only light coming from the doorway. There are three-tiered bunks made of wooden planks against one wall which serve as beds, when they can snatch a few hours sleep between fishing trips.

The roof needs repaired. Inside is full of winter debris. The fire must be lit, a meal cooked. Magnie organises the men while he goes off to stow their gear – buoys, sinkers, *gansies* (jerseys), lines and kreels – in the *sixern* (a six-oared, square-sailed, light and easily manoeuvred Viking-style longboat). He meets up with others also getting their sixerns ready, and they share thoughts on the likely trend of the weather over the next couple of days. Magnie is for getting off as soon as possible while it's fine.

Like other haaf (deep sea) fishermen, Magnie has left his wife and children with the day-to-day running of the croft (sheep-lambing, cow-milking, and crop-tending) while he goes in search of large cod and ling. He has rented this croft from the landlord, on the understanding that he will fish for him, during the summer months, at the fishing station.

The bay here at Fethaland is sheltered with a long shingle beach, good for drying fish and pulling up boats, which has helped make it one of the largest stations on these northern islands, close to rich fishing grounds. The landlord's factor manages the busy station, weighing and recording each boat's catch when it comes in and employing curers to salt and dry the large cod and ling. Young boys from the crofts, known as 'beach boys', start working for the curers when they are twelve, washing the fish when they come in, putting them in vats, layering them with salt and spreading the salted fish out on the beach to dry – among other chores.

Magnie goes back to the lodge to join the others for a bowl of thick broth. They sit on wooden boxes supping the steaming broth from their large wooden bowls. It will be their last hot meal for two days, maybe three. Magnie gives the beach boy, who's sharing their lodge, his orders to damp down the slow-burning peat fire and be sure and keep it going while they're away.

A gang of beach boys helps slide the boat down into the water and they head out on the long row, thirty or so miles to the fishing grounds.

At first light, the fishing begins and the long lines are shot. All Magnie hopes for is a good catch and fair weather. He's had some lucky escapes, but others have not. When a summer gale blows up they are in trouble in this small open boat so far out. There is also a problem if the boat is capsized by a surfacing whale.

All well so far, though, and the boat is filling up with good-sized fish. He keeps changing the crew round as they work, so those pulling in the lines get a break. There is gutting and de-heading to do as well as re-baiting the lines. At this time of year, this far north, there is the *simmer dim* (daylight all night) so they fish through the night, taking turns at curling up in the bottom of the boat for a sleep. They survive on a supply of brunnies (girdle bannocks), croft cheese and a keg of *soor blaand* (fermented whey).

It's late Tuesday night when he turns the boat, returning safely to the fishing station early Wednesday morning. The catch is weighed and noted in the factor's ledger. After a bowl of more broth and a few hours in their bunks, they are up again baiting lines for the next trip.

Weather permitting, he will be off again Thursday night to Saturday morning. Then he can get home for the weekend, see his family, go to the Kirk on Sunday.

But before he leaves for home at the end of the week, he shares out the 'house fish' among his crew. This is the fish which the curers don't want – large halibut and skate, and fish too small to cure. The haaf-fishers' perks also include large cod, ling and tusk heads, as well as the innards: livers, *rhans* (roes) *muggies* (fish stomachs), and *soonds* (swimming bladders), which Magnie's wife is an expert at transforming into tasty meals.

Shetland crofter-fisher families in the 1800s had an unbroken history connecting them, more intimately than any other communities around the Scottish coast, to the harvest of the seas. Nowhere else, possibly in the world,[119] has a community shown such ingenuity when using up the odds and ends of the cured white fish industry. No other coastal communities in Scotland became as tied to the cured white fish industry as the Shetlanders.

Fethaland haaf station with a sixareen launching from the shore while another rows out. At the head of the beach are the salting vats and other sixareens. There is smoke rising from one of the bøds (summer lodges) (© Shetland Museum).

Certainly they had the advantage of nearness to the best fishing grounds at the edge of the continental shelf. Their problem was distance from markets and lack of resources which led, during the late medieval period, to exploitation by other Europeans, who not only fished their waters extensively but also established a monopoly in Shetland-cured white fish. This began to change in the 1600s, as conditions in Shetland, described as 'one long crisis', deteriorated.[120] As well as a collapse in the structure of government on the islands, there were repeated harvest failures and epidemics, leading to poverty for the people and bankruptcy for the landlords. But in an atmosphere of recession in Europe at the end of the seventeenth century the foreign merchants, mainly Germans, began to withdraw. Then, in 1712, the UK government brought in a salt tax which made it even less attractive for foreigners to continue trading in Shetland-cured white fish.

It took the local landlords some decades before they were financially able to take over the development and promotion of this lucrative commercial fishery. An important incentive was the government-sponsored system providing an export bounty for cured fish, which was introduced in the 1720s, guaranteeing three shillings for every hundredweight exported. Once haaf-fishing became established in the second half of the 1700s, there was an increase in the Shetland population. Though some stations were much smaller, at a large haaf station about seventy boats might gather with their crews, which could number around 400 fishermen plus a curing staff of about seventy, including beach boys, factors and storekeepers, all resident at the station for the summer season.[121]

The organisation and investment came mostly from the landlords and merchant traders who managed the curing process. The landlord bought boats, set up fishing stations at suitable coastal locations and ensured that the tenants on his land became his fishermen. Only if they agreed to deep-sea fish for large white fish were they given tenancy of a house and croft land. Only if they sold their fish exclusively to the landlord, or merchant, for a price decided by him, would they keep their house and croft land. Only at the end of the season would they be paid a price decided by the landlord.

This landlord-tenant relationship was known as a 'fishing tenure',[122] and in addition to the compulsory haaf-fishing, the tenant was also required to pay a cash rent and a percentage of the croft's produce – grain, butter, etc. Anecdotal stories of unsympathetic landlords abound. Whatever financial risks the landlords took setting up fishing stations and finding a market for the fish, the crofter-fishers risked their lives and often failed to make a profit.

The loss of life at sea, caused devastation for whole communities.[123] When summer storms blew up suddenly, when the fishermen were far out, the agonising decision had to be made: whether to ride it out, and risk death, or cut the lines and head home, which would mean wiping out their profit for the season. Those who cut their lines had no hope of getting back into profit till the end of the following season, by which time they would probably be so badly into debt that their profit would be wiped out for a second year.

> I shall never forget the looks of despair that the men expressed, when they had to relate their story [of cutting the lines in a storm] – how the hopes of supporting their family with independence were thus blighted.[124]

It was fairly common for haaf-fishermen to live in a perpetual state of debt. Gear and supplies, at the beginning of the season, were bought on credit when they had no idea of the price they would get for the season's catch. This would be decided at 'settling time' in the autumn, when the merchants sold the dried fish. Often the credit they had run up would exceed the price they got for their fish and the debt would be carried over to the next year, and so on.

As the debt increased, the family would live under the constant fear of eviction by an unsympathetic landlord.[125] Known as a 'truck system', it meant that there was little money in circulation, since transactions were done in ledger books, and traders and merchants had near-monopoly power over the fishermen.[126]

An alternative to this system, offering opportunities for the next generation of Shetland fishermen, had begun to develop when larger boats were built which could sail even further out to sea to the cod-fishing grounds around the Faroe Islands, Iceland and Rockall. Foreign fishermen had initiated this development around 1600, when they gave up their old hard-dried stockfish method and started salting their cod catch in barrels.[127] This initial salting, which extracted much of the moisture from the fish, was done on board ship, which meant that bigger boats could stay out longer and go further.

Known as 'cod smacks', these bigger boats' development was encouraged, in the early stages, by government bounties. The boats could make two or three trips in the summer season, returning to cod stations on Shetland with their partly salted catch, which would then be dried out on the beach. The cod smack fleet eventually increased to around a hundred boats, employing over a thousand men. The other alternative for young men was to join Shetland's expanding herring fleet, which had begun to develop, as the East coast herring fishermen began buying bigger boats and Shetlanders began buying up their old boats.

Not until the government began their inquiry into the crofters' plight in 1883 was there any opportunity to express grievances against landlords and merchants without fear of retribution. The outcome of the inquiry was the Crofters' Act of 1886, giving crofters security of tenure, reduced rents and compensation for improvements they made to the croft. But it was too late for the haaf-fishers. By now the communities were no longer prepared to risk needless loss of life in summer gales. A year after the crofting act, there were just ten sixerns fishing out of Fethaland.

If the young men had not joined a cod smack or a herring boat, they went off to start new lives on the UK mainland, or across the Atlantic. In 1903 the haaf-fishing was at an end, with just one boat and crew left at Fethaland. The skipper,

Charles Ratter, at the age of sixty-eight, continued to fish with his crew for a few more years before he finally gave up. When he died in 1930 at the age of ninety-five, he was remembered for 'his great love for the work [haaf-fishing] and [that] for many years after he gave up fishing, he kept his old fishing lodge in good repair.'[128] Despite the hard life and its perils, for many summers in his old age, he went back to sit at the door of his lodge, puffing on his pipe, looking out to sea, and remembering.

The catch from the sea had been an essential means of survival, since prehistoric times, for all who lived on these remote islands with their extensive coastline and minimal area of fertile land. And it remained important to the crofter-fishing community, despite the demands of the haaf-fishing, from the early 1700s to the late 1800s. They might have to fish for the landlord in summer, but for the remainder of the year they continued to pursue their subsistence fishing which had provided them with their fish-based diet for so many thousands of years.

Despite good supplies of shellfish, little was eaten, since it was used as fishing bait. Shellfish 'were put on a hook rather than on the table'.[129] And when the haaf-fishing was over in August, the men went out on fine nights for a few hours of *eela* (rod and line) fishing, hoping for a good catch of lively *pilticks* (two year-old saithe) or some herring or mackerel if they happened to come into the bay. While one man rowed slowly round the local bays, rocks and skerries, others managed the rods and lines with a 'lure' (something which flashed in the water like feathers) attached to the hook. Boys started going out when they were as young as seven, learning to understand the weather, recognise the landmarks, locate the fishing grounds, tie the knots and read a compass.

When the summer fishing was over, they carried on through the winter, when shoals of *sillocks* (very young coley/saithe) were 'so thick in winter *voes* [open sea lochs between islands] that a bucket is easily filled'.[130] Saithe was available all year round. It was fished at every stage in its growth up to a *ruthin*, three year-old, and a *skoorie*, a fully grown fish around four years old.

Two-year old pilticks made a very good meal for one, floured and roasted on the brander (iron grid put over the fire), then eaten with melted butter and potatoes for dinner or with bannocks for breakfast. Their liver was used either for food or oil, which was used for lamps before other alternatives were available.

The winter inshore fishing, a few miles out to sea, was done with long lines, shorter than the haaf lines; but still there were hundreds of hooks to be baited, often with the help of children. Here, they hoped to catch larger saithe as well as cod, haddock, ling, whiting, hake and tusk. In late April, they began to keep a lookout for signs of disturbance, flashes of silver and excited birds circling an area, which was the signal to get out the herring net. Mackerel were around for a briefer period from July through to early September, when the herring was getting scarce.

Even if the Shetlanders failed to see the eating potential of shellfish (unless they were starving) a yearly cycle of different types of fishing for different types of fish provided huge variety in their diet. Add this to their frequent and original ways with roes, livers, stomachs, sounds and leftover heads, and the Shetlanders' seafood heritage is unique.

2 North West Coast and Islands

Isle of Barra crofter-fishers, taking fish to market, early 1800s

Rowing and singing to themselves, the four crofter-fishers make their way out of Castlebay in their heavily-laden fishing boat. Out in the Minch there is a fine breeze which takes them eastwards towards the Sound of Mull. Donnie, the *sigobair* (skipper), is the oldest and most experienced, his eldest son Murdo is with him and two neighbouring crofters. They take turns through the night, two having a short sleep while the other two manage the boat.

Donnie began preparations for this trip in March. Before the barley and oats were planted on the croft, he'd launched his boat and set off with Murdo to fish for large cod and ling. They were the most valuable fish, especially cured. But other fish took the bait on the long lines too – dogfish (good to eat and a useful source of oil for lamps), skate (only for their edible wings) and halibut (very good to eat but useless for salt-curing).

His wife cooked these fish fresh, either roasting them on the gridiron over the fire when they were the right size and shape, or cutting up the larger or more awkward-shaped fish and adding them to the broth pot. After a long winter of salt-cured fish, these first tastes of fresh fish were the greatest treat, their own croft butter melting into the lightly cooked fish.

All the good-sized cod and ling were salt cured and dried till they became *sailte iasg* (salt fish), light and hard as a board. They were the largest volume but least heavy part of their valuable cargo which included fish oil, croft butter and some baskets of croft eggs packed between layers of straw. Four other boats, similarly laden, had left Castlebay a few days ago, also en route south, as they were, to the market in Glasgow.

Besides singing lyrical Gaelic boat songs as they rowed, they were always mindful to sing a psalm. Donnie had a fine singing voice and led with a rhythmic chanting of each line which the others repeated. They prayed for deliverance from whatever dangers lay ahead. Some years earlier, five boats had left Barra for Glasgow but only one returned. It was a devastating loss to the small island community.

Thankfully, the breeze was still with them as they turned into the Sound of Luing, when Donnie decided it was time to stop for fresh water and to stretch legs. He found a quiet inlet on the island of Luing with rocks where they tied up the boat and jumped ashore. While he went off to visit a croft to barter some fish for fresh supplies of bannocks, the others found a burn to fill up the water flagons.

They are not far now from Crinan, and the start of the canal which will take them into Loch Fyne, then through the Kyles of Bute and into the Firth of Clyde. They will be in Glasgow in no time.

There had been a fish market here beside the river since the 1500s, and now that Glasgow was such a hub of trade with the New World, there was no problem selling their Barra-cured fish, which was in great demand both at home and abroad. It was their most important source of income. The butter and eggs, which they took to the general market to join the mature clothbound truckles of Ayrshire cheese, all fetch good prices too, but not as much as the fish. They speak hardly any English, but it's not a problem since there are plenty of Barra relatives here in Glasgow, who are now fluent in both English and Gaelic.

Once everything is sold, Donnie goes off to get supplies of fishing hooks and hemp for making lines. Then they all indulge in some packets of tea and sugar, and some tobacco. His wife wants a new iron girdle which he picks up from an ironmonger. He is not keen to linger too long. Glasgow is not the safest place in the world, as he's discovered from previous visits. The sooner he gets the younger boys into the boat and heading back to Barra the better.

Intrepid seafaring[131] was an inherited talent among the people living on this coastline. For both the Gaelic-speaking Celts, who came from Ireland preaching Christianity, and the Norse-speaking Vikings who invaded and ruled briefly, the seas were an open road. In an area of many islands, some very remote, and a mainland frequently indented with fiord-like sea lochs and dominated by high mountains, those who could build seaworthy boats and navigate the seas successfully were always at an advantage, as were the members of the MacDonald clan, led by their chieftain, the Lord of the Isles.

The MacDonalds' control of these seas had begun in the 1300s, creating a separate kingdom of all the islands and large parts of the Highland mainland. All spoke Gaelic, and were ruled from Finlaggan on Islay. At one time this powerful dynasty might have emerged as the rulers of all Scotland, had history been different. Instead it was the Lowland Stuarts, after much skulduggery on both sides, who claimed that prize.

Despite the unification of the country, a divide in culture, language and geography remained a barrier between the Gaelic-speaking people of the Highlands and islands and the Scots-speaking Lowlanders. This would continue, so long as communication was restricted, and the main open road into the area was the sea, navigated in small open boats, often in precarious weather conditions. Not until the late 1800s when adequate roads, a rail network, and passenger steamers arrived, would the physical division become less of a problem. Until then generations of seafarers – like the Barra crofter-fishers – continued to use the rich source of food from the sea which was an essential part of their self-sufficient lifestyle.

With such assets, it might be assumed that the area was set for a successful future reaping rich rewards from a seafood industry. In the late 1500s the Stuart king, James VI, had ordered two surveys of the resources of the Western Isles. No doubt his intention was to check the taxable wealth of the area which had, after all, been a rich resource for the Lords of the Isles. Its assets, he was told, were some fertile areas where corn could be grown. There were whales which could provide valuable oil, plenty of birds whose feathers would be useful, also there were pelts from wild animals and young falcon for hunting. [132]

Surprisingly, only whales were the considered an asset from the sea. But the clansmen in these parts, who followed their chief into battle, also followed him into the wild places to hunt deer, hare, grouse and ptarmigan. This was the noble and challenging occupation of the warrior, who also indulged in frequent skirmishes between rival clans. Fishing had none of this allure.

Then the prospects of developing a successful fishing industry, from the rich seafood resources in the area, became even more remote when the Stuart dynasty, now reigning over both Scotland and England, was deposed in the 1700s. After two unsuccessful and costly uprisings, both in loss of life and in economic terms, the Jacobite clan chiefs from this area who had supported the Stuarts lost their lands and their source of income. Neither the clan chiefs who had backed the winning side, nor the aristocratic proprietors who took over the lands of the dispossessed chiefs, were as interested in trade as the merchant lairds on Orkney and Shetland. Many of the Highland and island landowners, post 1745, preferred to live for most of the year in London, or Edinburgh, employing tacksmen or factors to run their estates while they were away.

Yet another blow was struck to harvesting the rich fish and shellfish resources from the sea in this area was when kelp-making from seaweed developed as an alternative occupation for coastal communities. The commercially minded merchant-lairds on Orkney were the first to see the potential of kelp, beginning production around 1722,[133] and becoming a major producer in the next couple of decades.

By 1750 landowners in the Highlands and Islands had also cottoned on to the advantages, and the industry was soon common on the islands of Lewis and Harris, North and South Uist, Barra, Tiree, Coll, Jura, Skye, Mull and Morven on the mainland. The entire coast of the north and west had the richest seaweed resources in the UK.[134] Gathered and burnt in a kiln, it made a hard block of valuable chemical-rich alkali, essential at this time for bleaching, soap and glass-making.

From June to August – peak fishing months – thousands of seafaring crofter-fishers, and their families, spent hours every day up to their waists in the sea cutting seaweed.[135] For fifty years, from 1760 to 1820, foreign wars had made importing kelp more expensive than making it at home and profits from the home-based industry soared. Such was the scale of the profits, in these boom years, that many landowners set about increasing the population.

They needed more labour, which they achieved by dividing-up crofts into smaller areas of land, at a time when most crofts could hardly provide enough food to support the existing population, but it meant more families could be housed. The recorded population increase from 1755 to 1811 varied from one area to another, with the greatest increases on the North and South Uists of over 100 per cent.[136]

Another common action of landowners was to remove their tenants, living in the fertile glens, to areas at the coast where the land was minimal and often less fertile, but where they could be employed in the kelp industry. Meanwhile, the landowners had discovered another source of income: farming sheep on the cleared land. Of course, it was always recognised that the prosperity from kelp depended on the continuation of foreign wars. When they ended, the boom years of kelp-making would be over.

While attempts were made by those who saw that fishing the seas offered a better prospect for long term prosperity than making kelp, the problems seemed insurmountable. [137] The intrepid Barra crofter-fishers, making their trip to the Glasgow market, were part of a seafaring culture which had harvested the seas for thousands of years but were now being left behind. The state of the people at the bottom of the heap here was described by Sir Walter Scott on the first of two trips he made to the Hebrides, visiting Iona in 1810, en route to Fingal's Cave on Staffa.

> Iona is a very singular place . . . The inhabitants are in the last state of poverty and wretchedness. Fisheries might relieve them, but I see no other resource, for the island, though fertile, considering all things, does not produce food for the inhabitants, and they have neither money nor commodities to induce importation of provisions. [138]

In 1784 an account by Archibald McDonnell, a crofter-fisher from Barrisdale on Loch Hourn, also illustrates the problems. Of the weather, for a start: 'being out to the extremity of his district', seventy miles north of his own house in his open small yawl with four hands, he was 'detained here for five days in one place, without being able to stir either backwards or forwards from the violence of the weather'.

On his way home, he saw a shoal of herring, but the weather was still too rough for him to risk setting a net from his small boat. There was more frustration back in Loch Hourn, when a huge shoal of herring followed him into the loch. Planning to go out and set his net, he discovered that the salt he'd ordered had not been delivered. So yet another opportunity was lost to make some profit from this rich, but highly perishable, resource. [139]

Though the British Fisheries Society was set up in 1786 to invest in this area, with the exception of Ullapool, it failed to develop a successful fishing industry. [140] By the early 1800s, it had turned its attention to the north east coast, at Wick, where there were fewer obstacles. What happened on the north and west coasts, were sporadic commercial fishing enterprises set up by landlords, often absent, who provided the initial finance to build fishing stations which they then handed over to managers to run. The incentive for landlords was a bounty (monetary bonus) paid on barrels of all cured herring passed and registered by Customs Officers.

The saga of a fishing station set up by Kenneth Mackenzie of Torridon, on the inner loch at Ardmore in 1787, sums up some of the problems these enterprises faced, and some of the reasons they failed. Mackenzie had employed an enthusiastic Lewisman, Donald Morison, who was a cooper by trade, and promised him finances for the enterprise, and remuneration for himself, but delivered neither.

When John Knox, advisor to the Fisheries Society, visited Morison's curing station, he claimed it to be the first of its kind built in Scotland.

> A large and commodious curing-house after a model of those on the coast of Labradore [sic] and other northern parts of America. The principal design of this building is to dry cod and ling, in any weather, under cover; an improvement of the greatest importance in that watry [sic] climate . . . The buildings have likewise all manner of conveniences for curing herrings . . . nature has formed a creek where some hundred boats may lie in perfect safety, in any winds, from whatever quarter they blow.[141]

Morison found it a 'great hindrance' that the Customs house where he had to register his barrels of herring was north of Ullapool, some 40 odd miles away. There were other 'red tape' problems and he left very soon after Knox's visit. The curing station, however, continued in use, possibly up to the late nineteenth century.

Wild salmon was another important fishing asset in this area and had its own fishery, originally owned by the Crown, though these rights were now often in the control of landlords. Compared with the huge volumes of salmon caught in the large east coast rivers and estuaries, the rivers were smaller here and there were fewer salmon caught. Until the advent of railways and steamers, the only fast transport to market for fresh salmon from this area was by sailing boat. While ice houses were built beside east coast salmon rivers, none were built here where the volumes were not sufficient for such a costly investment.

Many salmon found their way onto the laird's table where there was no shortage of seafood. In 1704, on the Duke of Sutherland's estate, the monthly total of fish received in lieu of rent from his crofter-fisher tenants in May was 1,676. The number was noted by the Duke's factor, who kept a record, describing them as 'great or small'. The 'great' fish were most likely salmon from the River Helmsdale.[142] Surplus fish would have been salted and smoked (kippered), or pickled in a barrel with spices to put in store for winter.

A catch of cod, halibut and ling laid out ready for auction on the quay at Stornoway, Isle of Lewis, 1906 (National Museums Scotland, licensor www.scran.ac.uk).

Another sporadic fishery, with a future, was lobster creel-fishing. As on Orkney, this fitted in better with the crofter-fisher's land work than going out to sea for several days for white fish. The London fish merchants sent their well-smacks (boats with salt water wells where the shellfish was kept alive) north to Orkney for lobsters, and collected them from this area too. The great advantage of the lobster was that it could be kept alive until it reached the market, no matter the length of the journey.

With a coastline rich in other kinds of shellfish, it might be imagined that this asset was developed to the crofter-fisher's advantage. There were plentiful supplies of crabs, mussels, whelks, cockles, scallops, limpets and crabs, as well as some oyster beds. Yet none of them became commercially viable until fast transport was able to get such perishable food from this remote area to market quickly. Unlike the Shetlanders, who mostly regarded shellfish as poverty food, this area made more use of them and of seaweed. Seaweed was used as a flavour addition to broths. Purple *duileasg* (dulse) was popular in a mutton broth, its salty-iodine aroma adding character and its soft texture breaking down and mingling with other ingredients. Some seaweeds were gathered from the beach and carried on the people's backs in wicker creels to be spread on the land as valuable fertiliser. The holdfasts (stalks) of dulse were chewed like sticks of rock by the children.

In summer, like the Shetlanders and Orcadians, the crofter-fishers craig-fished from the rocks. They also fished in their small boats, close inshore, for saithe and other white fish. As in Shetland, the habit of using the valuable white fish livers, and other innards, was also widely practised. Like Orcadians, they also dried white fish outside in a brisk wind for a few days for *blawn* (wind-blown) fish. They also put out a net when the herring came into the loch, taking just enough for a few meals of fresh herring – coated in oatmeal and fried in butter – with the rest salted in barrels in the barn for the winter.

At some locations where there were bird-nesting cliffs, they also caught sea birds, which were a valued food resource. Sometimes the birds were caught at sea using trailing devices with a bait and a noose attached. The more dangerous activity, by far, was scaling down cliffs where the birds were nesting and catching them with a pole and noose. Though a variety of sea birds were caught, the most productive and the most valued was the young gannet, known by its Gaelic name of *guga*.[143] While there is early evidence of catching guga both in Orkney and Shetland, and on remote islands like St Kilda and North Rona, records of the annual guga hunt – still active in 2010 – by the *Niseachs* (men of Ness at the northernmost point of the Isle of Lewis) are the most detailed.

The location of their hunt was the remote and uninhabited island of Sulsgeir, forty miles north of the Butt of Lewis, half a mile long and with cliffs a mere two hundred feet high, compared with those over a thousand feet on St Kilda. On Sulsgeir, a few sheep scraped a living from a small area of rough grazing, and there were the ruins of a beehive-shaped, early Christian hermit's cell which the hunters called the 'Temple'. In the 1800s, a visiting archaeologist described the island as 'barren and repulsive', while another visitor notes its 'ghastly loneliness'. A travelling churchman, however, is one of the first to record the activity on the island by the Niseachs in 1549. There are other accounts, one in 1797 which notes that: 'There is in Ness a most venturous set of people who, for a few years back, at the hazard of their lives, went there [Sulsgeir] in an open six-oared boat without even the aid of a compass'. During the first half of the 1800s, the Niseachs began building bothies with drystone walls on the island so they could stay, more comfortably, for several days.[144]

Today, there are five bothies on the island and methods of catching and salt curing have changed. What remains unchanged is the spirit of the Niseachs and their passion for this seafaring adventure. Testing the mind, body and spirit when out on the rock, young men discover their strengths and weaknesses and how to work in a team. Yet this is not the only reason for keeping the guga tradition alive, as Niseach Donald S. Murray explains:

> It is one of the few foods we are likely to consume today that binds us to both a place and the practices of our ancestors. When we consume it, we are no longer the 'unrooted' disconnected people into which we have been transformed by progress and our modern consumer society. We are at one with those who have gone before us, people who at one time scoured the cliffs and crags of the coastline for such or similar food.[145]

3 South West – Argyll, Firth of Clyde and Solway Firth

A trip 'doon the watter' – Glasgow 1920

They had never been this far into the Highlands before. The changing landscape and distant mountains, the fresh sea breeze on their faces and the thrill of gliding through the water in this new Clyde steamer was their idea of heaven. Home, for sisters Katie and Flora, was a cramped two-room-and-kitchen with a communal *cludgie* (toilet) on the *stairheid* (outside landing) in a tenement in the city's East End. Flora worked as a French polisher in Bow's Furniture Emporium in the High Street, while Katie was a clerkess in the Grocers' Supply Company in Cambridge Street.

Today they were on holiday, up at the crack of dawn, dressed in their Sunday best, as they set off to walk along Argyle Street to catch the train from St Enoch station, which would take them to Princes pier at Greenock. Now here they were, sailing through the Kyles of Bute and into Loch Fyne. The steamer would stop soon at Tarbert and they could get off for a look round.

As the other passengers wandered off into the village, Katie and Flora stopped to watch the goings-on at the pier. Herring boats, back from the night's fishing, were unloading. It was all buzz. Wicker creels, overflowing with silvery fish, were swung across from boat to pier as squawking gulls dived. Quaint old men puffing pipes sat mending nets. Very fanciable, rugged young fishermen in navy blue jerseys and jaunty caps were leaping about the boats . . .

Then they noticed some young girls, about their own age, with their hair tied up in head scarves, wearing welly boots and thick rubber aprons covered in blood and fish scales. Their fingers were tied up in what looked like filthy bandages, yet this didn't stop them working at the speed of lightning, cutting the herring open and removing the guts. Flora and Katie had never seen anything like it. How could they do such a job?

Every so often a man would take the full creels of fish they'd gutted over to a shed.

'I think they're making kippers,' said Katie.

Ever since their mother had been sending them to do the *messages* (shopping) they'd been told to make sure they bought Loch Fyne kippers at the fish shop. They were the best. How their mother would love to have seen all this.

They watched the man take herring out of a large wooden vat, where they seemed to be soaking in something, then stretch the opened-out fish over hooks on a long wooden rod. When the rod was full of fish he opened a shed door, and they got a glimpse of its dark interior and the rows of burnished copper herring hanging in the smoke. A sign propped up against the shed said: 'Freshly Kippered Loch Fyne Herring for Sale'.

They bought four pairs and the curer wrapped them, first in waxed greaseproof paper and then in thick brown paper. Finally, tying the package up securely, he made them a string handle for carrying.

'Maw'll be real pleased,' said Flora as she paid him. 'There's nothing she likes better than a kipper for her tea.'

The steamer was hooting for everyone to return to the boat. Next stop Inveraray.

Plentiful herring catches in this area lasted into the early 1900s. Wealthy Glasgow merchants had made it their business to capitalise, more than a century before, on government bounties given for cured herring for export, with the intention of displacing the Dutch invasion of herring factory-ships from Scottish waters. Compared with the problems of establishing fishing communities in the more remote Highlands and islands to the north, this area was more fortunate. Dynamic fishing communities had been established by the time the Dutch domination eventually declined and the era of industrial Glasgow began.

Here – the birthplace of steam power – steamers and railway engines were now being built which would provide an extensive steamer and rail network into its scenic hinterland. While the new inventions allowed Glasgow's citizens to be transported by the thousands, many exiles nostalgically back to the spectacular mountains and lochs of their homeland, the fisherman's fresh-caught fish was also transported in the opposite direction to the urban market.

Until now, fresh fish had been an expensive luxury for only the very rich. Now it was affordable for everyone. The less affluent, growing up in Glasgow in the early 1900s, began to eat more fresh fish, especially herring, than any urban population in the past. It could be caught for most of the year, which was not the case in other areas where fish was more seasonal. Also, fishing was less affected by bad weather

Promotional postcard from 1906. The message from the fishmonger reads: 'Sir – Loch Fyne Kippers, Bloaters & Haddocks are now in prime condition, sold in boxes: 2/-, 2/6d & 4/-'. The barrels in the window are of salt-pickled herring (Argyll and Bute Council, licensor www.scran.ac.uk).

in the sheltered sea lochs, though not all the local herring boats stayed within this area and some followed the herring into the Minch, landing their catches at Mallaig or Oban where there were also rail connections.

The system of transporting fresh fish to link up with a rail network in Glasgow, meant it could also be sent on very quickly to markets in England. While the trade in fresh fish was developing, the trade continued in salt-pickled herring, sold in barrels for export. Some Scots continued to eat the heavily-salted herring, boiled with potatoes in their traditional *tatties 'n' saut herrin*, but tastes were changing. A fresh herring coated in oatmeal and fried in the pan with butter – *fresh herrin 'n' oatmeal* – had become just as popular. And they were also in love with the new, lighter-salted and more delicately smoked cures, especially the tasty kipper, which was the curer's response to changing tastes as speedy transport reduced the need for a long-life cure.

While curers in the north east coast of Scotland had pioneered finnans and smokies, the new, shorter-shelf-life smoked herring cure was first made by John Wodger, a fish curer at Seahouses on the Northumberland coast. He began experimenting in 1843, deciding to copy the old method used for kippering salmon.[146] His method involved splitting the herring open. This was an innovation since all previous smoked herring had been 'closed' fish.

The opened out fish gave a larger surface to absorb the salt and smoke, making it possible to reduce the smoking time. The light brining gave it a protective gloss on the surface which lengthened its shelf life. Kippered herring were put into cool smoke from smouldering sawdust for six to eighteen hours, depending on their position in the kiln and the volume of smoke. Though Wodger sent his first boxes of kippered herring to the London market in 1846, Scots curers were slow to adopt the English cure. They were, in 1849, still making the old 'closed' red herring and another less heavily cured version but not yet, it seems, the 'English' kipper.[147] The first record of a Scots-cured kipper is in 1885.[148]

East coast kippering ports included Eyemouth, Peterhead, Fraserburgh, and Wick. Herring were also kippered in Glasgow. The extra shelf-life of the kipper made it possible for remoter ports like Lerwick, Scalloway and Stornoway to kipper herring too.[149] And small pierside smoking sheds could always be found at small ports, like Tarbert on Loch Fyne, wherever there were regular herring landings. There were subtle differences between the cures, defined by the quality of the herring and the curers' smoking methods. Besides the large plump Loch Fyne kippers, which Glasgow rated the finest, a smaller-sized kipper smoked at Mallaig was also very popular.

In 1914, annual Scottish kipper production had reached 20,000 tons.[150] The years prior to World War I were peak years for the curing industry, with the volume of all cured fish amounting to around three-quarters of the total fish production.[151] Short shelf-life cured fish was here to stay. Long shelf-life cured fish gradually declined, though there was still an export market in Europe, where traditional tastes for heavily salted cures meant they remained very popular. There was also a demand where communities continued to eat their traditional foods. Despite innovations and new fashions, this remained an important part of their identity and culture. In the Highlands and Islands, pots of floury tatties and salt herring are still – like the Hebridean guga – meals which evoke a sense of belonging to a place: being 'at one with the people who have gone before us'.[152]

Meanwhile the most important development for urban fish eating habits was the plentiful supplies of fresh herring and white fish. Specialist fish shops were appearing on every high street. Italian immigrants who had come, first to sell their *gelati* in the summer, were now investing their profits in deep-fat fryers as they married the battered haddock with the chipped potato which had become such a popular warming winter street-food, deep fried in lard, at street markets in the late 1800s.

From 1894 to 1946, national fresh fish consumption quadrupled.[153] But post World War II, west coast herring fishermen had a problem. For decades they had been, first and foremost, herring fishermen. Chasing the silvery shoals was their life, but the big shoals were disappearing. It was a problem which had its origins in a change in fishing methods in the 1830s.[154] The old drift-net, hanging like a curtain in the water, caught only parts of a shoal, but the newer, more efficient, ring-net encircled practically a whole shoal, leaving the remainder both vulnerable to predators and unable to reproduce successfully.

One of the early repercussions of this hoovering-up of the shoals was that fewer herring were coming into the long narrow sea lochs like Loch Fyne. To save their livelihoods, herring fishermen and kipper curers at the head of the loch at Inveraray fought an acrimonious battle against using the more efficient nets, but lost. Conflict between the drift-netters of the inner lochs and the ring-netters was at its peak throughout the 1840s and 50s.[155]

The damage to herring stocks continued, so that out-of-work herring fishermen began to harvest other species which previously they had often tossed back into the sea. Saithe (coley) and lythe (pollack), both members of the cod family, had been an abundant and easily caught food supply in previous centuries. During the food shortages of World War II, saithe became so valuable to Campbeltown fishermen that they renamed them 'goldfish'.[156] Their less than white flesh did not deter those who enjoyed their fine flavour and meaty texture. Lythe did not migrate offshore as it matured, but stayed close in around rocky coasts and kelp-covered offshore reefs, so it was more difficult for the trawlermen to catch, but it could be caught with long lines. Post World War II, cod, haddock, whiting and hake were all caught by trawlers in this area.

The revealing log books of a herring ring-net skipper, Donald McDougall, for the third week of February 1953, confirm that the herring fishery was poor, with only the 'odd puckles [small amounts of] good quality got'. Prospects, it appeared, were even poorer at the herring spawning fisheries around Arran and off Ayrshire. Most of the fleet had gone scallop (clam) dredging or had resorted to the old method of fishing with long baited lines for large white fish: some were having 'good fishings with lines of hake'. By the end of March, most of the Tarbert fleet was 'tied up, or at lines', but now hake were 'getting very scarce owing to big fleet at lines'.[157]

Halibut and turbot were rarely caught in these waters, though there were catches of A-list lemon and Dover sole as well as the B-list plaice and flounder. There were also skate and ray, but these were of such little commercial value that they were usually thrown back. Anglerfish (monkfish), red gurnard, ling, pouting, ballan wrasse (known in Kintyre as *creggag*), dogfish, John Dory, squid and conger eel were around too. As was mackerel, though locals, and most other Scots at this time thought it a 'dirty eater' and boycotted it.

An Irish skipper was the first to recognise the value of scallop dredging in 1935.[158] It was a previously ignored shellfish which would later become a major fishery, especially off the Solway coast, where the scallop fishermen's breakfast on board was fried scallops and bacon with scrambled egg. On the Solway coast too, there were salmon fishers with ancient netting rights, and salmon-curing businesses. But they were separate from the rest of the fishing communities who were superstitious about salmon and never used the word, calling them a *billy* or *a queer fellow*. Other valuable seafood resources in the Solway area included cockle beds, which were also commercially exploited.

But it was the Norway lobster (*Nephrops norvegicus*), originally misnamed a 'prawn', now often called a langoustine, which realised the greatest commercial potential for fishermen of the entire area, when they stopped throwing them back into the sea in the 1950s. Lobster-fishing with creels had been the most lucrative shellfish here since the 1850s and continued to be profitable. It was not until the 1980s, however, that the value of crabs (partans and velvets) was realised and they stopped throwing them back into the sea too. Squat lobster, whelks (winkles) and mussels also added to the incredible variety in these seas, which scientists had begun to research in the 1860s. One of the first Marine Biological Stations was established at Millport on the island of Cumbrae off the Ayrshire coast in 1897.[159]

Fishermen in search of a living, and academic scientists attempting to uncover the mystery of what actually goes on beneath the seas, were not the only ones aware of the seas' hidden riches. At a rocky promontory, known to the local people of Machrihanish and Drumlemble on the west coast of Kintyre, the patient fisher had high hopes of a seafood bounty for free. Here there was the chance of good catches of many varieties of fish as well as crabs, lobsters, winkles (whelks) and limpets. Angus Martin, a native of the area, has recorded an invaluable oral history from local people who fished here, and whose memories span the period from the late 1800s to the present day.[160]

Rock fishing was a common activity all round the Scottish coasts, but this site had some unique features, making it not just a destination for keen fishers but also a popular picnic place for whole families. Children could discover here how to scramble over boulders safely and respect the dangers of the sea, when tides turned or big waves threatened to wash you off a rock in a flash.

The area was known as *Leac Bhuidhe* (yellow slab) after a large flattish rock, but the people just called it 'The Lake'. One of its main attractions was a natural swimming pool in the huge rock pool area of the largest boulder. Also, beneath the whole area of rocks was a network of interconnected tidal passageways and pools. There were four or five good rock-holes where the fisher could either dangle a bamboo cane with some bait on a line to catch a fish, or sink a *bait-bag* with a snare made from a loop of copper wire attached to a length of fence-wire, and catch a lobster or a crab. The bait-bag was filled with a tasty bait, often limpets or herring, and weighted with a stone. The fisher hung over the edge of the rock hole waiting for a hungry lobster or crab to enter, when the snare would be pulled quickly. Martin records that local-born Davie McVicar's best day's catch was eight lobsters, which he divided among his companions. Small lobsters were always put back, as were any females with eggs.

Some parents were sufficiently confident that their children would observe the rules that both boys and girls were allowed to go on their own when they were around eleven or twelve. They had been well-drilled about out-of-bounds areas and there were no recorded accidents with children, though one adult was almost taken away in a wave while fishing off a dangerous area.

During World War II and afterwards, when food rationing lasted till 1954, all kinds of food for free were greatly valued. Children, off for a wander on the shore, would be told to bring back winkles (whelks) or limpets by their mothers or grannies to make soup. Winkle soup was thickened with oatmeal; the limpet version was flavoured with onions or watercress.

Willie McMillan, of Coalhill Drumlemble, who began going to the Lake with his friends when he was eleven in the early 1940s, remembers the day they caught and killed a rabbit by 'diving on it', gutting and skinning it on the hill. Once at the Lake, they gathered firewood and lit a fire at the special cooking area which was called the Kitchen. Here, in among the rock ledges, were secreted pots and pans as well as cutlery and plates for communal use, everything cleaned and returned to the shelves before leaving. The boys had each put a few potatoes in their pockets before leaving home and had picked up a turnip and some carrots in passing from a farmer's field. While the lines were baited, the rabbit stew was simmering in the Kitchen. Food was eaten at the Table (the yellow slab).

If there was no rabbit, they would have to wait till someone got a bite from a fish. They always lit a fire when they arrived and put on the kettle, or the potatoes were put on to boil. Lythe (pollack), which liked to stay close inshore were the most commonly caught fish, but a record lythe of twelve pounds weight was once caught, though usually they were smaller. When they started 'taking' the bait, a shout would go up: 'Get the frying pan on.'

And out would come a cast-iron frying pan from the rock shelves. It was large enough to hold four or five fish, gutted and cleaned in seawater, and 'so sweet' when fried. Not all fish was fried in the pan, surplus were carried home and divided out among the community. Sometimes, other more exotic looking fish would be caught, as on the day Willie Allan, was heard shouting: 'A've caught a *creggach*! Rid (red) as hell, an' armour-plated.'

This was the very handsome ballan wrasse, which was 'quite plentiful' off rocky coasts. A prize to be taken home to admire, though not a great fish to eat with a lot of hidden bones. To hardened anglers it was only good for chopping up into bait.

While there were those on this coastline making an intimate connection with the sea, and the pleasures of its rich food resources, there were others, like Flora and Katie in a Glasgow tenement, with less opportunity to fish and forage and connect with their native seafood potential. Some might not know what a whole fish looked like, since they only ever ate fish in batter from the chippie. A fish eye staring up at them on their plate could be such a scary sight that it put them off eating fish for life.

Fish from the high street fishmonger came in a limited range and was dominated by the demand for convenient fillets of white fish – preferably haddock – whiting if cash was short, sole if it was not. It gave a very limited picture of the country's seafood resources, and city dwellers missed out on the unique tastes and flavours available in the wide range of seafood around the coasts.

This was not a regional variation, peculiar to this area, but a national divide between coastal communities and urban dwellers. Looking at a fishmongers' slab in the city, it might appear that no more than about five or six different fish were to be found in Scottish waters, and no shellfish. So fishermen looked elsewhere for buyers and found them easily, in a lucrative export market.

This problem continued throughout multiple retailing revolutions when high street fishmongers began disappearing. By the 1990s, however, various developments have helped to kick-start a reversal of this situation. Scots travelling abroad and seeing how highly others rate their exported Scottish seafood – and having a go at cooking it themselves – have helped. So have trailblazing fishmongers making a wider choice of seafood available. Chefs, in both prime seafood areas and urban restaurants, have made an attention-grabbing flourish of it on their menus, some opening special seafood restaurants. Fish festivals and farmers markets have taken seafood to the streets. Pierside fish stalls sell fresh-off-the-boats seafood. And not forgetting the fabulous kippers which are still smoked at Tarbert, Loch Fyne.

REGIONAL FOOD TRADITIONS

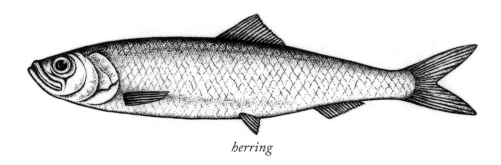

herring

A food 'tradition' gets its authenticity from being around for at least two or three generations. Many have been around for a lot longer. Many of Scotland's seafood traditions are to do with drying, salting and smoking, firstly for long-life, then for shorter shelf-life. This led to an east-west divide with east-coasters becoming skilled at smoking white fish, and west-coasters at kippering herring.

There is also distinct regional variation in a seafood version of the haggis (waste nothing) culture. The trick is to know how to create good tastes, textures and flavours out of the odds and ends of the animal or fish, as in *krappin, croppin or crawpeen* – a fish head stuffed with an oatmeal and high food-value fish-liver mix – made by a Shetlander or a North West Highland or islander, or anyone else in the know, and not to be judged by its looks. A tribute to its unique value appeared in the 2010 edition of the Lonely Planet Guide when it was listed in the world's 1,000 greatest experiences. Maybe one day a poet will immortalise it in a poem.

Another distinct regional variation is when there is a specially rich source of seafood in a particular area. The development of this tradition has often been held back by the economic need to export these valuable local assets, though this is now changing.

The following regional recipes are by no means a definitive collection, but a selection of a rich resource. Not just of regional variation, but also of family variation as tastes and habits create individual likes and dislikes.

Regional Recipes

Hairy Tatties

Bring me a ling fae the Viking Bank,
A tusk fae the Patch or Reef,
Or catch me a cod on the Buchan coast
An I'll greet nae mair for beef.
Steep her in saat for a three-fower days,
Then dry her slow in the sun
In the month o Mey, fin the safter win's
Bring the green growth up thro the grun.

Bring me a bile o the finest Pinks
Fae a craft on Mormon Braes,
At the tail o the hairst, fin the first fite frost
Tells a tale o winter days.
Peel them an bile in a fine big pot
Wi my bonny fish in anither;
Bree them baith when ye think they're richt
Syne ye'll chap them baith thegither.

A knottie o butter an a glaiss o milk –
Ye've a feast that's weel worth a Grace;
Then waste nae a meenit as ye fill yer speen
An stap it into yer face.
Bring me a tusk fae the Patch or Reef,
Fae the Viking Bank, a ling;
Or catch me a cod on the Buchan coast
Then I ken I'll dine like a king.

From *Collected Poems and Short Stories* by Peter Buchan (1917–1991),
(Gordon Wright, an imprint of Steve Savage Publishers, © the Executors
of Peter Buchan)

Patch and *Reef:* fishing areas, *greet:* weep, *safter:* softer, *Pinks:* Kerr's Pinks, Scottish variety of floury potatoes, *craft:* croft, *hairst:* harvest, *fite:* white, *bree:* drain, *chap:* mash, *baith:* both, *knottie:* small lump, *speen:* spoon, *stap:* put

EAST

East Coast

1785: Speldings – Cured White Fish

On their way north after leaving Edinburgh, James Boswell describes them in his *Journal of a Tour to the Hebrides with Samuel Johnson* in 1785:

> I bought some speldings, fish (generally whitings) salted and dried in a particular manner, being dipped in the sea and dried in the sun, and eaten by the Scots by way of a relish.

1862: Finnan Haddock [161]

> Finnan Haddocks should be skinned, broiled over a quick and clear fire and served in a napkin. Those of the best quality are of a creamy-yellow colour, and have a peculiar odour, from the nature of the material used in preparing them. When kept above forty-eight hours they lose much of their delicacy. Broiled haddocks, whether fresh, rizzared, or as Finnans, are held in great esteem by those who relish a good breakfast. Finnans are regularly forwarded from Aberdeen to Edinburgh and London by railways and steamers. They may be dressed in a bread-toaster before the fire, or in a Dutch oven.

> 'A Finnan haddock,' writes Sir Walter Scott,[162] 'has a relish of a very peculiar and delicate flavour, inimitable on any other coast than that of Aberdeenshire. Some of our Edinburgh philosophers tried to produce their equal in vain. I was one of a party at a dinner where the philosophical haddocks were placed in competition with the genuine Finnan dish. These were served round without distinguishing whence they came; but only one gentleman out of twelve present espoused the cause of philosophy.'

1862: Moray Firth or Cromarty Bay Haddock[163]

> Rizzard Haddocks – This recipe we consider the ne plus ultra of haddock-cookery. Clean thoroughly a Cromarty Bay or Moray Firth moderate-sized haddock. Rub it with a very little salt. Hang it on a fish-hake, and next morning cut off the head, take out the back-bone, skin, dust with flour, and broil it and serve with slices of fresh butter. In two days its flavour will have deteriorated.

1862: Plain Scottish Fish and Sauce or Fish Soup (East Coast)[164]

This is a popular preparation all along the eastern coasts of Scotland, where fine haddocks are got quite fresh. This is, in fact, just a good fish soup; and for such soups the fish must be very fresh.

Make a stock of the skins, heads, points of the tails, bones, fins, etc., or where fish are cheap, cut down one or two to help the stock. Boil green onions, parsley and chives in this, and some whole pepper. When all the substance is obtained, strain it. Thicken with butter kneaded in browned flour, but only to the consistence of a soup, and put in the fish (generally small haddocks) cut in three, or divided. Boil the fish ten minutes, add catsup, and serve them in the sauce, in a tureen or soup-dish.

1929: Cullen Skink
A Cottage Recipe from the Shores of the Moray Firth[165]

Finnan-haddie, onion, mashed potatoes, butter, milk, pepper and salt

Skin a Finnan-haddie, and place it in a pan with sufficient boiling water to cover it (no more). Bring to the boil and add a chopped onion. When the haddock is cooked, take it out and remove all the bones. Flake the fish and return all the bones to the stock. Boil for one hour. Strain the stock and again bring to the boil. Boil about a pint of milk separately and add it to the stock with the flake fish and salt to taste. Boil for a few minutes. Add enough mashed potato to make the soup a nice consistency, with a tablespoonful of butter, and pepper to taste, and serve.

1929: Finnan Haddie – Fisherwife's fashion[166]

Skin a finnan-haddie, and cut it into pieces. Lay these in a stew-pan with a dessertspoonful of butter. Put on the lid closely and steam for five minutes. Now break a teaspoonful of cornflour with a little milk and add more milk – about a breakfastcupful in all. Pour over the fish and butter, bring it to the boil, and cook for a few minutes. Take out the pieces of fish, lay them nicely on a dish, and pour the sauce over them.

1972: Finnan Haddock: Mary Annie's Method[167]

Cut the haddock into portions and cook gently in a saucepan with enough milk to cover them. Add pepper (salt if needed) and a shake of celery salt. While the haddock is cooking – and it will not take long – take a piece of butter about the size of a small egg and work as much flour into it as it will take.

Lift the haddock onto a warm ashet, take the pan away from the fire, and drop in the ball of buttered flour. With a fork beat until it is smooth and put back on the fire to come through the boil. Serve the sauce in a warmed sauceboat.

Jessie's Jeems' Favourite[168]

Take a 'wise-like' (decent size) finnan haddock and give it a trim. Dip it in flour and cover it well. Fry it slowly in a spoonful of good dripping, then put in a cupful of milk and a good shake of black pepper.

Put a lid on the pan and cook the fish slowly until it comes clean from the bone.

('Jessie's Jeems' is a 'tee' name, a form of identification used in fishing villages where there are very few who are not of the same surname.)

Findon Fish Pudding (anonymous)[169]

Found written on a piece of paper among the pages of an old cookery book from this area. Described as 'very convenient'.

2lb potatoes; 1lb 4oz Aberdeen fillet; 1oz butter; 2 tablespoons milk or cream; 1 tomato; 1oz grated cheese

Peel the potatoes and put on to boil. While they are boiling put the fish onto a greased baking tray, dot with butter and sprinkle with milk. Cover with a piece of paper and bake in a moderate oven for 20 minutes. Remove from the oven and leave to cool.

The potatoes can now be drained and mashed. Drain the cooking liquor from the fish into the potatoes, then flake the fish on top. Mash all this together and season well. Put into a greased 2 ½ pint pie dish. Put sliced tomato on top and cover with grated cheese. Heat through in the oven and serve with leeks in a cream sauce.

1929: Tweed Kettle (Salmon Hash)[170]

Fresh salmon, shallot or chives, parsley, salt, pepper, mace, wine vinegar or white wine, water

Cut a pound of fresh salmon, freed from skin and bone, into one-inch cubes. Season with salt, pepper and a tiny pinch of mace, and place in a fish-kettle or saucepan with a minced shallot or a tablespoonful of chopped chives. Add half a cup of water and a quarter cup of wine vinegar or white wine, bring to the boil and simmer very gently for about thirty-five minutes. Add a tablespoonful of chopped parsley shortly before dishing up.

A few small mushrooms, chopped and cooked in butter for ten minutes, may be added, or a few cooked shrimps, or one or two chopped hard-boiled eggs. Another variant has a dash of anchovy sauce.

Serve hot with fresh girdle scones or a border of creamed potatoes, or cold garnished with cress and cucumber.

In Edinburgh, in the mid-nineteenth century, 'in a house down a stair in Broughton Street, much frequented by booksellers' clerks, one might obtain, at the modest charge of seven pence, a liberal helping from a succulent dish called "salmon hash", better known as "Tweed Kettle", and it could be obtained all day long, hot or cold to taste. . . . it could be got all the year round and always excellently cooked. The landlady, being a Kelso woman, was familiar with the fish and its capabilities.'

James Bertram, *Books, Authors and Events.*

Firth of Forth

Not only available in the streets and taverns of Edinburgh by the hundred, Firth of Forth oysters also appeared on the dining tables of the gentry in the 1700s, sometimes by the two hundred, as in this recipe which appears in Scotland's first published recipe book.

1736: To Frigasie [sic] Oysters[171]

Take two hundred Oysters, stew them in their own Liquor and wash them therein from the shells, then strain the Liquor, and put the Oysters into it, with some white wine, pickled Mushrooms, and some Capers, sweet Butter rolled in flour, grated Bread, some Lemon Peil [sic], stew them a little in the Pan with a little Pepper, beaten Nutmeg and Mace, then take the Yolks of four Eggs beat very well, put them into the Pan, and toss all round lest the Eggs curdle, till they be near boiling, then put them into your dish, and garnish it with sliced Lemon, Mushrooms and Pickles.

1791: Beef Steaks with Oyster Sauce[172]

Cut your Steaks off any under Part of the Beef, flat them with your chopping knife, and put them on to a hot clean Brander on a clear quick fire, turning them often that the Gravy does not run out; have your sauce ready, make up thus: Scald your Oysters, and wash them clean in their own liquor, then strain the liquor into a saucepan, put to it a piece of butter worked in flour, two or three shallots, pounded pepper, Cloves, and Nutmegs, salt it to your taste; put a Glass of white wine and the rind and Juice of a Lemon in it; So pour it on your ashet of Steaks boiling hot. Garnish them with pickles.

Another variation of 'surf and turf' is the Musselburgh Pie, a beef steak pie with added mussels.

1826: To Serve Oysters in the Shell[173]

Let the opener stand behind the eater's chair, who should make a quick and clean conveyance. If not so placed, wash, brush and open and beard the oysters, and arrange them on rows on a tray; or if pinched for room, heap the shells in piles; the fresher from the sea, and the more recently opened the better. The French serve lemon-juice with raw oysters; we serve this or vinegar, pepper and toasted crusts.

Orkney

The Orcadians were as keen on salt fish as the Shetlanders, and certainly in Stromness and Kirkwall there was a busy trade in large fish such as cod, ling and tusk, hard salted for export. The most popular way with salt fish was boiled and eaten with a sauce of Orkney butter and a floury potato.

Early 1900s: Home-Made Soups[174]
Thelma Rendall, Stronsay

Dinnertime it was just home-made soups – there was no instant food then....
. . . You usually had meat or fish every day and at teatime then it was a time when you very often had your own eggs, it was time for something simple.

1929: To Fry Sillocks[175]

(Sillocks are the fry of the saithe or coal-fish, a variety of cod)

Sillocks, salt, oatmeal, butter

The perfect dish of sillocks must be caught and cooked by the consumers. When the moon rises on a late summer's night, you must fish far out on a sea moved only by the slow, broad Atlantic swell. And the little mountain of sillocks, the reward of cold but exciting hours, must be 'dite' cleaned in a moonlit rockpool. Then home at cockcrow.

Around the kitchen fire, while the rest of the household sleep, come the happy rites of cooking and eating. Each tiny, headless fish, wrapped in a stout jacket of salted oatmeal, is popped into a pan of hot butter. There they bounce and spit while the fishers, ringed round pan and fire, exquisitely thaw. At last, richly browned and curled into fantastic shapes, and so tender they almost fall to pieces, they are dished.

Sillock-eating at the kitchen table dispenses with knives and forks. You lift a sillock gently between thumb and forefinger, snip off the tail, press the plump sides – and the backbone shoots forth! The delicious morsel left – hot crisp oatmeal and sweet, melting fish – you eat on buttered bere (barley) bread, a darkly brown, flatly sour scone.

Note – This recipe won a prize many years ago in a competition in Everyman.

1988: Salt Cuithes and Keppleton Kidneys[176]

Mary and Robert Leslie on the Isle of Shapinsay

4 salt cuithes; Keppleton kidney potatoes, or Sharps Express or Record; melted dripping

With a sharp knife, cut a thin sliver from the edge of the cuithe back removing the back fins. Cut another sliver from the belly edge also removing the fins. Peel off the papery dried skin which should come off easily. Put the fish into a pan, cover with water and simmer for about 20 minutes. Meanwhile, wash the potatoes and put on to boil in another pan. Drain when cooked. Drain the fish and eat with melted dripping and potatoes.

WEST

Shetland

The fish taken home by fishermen included leftover heads, bones and innards from fish curing as well as any unwanted whole fish. White fish innards included: *rhans* (roe); liver; *sounds* or *soonds* (swimming bladder); and *muggies* (stomach). For oily fish it was the roe or milt.

1925: House Fish[177]

Surplus 'house fish' might be salted or preserved in other ways:

Reested – when the fish was hung up on a rafter (reest) above a central open peat fire in the croft house. As the smoke wafted upwards it dried the fish, giving it a smoky flavour. Left too long, it became very dark with smoke and a very smoky flavour as well as very hard, requiring much soaking to make it palatable. When fires were moved to a gable end with a chimney, the fish was hung up near the fire to dry, sometimes it was hung inside the chimney. Or it might have been simply hung over a rafter in the old way to dry out, without the added smoke flavour.

Blawn – also known as stockfish – the fish were washed in salt water and then hung up on a wooden frame attached to the side of the croft-house on its windy side and left to dry out.

Grozened – this was when fish had been gutted, de-headed and filleted. It was washed in salt or sea water and stretched out on a south-facing rock, preferably with a slant to catch the full rays of the sun. On a very hot sunny day the fish dried out and 'cooked' in the sun. It was then eaten without cooking.

Skaraefish – This was fish dried in the sun without being salted.

Shetland dishes of: Rhans (Roes); Livers; Muggies (stomachs); Sounds (swimming bladder)

Using Rhans (roes)

Slott, a kind of cod roe dumpling, was made with uncooked roe. It might be made with just cod roe and flour in one area while in another it might also have some cod liver added.

1914: Slott[178]

Slott was fish roe (uncooked) beat with a spoon till it was like cream, a little flour with salt was added, and the slott, roughly shaped into balls, was dropped into hot water and boiled a short time. When cool it was sliced, fried in butter, and eaten hot.

1925: Slott (with liver)[179]

One Cod Roe [uncooked]
One quarter of a Ling Liver
One cupful of Flour
Pepper and Salt

Skin the roe, add liver and enough flour to bind; beat well together until thoroughly mixed. Have ready a pan of boiling fish broe [fish stock] or boiling salted water; with a saucer dipped in hot water lift out a portion of the slott, drop into the boiling water and cook for 20-25 minutes. The boiling water will cause a coating to form on the outside of the slott and keep the portions from breaking. Serve very hot.

Note: as a rule the taste of the liver should not be pronounced. Sometimes more flour was added, but the mixture must not be of too stiff a consistency. To get the correct saltiness, a pan consisting of half sea water and half fresh water was generally used. Sometimes the slott was dropped into a ladle in boiling water, and the ladle withdrawn after it had formed its shape.

1978: Slott (without liver)[180]

There are several recipes, but try this one. First beat the roe till creamy, add a little flour and salt to make it into small dumplings. Drop them into boiling well salted water (or sea water). They will rise to the top when done. Eat hot or, when cold, slice and fry in butter.

1978: Cod Rhans (Roes)[181]

Wash roe and tie in muslin (it breaks easily during cooking). Cover and simmer 30 minutes. Skin when still warm. If the rhans are peerie (small) fry in butter for a few minutes only and eat hot.

Using Fish Liver

Using the fish livers in a mix with meal (beremeal, oatmeal or wheat flour) for a stuffing or dumpling mix was not unique to Shetland but was common wherever there was a surplus of innards when large white fish were being caught, usually for curing.

The stuffing was often cooked in a large fish head, regarded as the most delicious method since the dumpling absorbed all the flavour from the head. It might also be cooked as a dumpling, boiled in a cloth or steamed in a pudding bowl. More modern methods suggest wrapping the stuffed head in foil and baking it in the oven. The liver dumpling was usually served with some lightly poached fillets of white fish.

It can also be made into small dumplings, the mixture divided into small rounds the size of a large egg and cooked in boiling salted water like slott, or put on top of a fish soup or stew.

This seafood equivalent of the haggis culture of wasting nothing, might sound like a recipe for less than delicious fare but, as with haggis, the trick is in the know-how. Those who know *krappin*, *croppin* or *crawpeen* with its high Omega 3 oil liver mix, made by a Shetlander, West Highlander or islander, will know its worth and will not be surprised that others beyond these regions also value its unique flavour and waste-not credentials. So much so that it appeared in the 2010 edition of the Lonely Planet Guide's listing of the top 1000 of the world's greatest experiences: 'It's surprisingly tasty and healthy, with miracle-cure fish oils and plenty of protein,' said the guide. 'The best flavour is achieved by boiling the head in seawater.'

1925: Krappin (also known as croppin, or crawpeen)[182]

One pound of liver (or two cupfuls); Quarter of a pound of Flour (one cupful); Quarter of a pound of Beremeal or fine Oatmeal; One teaspoonful of Salt; Pepper

(1) Put all into a basin and, with the hand, thoroughly mix together, breaking down the liver until the mixture forms a ball and holds together. Thoroughly

wash a fish head, remove blood and gills and stuff with the mixture. Cook in boiling salted water for 20-30 minutes.

(2) Put mixture (as above) into a clean dry white paper bag and put this inside another bag; tie around with string, plunge into boiling water and boil for half an hour.

None of these recipes make it clear how the stuffing stays in the head while cooking. In the North West Highlands, they tie up a large fish with string. Firstly the jaws are tied together with a sort of noose so the stuffing stays in at that end. Then the string is taken round the back of the head with another loop and then another loop is taken over the top of the head, tying it all up like a parcel.

Modern variations: Shetland fisherman and galley cook, Charlie Simpson, wrote extensively about Shetland fish-eating traditions in his column *In Da Galley* in the *Shetland Fishing News* during the 1990s. Here he describes how he cooks livers now, in the oven.

Three dishes in all – the stuffed heads, a dish of livers and a dish of white fish – are his 'livery feast', when some of the white fish are mixed through livers to make a dish of Stap.

> I was brought up to simmer the mixture of livers and oatmeal, wrapped up in a cloot, in a pan of water, as the written recipes still instruct. However, having tasted the delights of baked livers, I tried crawpeen the same way, wrapping the mixture in tinfoil and baking as for livers. The logical extension of this technique gives good results with crawpeen heids as well, so for a livery feast nowadays I cook it all in the oven; heads foil-wrapped on a tray, livers in a lidded dish and the cuts of fish in a greased dish, again foil covered.[184]

Using Fish Muggie (from Norwegian, *mage*, Old Norse, *magi*, the stomach). The ling muggie was regarded the best for stuffing.

1925 Liver Muggies[185]

ling muggies
ling (or other white fish) liver
Salt and pepper

Fill a pot with water and bring to the boil.

Wash the muggie carefully, taking care not to tear it. Tie a string tightly round the small end to make a bag. Slice the liver and season with salt and pepper. Stuff the muggie with the liver about three-quarters full since the muggie will shrink while cooking. Tie the other end of the muggie about an inch from the end. Add salt to the boiling water and add the muggie. Simmer gently for about 30 minutes. To serve as a main course: Remove muggie and serve hot with boiled potatoes. Both the muggie and the liver can be eaten.

To serve as a broth: Put muggie in a bowl and pour over some of the cooking liquor. Serve with bere bannocks.

Variations:

Hakka Muggies

Filling: a mix of fish liver, fish sounds and flaked fish. Put into a bowl and mix thoroughly by hand to break down the liver. Season well with salt. Use to fill muggies.

Krappit Muggies – (Fish Haggis)

The muggie (stomach) of some fish was cleaned out and filled with the liver and oatmeal well mixed with pepper and salt. This was called 'krappit muggies'.[186]

Stapp (from Norwegian dialect, *stappa*, v., to mash, pound, squeeze, cram, *n.*, a mash, of food, Old Norse, *stappa*, to pound)

1932: Stapp is the meat of fish-heads with the livers boiled, carefully mixed with seasoning, baked and served hot.[187]

2010 Stapp[188]

> *3 large Piltocks (Saithe)*
> *2–3lb of Piltock Livers*
> *Seasoning to taste*

Place livers in a covered, but not sealed, container, in a steamer for about 4 hours until most of the oil has come out of the livers. Drain the livers, reserving some of the oil.

Just before the livers are ready, boil the fish, then remove all skin and bones and keep fish warm. Roughly mash livers and fish together in equal proportions, adding salt and pepper to taste. If the mixture is too dry, add some of the oil from the livers.

Serve with boiled or steamed potatoes and butter. Any leftover Stap is excellent in sandwiches.

Margaret Stout[189] (and others) advises using haddock rather than saithe. She puts the livers into a jam jar which she covers and then simmers in a pan of boiling water for an hour. She poaches the fish gently till just cooked. She removes just one piece of fish, skins and bones it then adds it to the liver, chopping everything together in the jam jar. Then she seasons with salt and pepper and serves it in a separate pie dish with the fish.

1978: Liver Bannocks[190]

3 breakfast cups plain white flour
1 tsp salt
2 tsp baking soda and 1 breakfastcupful sour or buttermilk
Or 3 tsp baking powder and 1 breakfastcupful sweet milk
uncooked fish liver

Sift the flour and salt. Lightly fork in the uncooked livers. Add baking soda stirred into the sour/buttermilk (or baking powder and sweet milk) and mix to a dough. Put on an ungreased tin and bake in a hot oven until well risen. Eat on their own or with fish instead of tatties.

Always use fish livers very fresh: it is best to buy them for eating the same day.

Using Soonds (swimming bladders)

Cod Soonds Broiled with Gravy[191]

Scald the sounds in hot water, rub over with salt and blanch. Remove black skin, return to pan with cold water, bring to boil, and simmer till almost tender. Remove from pan, toss in seasoned flour and grill. Serve hot with white sauce or gravy around.

1950s: *Mackerel at Midnight*

In summer, when the midnight sun hangs low in the sky, the mackerel shoals come to feed round the Scottish coast. On Shetland, the islanders keep a watch for signs in the bay of jumping mackerel. Then they push out the boat and set off for a catch.

Meanwhile, others go off to dig up a pile of floury potatoes and put them on to boil. Another pot of boiling salted water is made ready when the fishers return with the mackerel. Poached for a few minutes over the slow peat fire, they are ready in minutes.

An unforgettable *simmer dim* (daylight-through-the-night) feast of fresh-out-the-sea mackerel, floury potatoes, farmhouse butter, bannocks and rhubarb jam is recalled by Ethel Hofman in her memories of a Shetland childhood, *Mackerel at Midnight* (2006).

'Without freshness it [mackerel] is nothing.' *Jane Grigson's Fish Book* (1973).

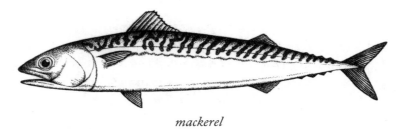

mackerel

North West Highlands and Islands

Many of the Shetland traditions of dishes created from fish innards also apply to this area, though they have not been so well documented. Distinctive traditions here are a more extensive use of both shellfish and seaweed.

Certainly, seaweed was seldom used in Shetland unless 'in cases of extremity'[192] when a family in poverty was known to live for a short time on seaweed. But in the west coast Highlands and Islands its food value and healing powers were well known and used widely. Long wavy fronds of seaweed were a valuable wild vegetable resource and became a vital part of the diet during the period in the 1800s when inland crofters were moved to the coast. Short of land, they learned to harvest the sea bed more intensively and about twenty Gaelic names were used to describe different seaweeds.

The more extensive use of shellfish here too has origins in poverty, when it was used when no other food was available. In the more remote areas, especially on islands with steep cliffs used by nesting sea birds, the birds and their eggs were also an important seafood resource in the self-sufficient crofter's lifestyle.

Since they like to taste the seaweed tang, many eat this just sweetened slightly and served with equal quantities of freshly whipped cream. Carrageen is its Irish name, Sea Moss its Scots.

1929: Limpet Stovies (Isle of Colonsay)[193]

Limpets, potatoes, water, pepper, salt, butter

Gather two quarts of limpets on the rocks at low tide. Put them in a pot, cover them with water, and bring to the boil. Take out the limpets, remove them from the shells, and remove the eyes and the sandy trail. Take three times their quantity of peeled potatoes, put a layer in the bottom of a large round three-legged pot, add a layer of limpets, season with pepper and a little salt, and repeat the operation until they are all used up. Then add two cupfuls of the liquor in which the limpets were scalded and put pieces of butter over the top, using about half a pound for that quantity. Cover it all with a clean white cloth well rolled in round the edges, bring to the boil and hang it high up on the crook above a peat fire. Let it simmer for at least an hour.

Fried Barra Cockles

These are collected from the beach where the plane lands. A rake with blunted points is the best way of pulling them out of the sand since they are often about an inch or two below the surface. Don't use any which are less than 2cm (1in) across.

Cockles; Butter; Salt and Pepper

Place cockles in fresh water and leave overnight. This will clear them of sand. Rinse them in fresh water. Place in a pan of boiling water and boil for a few minutes. Strain and shell.

Melt butter in a frying pan and toss the cockles over a gentle heat for about a minute just to heat through. Season with salt and pepper and serve.

1978: Cuddies (*The Hebridean Kitchen* © Willie Fulton)[194]

Cuddaigean – the young of the saithe or coalfish (member of the cod family). These small but voracious fish are plentiful among the rocks and by jetties etc. during the winter months.

They will devour almost any small bait, but now small feathers or sheep's wool tied onto two or three hooks and suspended from a long bamboo pole is the usual method. Around four or five fish 4 to 6 inches long, per person. Gut, clean, but retain the little livers.

Simmer fish and livers for a few minutes, till ready. Serve with spuds and veg. More often than not the juice is kept, milk, salt and pepper added, and a nutritious drink it is too, taken hot.*

*I prefer them fried in butter after rolling in oatmeal. Remove from pan after a few minutes, then the crisp little fish are eaten using the fingers.

1978: Rionach (Mackerel) (*The Hebridean Kitchen*)[195]

(Must be fresh and head removed and fish cleaned when caught.)

Mackerel; Brown Sugar; Salt; Vinegar

A fish much underrated – mackerel has a unique strong taste, when eaten fresh – plentiful in the autumn months, when they will take any bait, anything that shines on a hook.

Fillet fish by removing generous slices from each side. Place mackerel fillets, brown sugar, salt in alternate layers in a dish and leave overnight.

Next day, wash in cold water (the fish also) and boil in equal parts of vinegar and water till cooked. Leave to cool and serve with salad. Can also be treated as herring and fried in oatmeal.

1978: Ceann Cropaig – fish head, liver and oatmeal (*The Hebridean Kitchen*)[196]

Haddock or Cod's head; Fish livers; Oatmeal; Heaped teaspoon sugar; Pinch of salt

Catch large fish and when dead, remove head. Mix fish livers in a bowl with sufficient oatmeal to make a paste, which is not too dry. Fill head (fish) with paste. Boil, simmer for 30-35 mins. Remove filling from head and surplus meat from the fish. Eat hot or cold with boiled potatoes.

1981: Port of Ness Cod[197]

A simple way of serving cod.

750g cod on the bone; Salt and pepper; 1kg potatoes, boiled and mashed; 50g butter; 2-3 tablespoons milk; 1 tablespoon chopped parsley

Put the cod into a pan and just cover with water. Season with salt and pepper and bring to the boil. Simmer for 2-5 minutes, depending on the thickness of the cod. Remove cod from the pan, skin and bone. Put flakes into a large heated ashet and put pats of butter on top. Moisten with a little of the cooking liquor and sprinkle with chopped parsley. Add the milk and a little of the butter to the potatoes and beat them till creamy. Serve round the fish on the ashet.

1981: Lewis Way of Frying Brown Trout[198]

The small speckled brown trout which are found in the many lochs, burns and rivers have a delicate sweet flavour.

4 trout about 250g each; Salt; Milk; 50g seasoned oatmeal; Oil or fat for frying

After the trout have been gutted, salt them inside and out. Cover and leave in a cool place overnight. The next day, wipe the fish and split them open to remove the bone. Dip the fillets in milk and coat thickly in seasoned oatmeal. Heat oil or fat in frying pan and place in fillets flesh side down, turning once. Serve with butter.

2008: Taste of Guga by Donald Murray, Ness, Isle of Lewis[199]

The filleted fowl is washed carefully, making sure that not one grain of coarse salt remains. Sometimes the four portions (or ceathramhan) that the bird is cut into are scraped clean with the edge of a knife. After this it is boiled for an hour with a water change after 30 minutes. (Some people do this more than once through the process.) And accompanying the guga is a cup or two of milk or water and a serving of potatoes – boiled of course.

Most of the time, too, the people of Ness are even specific about the type of potato that should accompany the dish. It has to be the Kerr's Pink; its red jacket bursting open as it lies . . . oozing with melted butter.

The meat and skin are two quite distinct experiences. The former has been described in a number of ways by those who come to praise it. In my view, its taste resembles salt mackerel-flavoured chicken. Others claim the meat has the texture of steak and the flavour of kipper. Some rhapsodise over it, claiming it is like salt goose – one with very little fat. Those who have eaten 'reestit mutton' while in Shetland argue that there are certain similarities between the two foods.

Even its admirers, however, freely admit that in terms of its appearance, the skin has little to commend it. It has been said to resemble a dirty cloth employed only a short time before to clean up a grimy, dirt-engrained floor. Yet there are many citizens of Ness and elsewhere who believe that the skin is the most exquisite part of their native delicacy. Some liken it to tripe, what was at one time the central culinary experience of Britain's industrial past. Others enjoy it as a titbit, storing it in the fridge and nibbling a small piece at a time like Americans are said to do with beef jerky.

1990s: Cooking and Eating Guga

Stravaigin Restaurant, Gibson Street, Glasgow

The guga was already simmering and only a slight fishy-oily whiff hovered over the pot on the stove. It had been cooking for over an hour and the water had been changed, yet there was still lots of oil floating on the surface from the heavily salt-cured young gannet. Chef Colin Clydesdale, reckoned it was almost ready.

Never having cooked a guga before, this was a first for him. As it was for the eaters. We gathered round a table set with the traditional Lewis accompaniment of glasses of milk and a pile of bursting-out-of-their-skins, floury tatties. Chef brought in the steaming guga – about as visually attractive as a haggis – but appearances never tell the full story. He put it in the centre of the table and began dividing it up, removing the dirty-dishcloth-looking skin – we got stuck in.

First impression was complex – salty, meaty, fishy – none of them dominating; yet the combined effect was like a well-cured Iberian ham with a flavour kick that lingered pleasantly on, and on . . .

Chef wondered what to do with the skin? In its just-out-the-pot boiled state it seemed pretty inedible to us. But then he suddenly had the bright idea of chopping it up very small and deep-frying it. Could this be the Scottish twist on English 'scratchings'?

Off he went to experiment while we carried on with the guga feast. The milk and potatoes were the perfect foil for the intensely interesting guga. Like a salt herring, treated as a relish or piquant flavouring for mealy tatties, it was not made to be eaten in a large quantity.

Then the deep-fried skin appeared. Its texture was transformed and its flavour even more intensely fishy: the inedible made edible as we crunched on our guga 'scratchings'.

South West and Firth of Clyde

1826: Fresh Herrings as Dressed at Inveraray and the Highland Sea-Lochs[200]

The best herrings are obtained in these localities almost alive. Cut off the heads, fins and tails; scale, gut, and wash them. Split and bone them or not, dust the inside with pepper and fine salt. Place two herrings flat together, the backs outmost, and dip in toasted oatmeal and fry them for seven minutes. Serve hot. They are delicious; and in the summer, add much to the breakfasts in the steamers on the Clyde, and round all the north-east and west coasts of Scotland.

1929: Winkle Soup[201]

Winkles, oatmeal, fish stock or milk, water

Gather a small pailful of winkles on the rocks at low tide.* Put them into a pot, cover them with water, and bring them to the boil. Take out the winkles (preserving the liquor) and pick the fish out of the shells with a long pin. Strain carefully the water they were boiled in, as it is often sandy, and return it to the pot. It will probably be too salt, so it is an advantage to use equal proportions of the liquor and water in which fresh fish has been boiled; but if this is not available, a little milk and fresh water will do. When it comes to the boil, add enough oatmeal to make it of the consistency of thin gruel. The meal should be allowed to fall in a steady rain from the left hand whilst you stir it with a porridge stick or wooden spoon. When the oatmeal is nearly cooked (which takes about twenty minutes) put back the winkles and boil for ten minutes longer.

*Note: after picking, steep the winkles overnight in fresh water to remove sand.

1980s: Whelks at 'Ra Barras', Glasgow

A take-away bag of cooked whelks is the thing for all whelk-lovers on a trip to the Glasgow Barras. Never mind the hustle, find a place to sit and use your hat-pin-sized-picker (supplied) to twirl out the curly whelk from its shell and taste the sea in its chewy softness.

Why did Glaswegians – and some other Scots too – misname the grey-black, curly-shelled periwinkle a whelk or buckie? The true whelk, which these Scots call a dog whelk, has a whiter shell and flesh, also a longer, less curly shape.

SEAFOOD FUTURE

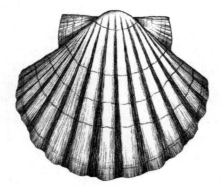

king scallop

1　Fishermen

Fishing for North Sea Haddock – October 2010

There are CCTV cameras on the deck of this deep sea trawler, fishing for white fish in the North Sea, which monitor the fishermen's activities. A screen in the wheelhouse relays what's going on outside. The skipper, for the moment, is watching from a wheelhouse window as the crew 'shoot' (launch) the net. His eyes shift about intently.

A new yellow float gets stuck as it goes over the edge of the boat and a crewman quickly goes to release it. For the next couple of hours he keeps an eye on the progress of over two hundred feet of net, dropping into the sea then being hauled back in. He's set its position to catch the fish in the depths below, after a careful study of the sonar screens in the wheelhouse.

They give him a picture of the seas beneath him of this Bressay Bank fishing area that he's in off Shetland, using multi-beam sonar technology and a global positioning system (GPS). Another type of sonar helps him find the fish. This high-tech equipment, besides showing him the lie of the 'land', and the rocks to avoid, also helps him to avoid straying into Norwegian waters. If he does, they will have a police boat alongside before he knows what's happened, and several officers will be on board inspecting the boat for evidence of illegal fishing.

His twenty-five metre trawler was built with the help of EU funds nine years ago in Spain, where he stayed to supervise its design. Besides its many innovative features, improving the quality of the fish landed was among the most important; reducing the 'hard graft' for the six-man crew was another.

When the net is fully out it encircles the fish. Now the winches pull in the haul which has swum into the 'cod-end' (the bag at the end of the net which traps them). As this nears the boat, the sea is a moving mass of silver. Frantic gulls are diving for fish. Small fish escape the net only to be gobbled by a gull. The nearer it gets to the boat, the shape of the net changes into a round ball of solid fish as it's winched out of the water and up the side of the boat. The crew position it over a hatch.

The fastening which holds it together is released and the fish fall down a chute onto a conveyer belt below deck. Some are still jumpingly alive, as they travel towards four crewmen who are waiting to sort and gut them. The skipper is here too, checking the catch. He's happy with the mix, plenty of haddock, some cod, and a few halibut. They are in good condition. A gutting machine deals with the haddock, the largest species in the catch. Once gutted, all the fish are washed.

Meanwhile, a crewman in the 'ice wing' is shovelling tons of fine ice – made onboard – into creels which go to a refrigerated 'fish room' where others are filling boxes with fish according to species and size. Layered between ice, they are packed neatly like sardines in a tin. Each box is weighed and labelled with details of the fish, time caught, and name of trawler.

While they box up the fish, the skipper turns the boat round to head for home. Of the boxed fish, it's this catch of North Sea haddock which has now been certified sustainable by the Marine Stewardship Council (MSC) which is the most important.

For two and a half years the Scottish North Sea haddock fishery has been undergoing MSC assessment by an independent certification body. It was a complicated process, but his family have been fishermen here for generations and he will do whatever he can to protect Scotland's fisheries for the future. His boat is one of seventeen in the Scottish demersal fleet. It has joined in a trial which has increased his catch quota on the understanding that all fish caught are also landed. The CCTV cameras are there to prove there have been no discards.

Sixteen hours sailing later – some spent in his bunk asleep – land is in sight. The Buchan Ness lighthouse at the entrance to Peterhead harbour is on the horizon.

'That's the most welcome sight in the North Sea,' he says.

Landing the haddock from this boat[202] and others which had also gained the MSC seal of approval,[203] did not pass without a congratulatory flurry of speeches and a presentation, as well as a delicious fresh-off-the-boat haddock lunch in the Boddam Inn attended by Alex Salmond, Scotland's First Minister, who is also this area's Member of the Scottish Parliament. North Sea haddock, the first Scottish demersal fish to be certified sustainable, is Scotland's fourth most valuable catch (worth £25m in 2009). Ten organisations, representing fishermen, producers and processors involved in the North Sea fisheries, worked together to achieve this certification. Their joint organisation, the Scottish Fisheries Sustainable Accreditation Group (SFSAG),[204] which was set up in 2008, is now in the process of attaining MSC certification for North Sea langoustine. Such is the passion to preserve the traditions of Scotland's fishing industry, against all the odds.

Over a century has passed since the invention of steam trawling sparked concerns about how this would damage fish stocks. Even at this early stage in the history of steam trawling, attempts were made to prevent fishing boats, both native and foreign, from sweeping their nets indiscriminately around the Scottish coast. Government regulations were put in place to ban trawling within three miles of low water mark and in the Firths. This was policed by the Fishery Board, reconstituted in 1882, and some trawlers were prosecuted for fishing illegally, with fines of up to £60 and prison sentences of up to 60 days imposed on masters of offending vessels. But the authorities did not have the resources to police every inch of the seas and many escaped prosecution.[205]

The Board, at this time, was also given powers to develop marine research, which would form the beginnings of a better understanding of what goes on beneath the seas. Early marine scientists studied, among other things, the effect of trawling on inshore grounds. They also worked with other marine scientists from other countries fronting the North Sea, and in 1902 the International Council for the Exploration of the Sea (ICES) was founded. It remains the advising body on the science of the seas and its resources, and is also responsible for recording and monitoring fish catches.[206]

After World War II, when there was a major effort to rebuild fishing fleets, largely with government help, the North East Atlantic Fisheries Commission (NEAFC) was set up to make recommendations on how fishery resources should be managed on the basis of marine research. Though it advised on mesh sizes and minimum landing sizes for each species to allow juveniles to grow to maturity, it lacked

First landings of MSC certified North Sea haddock, Peterhead Fish Market, October 2010.

effective power. Throughout the 1950s and into the 60s, however, it continued to contribute to the scientific debate, including the question of whether there should be formal conservation measures in the herring fisheries. Most believed herring stocks were not under threat.[207]

They were shocked, therefore, when it was discovered that stocks of herring, the most important single pelagic fishery in the North Sea, were in danger of extinction. A too-successful partnership of trawler, purse-seine net and power-hauled winch had more or less cleaned up this particular sea of the valuable herring. The purse-seine net was so large it could encircle whole shoals of fish. While its top end floated, its bottom end had a series of rings threaded with a rope which, when pulled, tightened like the drawstring of a purse, trapping a whole shoal of fish. A power-block on the boat could haul up nets containing several hundred tons of fish. In 1977 there was an international ban on herring fishing in the North Sea which lasted for six years.[208]

During this time a new force came into play, more powerful than any fleet of high-tech trawlers, as Britain negotiated entry into the European Union. Part of the UK's negotiations were about its unique position at the centre of some of the best fishing grounds in the world. How would this work as part of a Common Fisheries Policy (CFP)? And how could this national asset be protected, especially in Scotland, where there was the highest concentration of historic fishing communities?

The minority UK and Ireland lobby argued that they should retain their traditional fishing zones to protect their fishing industry. The more powerful Continental fishing industry, however, favoured a 'common sea' policy, with all member countries allowed to take a certain amount of fish each year, decided on a yearly basis. This is what prevailed.

There were some concessions for Scottish fishermen, with an allowance for 'historic fishing grounds'; the six-mile protected zone round all coasts was extended to twelve miles round Scotland's east coast, where the greatest concentration of fishing communities were established. There was also a six-mile protected shellfish zone round Orkney and Shetland, and another for demersal fish round Shetland, which was known as the 'Shetland box'.[209] Beyond these zones CFP rules applied, some relating to technical measures aimed at conservation, such as fish net sizes and allowable catch limits for endangered species. But the big issue was the allocation of how much each member could catch. These quotas continue to be decided at an annual meeting of fishery ministers of all members, which a recent report has described as a 'gladiatorial' battle over quotas, with fishermen coming off worst.[210]

Though Scottish boats were responsible for around 70 per cent of key UK fishing quotas throughout the latter half of the 1990s, they were represented at the yearly gladiatorial battle in Brussels by the Westminster government's fisheries minister. Even the revival of Scotland's Parliament did not bring with it the opportunity to have a Scottish fisheries negotiator attending the quota battle. In the early 2000s, around forty percent of the Scottish fleet was decommissioned, as Scotland's fishing industry paid a heavy price for losing its traditional fishing grounds. As the Member of the Westminster Parliament for the historic east coast fishing areas of Banff and Buchan from 1987 to 2010, how did Alex Salmond, now Scotland's First Minister, think this first period of the CFP will be judged in relation to Scotland's fishing industry?

'Very harshly,' he said. 'To me, the most significant comment, which has often been quoted, came from an official memo written by an obviously bitter Scottish Office civil servant. On the attitude of the Conservative Government's Ministry of Agriculture, Food and Fisheries, during the early CFP negotiations in the 1970s, he wrote: "In the light of Britain's wider European interests, they (the Scottish fishermen) are expendable." Which sums up what happened. It's only because of community and family resilience, that the Scottish industry survived this. What they need now is a reward in the form of additional quota for the work they're doing to conserve stocks. And there needs to be recognition, in terms of the price they're paid, for the higher value fish they're putting into the marketplace.'[211]

EU reform of the CFP is currently under discussion, with implementation due in 2013 as solutions are sought for, among other things, many complex issues of conservation, quotas and discards. Meanwhile many fishermen are working together with others in the industry to find solutions themselves to the problems which threaten their survival. Taking the high-value conservation route with MSC certification, they maintain their hope for the long term future of their industry.

They have also been cooperating on the problem of discards, which is caused by a quota system based on fish landed, not fish caught. This tempts fishermen to throw back large amounts of less valuable, as well as smaller fish, thus doing the opposite of conserving stocks. Iceland, with its own fishing rules, has a policy of 'no discarding': all fish caught must be landed. In February 2008, the Scottish Government, the fishing industry and the World Wide Fund for Nature (WWF) set up the Scottish Conservation Credit Scheme (SCCS) to find solutions.[212]

Discards had long been a WWF concern, and they wanted to put 'onboard observers' on the fishing boats to monitor what was actually happening, so solutions could be sought. Instead of a person on board, CCTV cameras were introduced on seventeen demersal boats as part of a scheme which increases their quota – provided they are monitored and throw no discards back. This Vessel Monitoring System (VMS) is just one of several actions taken by the SCCS to reduce discards.

Another move has been to make nets more selective so they don't catch unwanted fish. In the past there were frequent disputes between fishermen and scientists, but they are now working together, with fishermen reporting back to scientists where they find large stocks of cod, so the fishing in this area can be closed to prevent over-fishing. Described as Real Time Closures (RTC), this means that the area of high-density fish has a red box put round it on their sonar screen map in the wheelhouse, and all fishermen know to keep out of it. They must also keep out of Closure Areas from December to April, where it's known that cod are spawning.

Yet another effort by the SCCS to reduce discards is what they call 'increasing the market demand for under-utilised species'. In other words, get over your love affair with haddock and cod, and try an adventure with a dab, flounder, saithe, pollack, or even a squid.

'Scotland has been at the forefront of pushing for alternatives to the culture of discards, imposed by Europe's flawed fisheries policy,' said Richard Lochhead, the Scottish Government's Rural Affairs and Environment Secretary. 'It forces fishermen to dump good-quality fish back overboard, dead into the sea. This is a waste of a valuable food and economic resource . . . and will do nothing for cod recovery or deliver the main aim of harvesting fish stocks sustainably.'[213]

It's been judged that in 2009 a third of the Scottish catch, with a value of £33m, was discarded. Accountability provides the fishermen with proof of what's actually happening at sea. It can only help their cause, while those who don't throw the surplus back and sell them illegally as 'black fish', to dodge the quota system, only damage the fishing industry's reputation. At a meeting of Scottish, UK, Danish and German fishery ministers in 2009, these national representatives signed the Aalborg Declaration, which calls for all EU countries to adopt 'a system of catch quotas in a fully documented fishery, using onboard CCTV'.[214]

Despite the brutal changes following EU membership, Scottish fishermen continue to play an important role in the industry's survival. Close-knit fishing communities around the Scottish coast have had to cope with higher levels of competition in the last half century than at any other time in their history. Besides CFP problems, the oil boom in the North Sea has attracted young people in fishing communities away from a career on a working fishing boat. Yet there are others who are still motivated by their seafaring ancestry. For them, there are fishery courses at Buchan and Banff College in the North East and at Shetland's Scalloway College.

They provide hope for the future. As do those resolute skippers who have put their faith in the future by updating their boats, improving the quality of the catch, its sustainability, and the living conditions of their crew. They have also taken up the challenge of a frustrating quota system, and however unfairly they feel they have been treated, they continue to look for solutions. The heritage remains strong. At ports where fish are landed there are resilient families and supportive communities, determined to prosper, survive against the odds and carry on catching fish.

2 Seafood Farmers

A West Highland loch – 1975

He had come to this loch to farm Atlantic salmon. Just graduated as a marine biologist, he was delighted to get a job in the 'wild and wacky west', as he called it. His ambition was to hatch eggs from native Atlantic salmon, a procedure that salmon farming was pioneering. There might, he thought, be an opportunity to re-stock the west coast rivers where salmon numbers were falling.

In his newly built hatchery, the salmon eggs hatched and the young fish grew. But his hope that some might make it into the wild was not to be. He was, after all, not working for a concerned environmentalist but a commercial business with a distant corporate structure controlling the operation.

As time passed, he became more and more disturbed about the company's policy. Surely, he thought, there must be a less polluting method of fish farming. The cages had too many fish in them, so parasites were multiplying which required treatment with harmful chemicals. The sea bed, he could see, when he dived to clean the nets, was in a mess. He did not want to be part of trashing the planet. He loved living here in this unspoiled Highland landscape, but he was troubled.

In the pub one night he met three men who were trying out oyster farming further up the coast. As he talked to them, and listened to their problems, he decided they'd put the oysters in the wrong place. The loch he was working in would be much better for oysters, not so deep and with a better mix of salt and fresh water.

I could farm oysters here, he thought. But how?

Then one day a man in a faded fisherman's smock and a black Balmoral bonnet with a red toorie, appeared at the hatchery showing some interest in what he was up to. It was, he discovered, the local laird.

Some time later, after many conversations about fish, the village and the estate, it was clear that the laird was very impressed with his knowledge of marine biology. They became friendly, occasionally exchanging a bag of dived scallops for a bottle of vintage wine. Then one night, over glasses of whisky in the ancestral home at the head of the loch, they got to talking about farming oysters. The laird got very excited. The biologist got excited too when the laird suggested they have a go at farming them.

The laird, like the biologist, was also troubled. His worry was about how to save the ancestral estate from bankruptcy. There were people on the estate who depended on him for their livelihoods. He had tried to create jobs for the people, and income for himself so he could pay off inheritance taxes due from the death, recently, of his father, but nothing had been successful.

He was a benevolent and fatherly laird, liked by the people, a skilled communicator, witty and charming. He was also courageous and had vision. Funds were not plentiful, but he staked what he had on the oyster venture. The two men wrote out an agreement to share the profits equally.

The business would be built on respect for sea life and its habitat. Any impact of their activities must not harm the environment. They would aim to encourage others to enhance the biodiversity of the seas by insisting that all their suppliers fished with nature-friendly methods. They would improve the economy of the local community by providing skilled work. Local, independent businesses would be supported rather than multinational global brands.

The biologist grew oysters successfully. The laird turned out to be a brilliant salesman. The business flourished. Besides sending their west Highland loch oysters to customers around the globe, they also sold them to passing motorists from a shed at the head of the loch. Such was the demand that some old cowsheds were turned into an oyster bar with a car park, which became mobbed in the summer. Then a shop was opened selling locally caught fish, with nature-friendly methods (no damaging trawlers wrecking the seabed). The biologist researched the practices of salmon farms and bought fish from those who were, he judged, not in the business of 'trashing the planet'.

The guiding principles of their partnership remained strong, throughout its many ups and downs. When he died, the laird's estate was saved and passed on to the next generation in good financial health. Later, the biologist transferred his share of the business by setting up an employee-owned partnership, putting the power into the hands of the local people who had dedicated their lives to its success. Farmed oysters in Loch Fyne have a secure future.

This sustainable form of aquaculture, the laird[215] always pointed out when he was doing his charming oyster-lore chat, was a revival of a seafood tradition with an ancient pedigree in Scotland. Oysters, he enthused, had been a staple of the diet, eaten by all classes for thousands of years. They were a concentrated source

Johnny Noble and Andrew Lane at their oyster farm on Loch Fyne (© Loch Fyne Oysters)

of vitamins and minerals, fresh, pure and wild which had sustained the people wonderfully. There had always been plentiful oyster beds in the loch until they had been over-fished.

He was referring, of course, to European flat oysters (*Ostrea edulis*), known as 'natives', the slow-growing species with a four month spawning period, when they were not so nice to eat. Instead, the marine biologist[216] suggested they farmed Pacific cupped oysters (*Crassostrea gigas*) which were faster growing. Also, because the cold Scottish loch inhibited their spawning they were, conveniently, better to eat all year. Pacific or 'gigas' oysters have now become the most common farmed oyster in Scotland. Only a small amount, by comparison, of 'natives' are harvested from Scottish waters.

Gigas oysters are bred in hatcheries, then put into plastic mesh bags, fastened onto steel or timber trestles, and either fully submerged or submerged only during high tide. They must be constantly managed, graded as they grow, and the bags cleaned regularly. The best sites are sea lochs sheltered from the open sea, fairly shallow, and where there is a mix of marine and fresh water from a river. In some cases they are also grown where there is a Several Order[217] on a specific area, giving the shellfish farmer ownership of a designated species within the defined area. This allows 'ranching' of the sea bed without equipment, where the mature shellfish are laid loose on firm gravel ground.

Since such bivalves feed by filtering nutrients from many litres of seawater a day, they need no feeding and produce nothing to harm the environment. Over time, they absorb the natural flavour of the loch. And since no two lochs have an identical biological make-up, oysters from different lochs taste different. The same applies to farmed mussels and scallops grown in Scottish lochs which, like oysters, have provided valuable employment in the remote areas of the west coast and the islands, while sometimes also saving the laird from bankruptcy.

It was another form of fish farming, however, which saved Mrs Pauline Cameron-Head of Inverailort Castle from estate bankruptcy when she provided the location for the first farmed Atlantic salmon farming project in the early 1960s at Loch Ailort. By this time the Norwegians and the Swedes had perfected, not just hatching the eggs, but also the technique of growing the fish on to smolt stage quickly, making the young fish ready to go to sea much earlier than its natural life cycle in the wild. A wild salmon can spend up to three to four years growing to smolt stage in its native river before it goes to sea. By this time a farmed salmon will have been killed. Wild salmon remain at sea for another two to three years before reaching maturity.

After much resistance, the Loch Ailort project went ahead with a lease, held by Unilever's subsidiary, Marine Harvest. The first commercially grown Atlantic salmon from Scottish waters was sold, for the same price as wild salmon, on 28 February, 1970.[218] Unilever, uncertain whether to continue with Atlantic salmon, set up a research project to look at other possibilities. Dover sole, lobster, turbot, shrimp and cod were all rejected in favour of Atlantic salmon. The breakthrough was that salmon was not only easier to hatch than the others, Unilever had also found a way of transferring salmon smolts directly from fresh water to salt water, a process which they patented.

In these early days of salmon farming there were enthusiasts who saw it as a possible adjunct to crofting. Every crofter would have a few cattle and sheep, a potato patch, plus a fish cage in the loch growing salmon to improve his income. In the 1980s, the Highlands and Islands Development Board (HIDB) invested in this vision.[219] By 1985, there were 105 companies farming salmon on 128 sites. Some had been set up by individuals who had an interest – like the marine biologist – in the unpolluted remoteness of the marine environment and the unhurried lifestyle of the wild and wacky west. Some were, like him, not indigenous to the area. Others were. One had a rock band. Some had land, farming or fishing interests. Some lairds were keen. Others hated the idea, seeing it as a threat to rod and line angling, also to their privacy and the long established sporting traditions of Highland and Island shooting and fishing estates.

By 1985, of the 105 salmon farmers, independent crofters were in the minority. Marine Harvest, the Unilever subsidiary, which had started out on Loch Ailort had been joined by Booker (sugar, tea and other foods); Fitch Lowell Poultry (intensive chicken rearing) operating under its subsidiary Golden Sea Produce; Fison (fertiliser); British Oxygen; Blue Circle Cement; Shell; and BP Nutrition.[220] A complicated story of takeover and buy-out ensued among a plethora of multinationals, with fewer and fewer companies controlling more and more of the production. By 2010, of Scotland's 250 salmon farms, 98% were in the hands of eight companies. Of these, four were Scottish (22%) and four foreign (78%).

In the 1980s, increased volumes of fish and questions of quality, provenance and environmental damage prompted the setting up of Scottish Quality Salmon (SQS) in 1984. This operated a labelling scheme which guaranteed responsible farming practices, quality control and proof that the salmon was from Scotland, and not Norway, since its cheaper salmon was currently flooding the marketplace. Three years later, the Scottish Salmon Board (SSB) was set up as a joint venture between the Scottish Salmon Growers' Association and the Shetland Farmers' Association.

In 1991, Shetland decided to go it alone.[221] They reckoned they had a different product to sell compared to farmed salmon from the west coast sea lochs. Theirs were farmed in the fast-flowing strips of water between islands called *voes*. This, they claimed, made the fish use their muscles more, swimming against the tide, making a less flabby fish with a better body shape and a lower fat content. Also, they claimed to have fewer problems with parasites such as sea lice, reducing the need to use polluting chemicals to kill them.

In 1989 there was a disturbing fall in the price of Scottish farmed salmon, largely as a result of yet more cheap imports of Norwegian salmon, and fourteen small independent farms went out of business. Around this time, the industry spent between £2 and 3 million on a marketing campaign promoting farmed Scottish salmon.[222] Those reporting in the national media were invited on fact-finding press trips to remote salmon farm locations – sometimes transported across spectacular coastal landscapes by helicopter.

We got to see what they wanted us to see. There was the odd bag of fish feed left lying around with its list of ingredients which the more observant noted and asked questions about. The farms visited were mostly independently owned by well-informed conservationists, who seemed genuine in their arguments regarding environmental principals of preserving the purity of the seas. It was, they argued, their most important asset. Polluting with chemicals was not in their interests. The cages were not crammed full of fish. On a trip to Shetland there was a visit to a lab in the fisheries college in Scalloway where a scientist explained how they kept tabs on the nutrient and oil content of the salmon flesh. A lot was being done to improve the quality of the fish and to attempt to control the damage to the environment.

Yet two decades on, controversy remains. Thousands of farmed salmon continue to escape from cages into the wild, unavoidably breeding with wild salmon and causing hybridisation between the escapees and the wild fish and sea trout, which dilutes the gene-pool of native fish in an undesirable way and could threaten the survival of wild stocks in certain rivers.[223] Incidents of chemical poisoning still occur. How to monitor the irresponsible actions of some salmon farms is a difficult task for the authorities, but there are certainly plenty of official bodies around to prosecute if breaches are discovered. The Scottish Environmental Protection Agency (SEPA) is the body to notify if you happen to come across large, or small, numbers of dead fish anywhere near salmon farms or on council rubbish dumps (yes, it happens). While SEPA deals with chemical pollution, other people who will also take action are the RSPCA, Scottish Natural Heritage (SNH), Marine Scotland, or you can dial 999 for the police.[224]

To avoid some of these issues, others turned to farming Atlantic cod and halibut, but despite initial optimism many of the farmed cod ventures have not been successful. Halibut farmers, however, remain hopeful about the future. Halibut takes four or five years to grow to a marketable size, though they are up to four times more valuable than salmon. Of the freshwater fish farmed, American rainbow trout have been the most successful. Rainbows have the advantage of growing faster than native brown trout. They are also easier to catch, so are used to stock commercial fishing lochs and rivers. Though the water temperature in Scotland is too cold for them to breed, they do develop their own special character from their native environment. In a well-oxygenated Scottish loch or river, with good native feeding, they will produce a firm-fleshed, sweet-tasting fish. In less good conditions the quality will vary accordingly.

Arctic charr, a member of the salmon family, is another freshwater fish which is now being farmed. It was during the last ice age that charr from the Arctic migrated south from their native salty seas around Iceland and became trapped in Scotland's freshwater lochs. They were not unhappy in the chilly freshwater lochs, which became home for them as they morphed into freshwater fish. Now there are around two hundred wild populations, all with variable characteristics according to the feeding and habitat in the lochs, as well as the farmed Arctic charr.

These fish and shellfish farming ventures now make a very large contribution to the Scottish economy. Most notable recent increases have been in the volume of Scottish farmed mussels, scallops and gigas oysters. Native oysters, though only a small niche market, are on the increase too.[225] On the downside, cod, brown trout, sea trout and halibut have all decreased in volume. Arctic charr is the only other farmed fish, besides salmon, which has increased. And while farmed Atlantic salmon's production levels fell during several years up to 2008, there was an increase of 12 per cent in 2009.

'But the real story of this increase,' said Roseanna Cunningham, Scottish Environment Minister in 2010, 'is that the value of salmon in 2009 rose by 23 per cent with a new estimated value of £412 million.'

Despite an ancient history of wild fisheries, Scotland has now become a significant global player in farmed fish consumption. It's an issue which divides the country. Those who see farming seafood as the way out of the apparently insoluble problem of remote communities declining, from lack of employment, want it to succeed. Those who are opposed do not want to trash the planet in the process. Only the Scottish Parliament can resolve this vital issue.

A team of scientists have predicted that 2010 will be seen in the future as the milestone when, globally, there was more farmed seafood than wild eaten for the first time in history.[226] Whether this is true or not, there's no escaping the reality that since fish farming took off in the 1950s, its meteoric success has now brought it to the point of overtaking wild seafood on the world's dinner plates.

3 Buyers and Sellers

Where, what and who to buy from? 2010

Buying fish is the last thing on her mind. She has left her husband and children at their holiday cottage and has come to this town in the Highlands to shop for other things. She is walking along the high street when she passes a window with a man in a white coat standing at a table filleting his way through a pile of amazing looking fish.

Chalked-up on another window, she reads: 'Isle of Lewis mussels' – 'Orkney Island scallops' – 'Kyle of Tongue Oysters'... There is a notice, too, saying that wild fish is caught by a trawler off Scrabster on the North Coast where it's landed, and arrives the next day in the shop. Also, if you give the fishmonger an order he will do his best to get it for you.

She goes in. It's a big shop with more than just fresh seafood on offer. She browses for a bit. Then she asks about the pile of fish. She's never seen whole fish like this before. She asks him what this huge flat fish is.

'That's halibut,' he says.

'And what's that strange looking fish with the fierce head?'

'Catfish,' he says.

'Do you mean the catfish from Vietnam that they've been passing off as cod?'

'No, nothing to do with that. That's a cheap farmed fish they're buying in bulk frozen. This is a wild fish caught in the North Sea.'

The fishmonger explains that he has an arrangement with the skipper to take this kind of unusual fish so it's not a 'discard', tossed back dead into the sea. She discovers that its ferocious looking rows of teeth are for crunching a diet of sea urchins, crabs and clams, which accounts, the fishmonger thinks, for its good flavour. When skinned and filleted, its white flesh has a slightly pink tinge. The fishmonger cuts up the long fillets into thick steaks.

'I'll have some,' she says.

She also buys a bag of mussels which come from the Outer Hebrides, some dived Orkney scallops and a live crab. She's bought a lot more than she intended and spent a lot more than she can really afford. But it's been worth it. Scallops – a real holiday treat for her husband. Mussels – to keep the children happy. Plus a new fish for her to try. It will all be cooked in minutes too.

When she gets back to the cottage she tells the children she has a surprise for them. She takes them into the garden, then digs into her bag and carefully gets hold of the crab's back and pulls it out, laying it down on the grass. This is not the first live crab they've met, but they still squeal and jump out of the way as it gets onto its legs and does a sideways scuttle across the lawn.

Since prehistory the world's oceans have supplied wild seafood in plenty, coining the phrase: 'there's always plenty more fish in the sea'. So well-liked has it been that the world's population has consumed it in greater and greater quantities, reaching a peak in the 1990s. That a time would come when the supply no longer met this demand seemed unbelievable. Yet that time is now. In 2008, the UN Food and Agriculture Organisation (FAO) warned that, after decades of over-exploiting wild seafood stocks, eighty percent were either fully exploited, over-exploited, depleted or recovering from depletion. Most of the stocks of the top ten species, which together account for about thirty percent of world's marine fisheries caught for food, were fully exploited or over-exploited. The North-east Atlantic, which includes Scotland's fisheries, was one of three areas in the world which showed the highest proportion of fully-exploited stocks. [227]

Not good news. Yet with enlightened government action and precautionary fisheries management, stocks of wild fish can recover. It's happening with North Sea haddock.[228] It could be argued that the reason this fishery declined to worryingly low stock levels was simply because it was overfished. Ultra-efficient, modern fishing methods had taken their toll on a limited resource. It could also be argued that this happened because of the Scots love affair with haddock. For a large part of the twentieth century, haddock was the Scots' top fish choice. Fishermen met that demand, though catches in their nets contained all sorts of other fish which they could not sell to the Scots. So they sold it to other countries, threw it overboard, or found a trailblazing fishmonger who did something practical about encouraging Scots to eat other fish.[229]

But the Scots are not alone in this blinkered approach to fish choice. Spaniards are addicted to hake. Madrid's fish market, Mercamadrid (82 acres of purpose-built covered halls), is in the business of 'satisfying the capital's traditional demands' for hake (*merluza*).[230] Likewise Tokyo's Tsukiji fish market is in the business of satisfying the Japanese, and the world's, demand for tuna. Possibly the longest love affair with a single species, however, has been the Western world's passion for Atlantic cod.

Children admiring the fish display in an Edinburgh fishmonger's window, 1999
(Marius Alexander, licensor www.scran.ac.uk).

For centuries, long-life salt cod was the popular choice in Catholic Mediterranean countries when it was eaten on religious 'fish days'. Even when supplies of fresh cod became available, cured cod remained a popular choice. Its robust gamey flavour, often teamed up with pungent garlic and fruity olive oil, can be found in hundreds of traditional dishes from these areas. It was this huge demand for cod, both fresh and cured, which led to the spectacular collapse of the northern Atlantic cod industry in 1992, putting around thirty thousand fishermen out of work.[231]

It would be wrong to imagine that the collapse of a fishery in one part of the world's oceans means the end of this choice for the fish eater addicted to it. Cod stayed on the menu. It just came from another source. And so did hake. Charles Clover, investigating how the world's wild fish stocks are being squandered in his book *The End of the Line* (2007), visited Mercamadrid where he was surprised to find 'an awful lot of hake', since the information coming from scientists was that hake was on the verge of collapse in European waters. One of the reasons there was still hake in Mercamadrid was that Spanish fishing boats had moved south into the seas off West Africa and Namibia, as well as into the seas off Argentina, to fish for hake. The labels in the market proved that it came from these places.

What the labels did not say, though, was that when huge, high-tech European boats fish off the African coast they deplete the fish stocks for the impoverished indigenous fishing communities which are largely dependent on fish for survival. The documentary film made of Clover's book in 2009 provides graphic evidence of this.[232]

Another possible reason for plentiful amounts of hake in the Spanish marketplace, he discovered, was that Spanish fishermen have been found fishing it illegally. Evidence of fines imposed on the skippers who get caught is found in court records. One fishing company's fiddle over two years involved taking 'more than 25 times the amount of hake' than had been declared. They were fined a record £1.1m, though it was reckoned that they would already have made £1m in extra profit.[233] Illegal, unreported and unregulated (IUU) fishing is a significant cause of disappearing fish stocks. It is a global problem and an illicit trade thought to be worth between $10-23 billon a year, in some areas causing a loss of essential seafood for local communities in some of the poorest areas of the world.[234]

Aiming to capture the world's attention, and hopefully sparking it into action, regarding the damage to fish stocks by IUU fishing, a Taiwanese Greenpeace eco-warrior locked herself to the anchor chain of a blacklisted, blue fin tuna, factory-ship, preventing it from leaving port in early January 2011. Meanwhile, campaigners on land lobbied the Taiwan Fisheries Agency to investigate the ship's owners.[235] Greenpeace did not succeed in preventing the boat going off to kill more endangered blue fin tuna, but they did keep the issue alive in the world's media.

Headline-grabbing Greenpeace eco-warriors were ahead of other organisations in their concern for the oceans' endangered species when they took direct action against killing whales in the 1970s. They set off from Vancouver, where the organisation was founded, in the first Rainbow Warrior, on a mission to stop fleets of Russian and Japanese boats harpooning whales. Their current action against pirate boats and illegal fishing is just one battle in their war to change world demand for seafood in danger of extinction.

In total contrast regarding tactics but with similar aims, the world's largest conservationist organisation, the World Wide Fund for Nature (WWF) which works behind the scenes with governments and retailers, began discussions about declining wild sea stocks with the multinational Unilever in the mid-1990s. Unilever's interest at that time was as a major fish buyer for their Bird's Eye frozen fish brand. The talks were about how to secure the long term sustainability of global fish stocks and preserve the integrity of the marine environment. As a result, the Marine Stewardship Council (MSC) was set up in 1997 as an independent charity, with aims to provide individual fisheries with a guarantee that their fish is sustainably caught and effectively managed.[236]

The Western Australian rock lobster fishery was the first fishery in the world to be certified by the MSC as sustainable in March 2000. Since this time, other multinationals have joined Unilever in seeking to improve their sourcing of seafood, which many believe is an incentive to others.[237] The costs of achieving an eco-label for a fishery puts a premium price on the fish conserved for all businesses which source seafood, from multinationals to chippies. It's a reality too for every fish buyer. But every fish bought sends a message back to the fishermen that doing his bit to save wild fish for the future is important.

Nudging the fish-eating public into widening their wild fish buying options and becoming more adventurous in their choice, a variety of organisations began publishing information and sustainable fish guides in the early 2000s, when the first MSC fish became available. The Monterey Bay Aquarium in California was first off the mark with its Seafood Watch 'wallet card' for consumers in 2000, giving sustainable fish-buying advice.[238] In 2002, the UK-based Marine Conservation Society (MCS) began distributing similar sustainable fish-buying advice in a wallet card. They also published the Good Fish Guide to buying eco-friendly fish.[239]

The conservation-minded MCS had been created in the 1970s, with the backing of outspoken environmentalists like David Bellamy. Its aim initially was to protect the marine environment. It launched major projects and campaigns to clean beaches and seas, and to protect the sea's wildlife. It also became the UK's representative on the Seas at Risk, a watchdog organisation of nine European non-governmental bodies with a remit to protect and restore the marine environment in their common seas of the North East Atlantic, including the North and Irish seas. Besides its guides, it also provides up-to-date information on its website about all seafood and its sustainable status.[240]

Making a more direct attack on the question of seafood choice at the point of sale, the UK charity Bite-Back was set up in 2002 as a shark and marine conservation organisation, with a mission to halt the trade and consumption of endangered sharks. It is also active in promoting sustainable fishing, protecting ocean habitats and inspiring worldwide respect for the marine environment.

Now it is campaigning for direct action to protect vulnerable swordfish, marlin, monkfish, skate and warm water prawns (king and tiger). Encouraging action on its website, it provides information for consumers on how to to target supermarket fish buyers and ask them to remove vulnerable seafood from sale. It also gives advice on the best way to make a protest in a restaurant. Usefully, it provides 'intellectual' fish facts on the six target fish, while also keeping track of progress with 'follow-up' charts on each campaign.[241]

Yet another angle to saving the world's wild fish stocks for future generations has been setting aside areas of marine reserves, where seabeds and ecosystems are allowed to recover from the relentless ploughing-up by trawlers as they scour the seabed for fish and shellfish which bury themselves in the mud. The trailblazing Scottish organisation which has kept up its fight against this damage for over fifteen years is the Community of Arran Seabed Trust (COAST) which was set up in 1995 by two local divers concerned about what trawlers were doing to the seabed habitats.

In the past, Arran had been at the hub of a thriving fishing industry with over four hundred boats anchored in Lochranza Bay in the late 1800s. A hundred years later, there were only a few creel-fishers. Coast's aim is not only to manage and protect this area, but also to lobby the Scottish Government and the fishing and aquaculture industries to adopt non-destructive, sustainable fishing methods. In helping the seas to recover, and fish stocks return, they have a vision of the future which includes the revival of fishing so that it plays its part again in the life of the island community for future generations. One of its achievements has been establishing a No Take Zone (Scotland's first) in the autumn of 2008. Its aim is to protect valuable biodiversity and promote natural regeneration of all marine life which will eventually benefit commercial fishermen. While part of the bay is a NTZ, the remaining area is a Marine Protected Area (MPA).[242]

These MPAs are locations where the authorities have powers to limit development, control fishing seasons, determine catch limits and if necessary put a complete ban on removing marine life. In 2010 there were 5000 MPAs covering eight per cent of the world's oceans. In early 2011 the Scottish Government set up guidelines for a Scottish MPA network following new powers provided by the 2010 Marine (Scotland) Act.[243]

Another Scottish Government-led move has been setting up Inshore Fisheries Groups (IFGs). These are for those with fishing interests within the six or twelve nautical mile protected zone, and other stakeholders in the community. The aim is that they should work together to meet the goals of sustainable stocks and promote a healthy marine environment, as well as establish a profitable fishing industry which will support strong coastal communities. The first three pilot IFGs were established in the Outer Hebrides, the Clyde and the South East of Scotland in January 2009. The North West, Small Isles and Mull, and the Moray Firth IFGs were set up later in the year.[244]

So Scotland's fisheries have not actually reached the end of the line – yet. But the warning is out that it's time to change fish-buying habits, to adventure beyond the beloved species and get to know the rich choice of fish and shellfish to be found in plenty around the Scottish coast. It's also time to be aware of the knock-on effects of choosing fish from areas of the world's oceans where impoverished communities are losing their livelihoods while the more affluent world eats their fish.

4 Fisher-Foragers
Mountain burn fishing, 1969

Unscrewing the jar of juicy worms he'd dug up before they left, the gamekeeper gave one to the cook and they baited their hooks. Then, each finding a good place on the rock some distance apart, they kept their heads well back as they gently dropped their lines into the deep pool.

The keeper had seen this pool, with its convenient overhanging rock, on his way down the mountain as he returned with hotel guests out for a day's deer stalking on the high tops. It was August, and peak season for stalking and salmon fishing. Today, though, he had escaped from the arduous stalks and had joined up with the hotel's cook for some simple burn fishing halfway up a mountain on their Sunday off.

Now, the happy state of doing nothing until that tremor on the rod when the trout takes its first nibble. They made themselves comfortable and waited. Time stood still.

The cook, like the keeper, was not new to burn fishing with a worm and had been taken fishing like this since able to hold a rod around age four or five. In this remote and spectacular Highland landscape, though, it was the keeper who had the local know-how about this unspoiled wilderness area on the edge of Europe and its wild food potential. He had grown up here. Now he was passing on his skills and nature knowledge to those who returned year after year to join him in the hills.

The rod quivered. He had a bite.

Up the rock face he reeled in the wriggling trout, a nice half-pounder. A few minutes later the cook got one too.

The day passed in lazy exploration of the burn's fishing potential. Only as the sun began to sink in the sky did they think of packing up. With a good catch of brown trout, they made their way down to the lochside. Picking a sheltered spot they made a hearth with a few large stones; gathered some driftwood and piled it on top; then started the fire.

The cook was in charge now. Off to the lochside, gutting and washing some of the smaller fish, skewering them on sticks sharpened to a point. No condiments required – just trout and fresh air.

As the fire blazed, they sat reminiscing over their 'emergency' half-bottle of whisky while the sun dropped low in the sky behind the rugged outline of high mountains. And when the fire had died down to a white-hot ash, the cook began to grill the fish, balancing them between the hearthstones, turning them as if on a revolving spit. They were ready in no time, the skins brown and crisp, the pink flesh tasting of mountain burn.

The search for wild food for free can be traced back to the first settlers: hunting wild game, gathering wild food from land and seashore and fishing. The remains of their bones, found by archaeologists, provide evidence of the large amount of marine food in their diet and the long hours they must have spent wild fishing or foraging the seashore.[245] For them success depended, as it did for the keeper and the cook,[246] on being acutely aware of nature, senses sharpened to its dangers as well as its pleasures. They learned to respect it as a force which cannot be hurried, tuning into its sense of timelessness. They grew to know its potential as a food supply with a remarkable range of natural flavours, all of them pure and unadulterated.

By the mid-1900s this value system was under threat in some places and extinct in others. The great British Industrial Revolution of the previous century had caused a mass exodus from the country to the town. Those who migrated were no longer in such intimate daily contact with the seas, rivers and seashores. It became more difficult to pass on the knowledge of fishing and foraging from one generation to the next. Unique local flavours and textures from a wide range of seafoods and seaweeds were no longer such an important part of their daily food, while knowledge of their healing powers was another casualty.

Seaweed was at one time widely used in Highland folk medicine as a cure for a variety of ailments. Anecdotal stories from the past of the miraculous powers of a seaweed bath are numerous. It was also used for poultices on arthritic knees, or as a special plaster applied to the forehead to cure a headache. Dulse broth was given by the plateful, two or three times a week, for skin disorders which folk wisdom 'diagnosed as symptoms of general ill health'.[247] Science has now proved that these cures were not fanciful.[248] When serrated or toothed wrack or bladder wrack are added to a hot bath they release a mineral and vitamin-rich gel into the water, which is absorbed into the skin helping eczema sufferers. And seaweed's chemical makeup is such that several plates of dulse broth would certainly have done a lot to improve 'general ill health'.[249]

In the inevitable march of progress these wisdoms were not only lost by country people who moved to the towns, but also by country people still living in the country. It happened everywhere as new inventions of refrigeration and canning combined with improved road systems, railways and steam boats brought new foods to the most remote communities.

For a short period in the 1930s and 40s this progress was slowed down when economic depression, a world war and thirteen years of rationing all heightened the need to make the most of wild foods from the land and sea. But when these traumas were over, convenient new food inventions and convenient pills from the pharmaceutical industry were a more popular choice than inconvenient wild foods. It may have been progress, but it was also a separation from the natural world and how it worked. Though it might be imagined that those in remote areas like the Highlands and Islands would have kept in better touch with the natural world than urban dwellers, this was not always the case. Cut off by remoteness and inaccessibility, modern conveniences which took some of the effort out of their previously toil-weary lives were welcomed.

Tinned foods were considered a wonderful invention, adding a more attractive option to a monotonous winter diet of salt-preserved herring and mutton. In an ironic turn of fate, the people living on the remote islands off Scotland's west coast, where prehistoric hunter-gatherers first made camp so many thousands of years previously,[250] had now become rather obsessive converts to modern convenience foods. As a pair of mountaineers from Glasgow discovered when they landed on the isle of Rum to climb the tops.[251]

On their first night, they got their camp fire going on the beach. Always enthusiastic seashore foragers, they had done their hunt-and-gather-for-food and found enough mussels to fill their largest pot, which was just coming to the boil as some curious local children arrived to say hello to the strangers on the beach.

'Would you like some mussels?' they asked.

'No thanks,' said the children.

The climbers drained the pot, filled their plates and began to eat. The children eventually wandered off and the climbers thought no more of the incident, besides regret that the children didn't want to eat the fabulous mussels on their beach.

The next morning, as they were getting the fire going for the breakfast porridge, the children appeared again carrying several bags. They emptied the contents and said this was a present from their mothers. The campers knew the tradition, in the culture of crofting communities, of sharing with the less well-off. They imagined the scenario: the children going home and being questioned about the strangers on the beach. Yes, the men on the beach really had nothing else to eat but mussels!

The bags contained a supply of canned soups, beans and fruit in syrup. It was a generous gift which the climbers gratefully accepted. But they regretted this particular effect of progress. They been raised in hard times of food shortages in the early 1900s when the economy was in such a state that the government told people to get out and hunt-and-gather, or 'hedgerow harvest' as it was called. Scrimping and saving was the norm for the majority. For the Rum campers, a collapsible fishing rod was always packed so they could fish for their supper, if handy mussels on a beach were not available.

The generation which followed them, however, would grow up into a food culture where the pressures were not to scrimp and save or go wild food gathering. They were being invited to embrace instead a revolution in multiple retailing, moving hand in hand with a high-tech food industry. With mesmerising speed, between them they were creating more and more convenient foods, making it less and less necessary to think of the natural world as a source of food. This generation was in danger of becoming distanced from the origin of their foods: missing out on that benchmark natural taste of the pure and unadulterated, not to mention the great fun of a hunt-and-gather, and its excuse to escape life's stresses. They were at the receiving end of a food industry intent on standardising food supplies, more concerned with uniform colour, shape, taste and texture, and less with natural flavours.

There were voices suggesting an alternative to this development, among them, in 1972, the author of a small pocket guide to searching the natural world for *Food for Free*. Richard Mabey had begun writing it, he admitted, out of 'pure hedonism and historical curiosity'. But it had developed into a way, he said, 'of reconnecting with the wild' at all kinds of social, cultural and psychological levels.[252] Mabey was ahead of his time, as was Roger Phillips with his equally inspiring *Wild Food* in 1983.

The full implications of the revolution in multiple retailing and food industry innovations had still to unfold. It was the late 80s before evidence began emerging, that all was not well with this new system. 'Most of the egg production in this country, sadly, is now affected with salmonella.' said the Government's Minister of Health.[253] Had she said 'many of the eggs' instead of 'most' she would have been right and not lost her job. In the furore which ensued, everyone was alerted to some of this new food culture's more dubious practices. An investigative media, during the 90s, revealed more scandalous practices and disrespect for public health which had been allowed to develop in the pursuit of profit.[254]

In a counter-attack, writers began producing books on the benefits of returning to a more natural lifestyle. The movement towards reconnecting with both wild plant potential, and lost ancestral wisdom relating to natural cures, was gathering momentum.[255] Medical herbalism, bypassing the pharmaceutical industry, was still viewed sceptically by most of the medical establishment, but it had a growing public following.

Then a pair of characters took the movement to another level when they went back to the beginning and tried to work out how Britain's hunter-gatherer ancestors managed to survive on just wild foods. They gathered, cooked and ate their way through the wild foods they reckoned would have been eaten so many thousands of years ago. It made fascinating TV-watching as Ray Mears, bushcraft survival expert, joined up with Gordon Hillman, a professor of archaeobiology, in the series *Wild Food*.[256] It was an ambitious leap back in time as they imagined how the minds of the first hunter-gatherers would have been adapted to surviving in the wild.

Young fishers on Loch Torridon with their catch of mackerel, 1985.

Mears had been inspired by a veteran of World War II who had learned survival techniques in Burma, and who encouraged him with the mantra: 'You don't need equipment, you need knowledge to survive in the wild.'[257] His take on survival in the wild was that it was neither a battle against the elements, nor a sentimental re-enactment of the past, but simply an opportunity to reconnect with nature, a chance to escape from pressures in everyday lives, so that mind and body can be restored.

By the early 2000s, the wild food movement had entered a new era as more wild foods began appearing in shops and markets, as well as on menus in the smartest restaurants in town. Issues of sustainability arose. There could be no future if everyone went willy-nilly hunting and gathering without asking the question: Will I make this wild food extinct?

When Richard Mabey inspired an audience of food historians on the subject of wild food at the Oxford Symposium on Food and Cookery in 2004, he began on the subject of protecting wild foods from extinction, later endorsing this sentiment in his next edition of *Food For Free:*

'I've become more of a wayside nibbler than a heavy forager these days,' he said. 'I like serendipitous findings, small wayside gourmet treats . . . they seem to catch everything that's exhilarating about foraging . . . a sharpness of taste . . . a sense of place and season.

But it's the *finding* of them, the intimacy with the trees and the places they grow, a heightened consciousness of what they need to survive, that are just as important.'[258]

When wild foods are eaten in restaurants, or bought in shops, there is no intimate and personal 'reconnecting with the wild', no chance to ask the question – Will I damage the survival of this wild food? Mabey was not passing judgement on the commercialisation of wild food. Commercial foragers on seashores have, after all, been around since at least Shakespeare's day, when both rock and marsh samphire were sold in the streets, gathered from the seashore.[259] In seventeenth century Dublin, sweet Molly Malone sold her 'Cockles and Mussels, Alive, Alive Oh', also in the streets, while a common street cry for sellers of seaweed in eighteenth century Edinburgh was 'Dulse and Tangle!'

Today, collecting food from the seashore or anywhere else for commercial purposes is regulated by legislation in the Theft Act of 1978 and the Wildlife and Countryside Act of 1981.[260] It is not an offence to collect for personal use, but commercial foragers must comply with the law. In 2009, a commercial forager, Miles Irving, who supplies restaurant chefs with wild foods, also wrote a detailed and comprehensive guide for non-commercial foragers.[261] He was encouraged to write the book by restaurant owner and chef, Max Hix, one of his first customers.[262] And the first thing Hix has to say in the book's introduction is not how useful wild foods are for chefs looking for inspiration to add some zing to their menus but:

> Foraging should be a way of life for all serious foodies, whether you live in the country or in the city. Kids should also be encouraged to get out there and forage – even if it's only for blackberries.
>
> I remember my Gran, when making a pie or crumble with apples, used to send me out to pick blackberries and when it came time to pour over her lumpy custard I felt that enormous sense of achievement . . . that only comes from actually having been involved in creating something.[263]

It is, however, neither chefs, nor commercial foragers, nor television programmes, nor writers of inspiring books on wild foods, who will ensure the future of a meaningful reconnection with the rivers, seas and seashores and their natural tastes. It's anyone who knows how to alert children from the moment they become aware of the natural world: what food is for free; how best to catch or gather it; how the seasons change during the year; how to save wild foods for the future; how to deal with inevitable frustrations and disappointments, and how to create unforgettable memories of their own burn-caught trout roasted over an open fire on the beach.

SEAFOOD COOKING

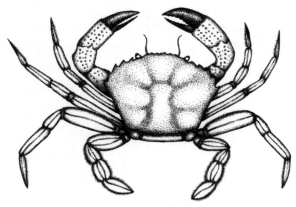

velvet crab

1 . . . basics

Buying; Knowing the Seafood Facts; How Much to Buy; Killing, Bleeding, Descaling, Gutting and Filleting; Cooking; Oven Temperatures; Metric Equivalents

Buying:
The look, the feel, the smell

What's the best buy?

- Finfish with its head still on to judge its freshness as shown by: eyes bright, black and convex, not cloudy and sunken. Gills which are a good red colour, not tattered, or faded to pale pink.

- Whole finfish whose skin is still glossy and taut, not dull and wrinkled. When pressed lightly, feels firm not flabby.

- Whole finfish whose stomach looks firm and intact, not soft and broken, which are signs of decay from the action of stomach enzymes and bacteria.

- Crustaceans which are lively when handled, and if they have a tail, it flicks back strongly when pulled out: *The Tail-flick Test.*

- Finfish, whole or filleted, which smells sea fresh. Strong 'fishy' smells come with age and deterioration.

- Finfish steaks or fillets which look full and glossy, not dried out or dull, or looking as though they might have been sprayed with water to make them look fresher than they are.

Where to buy?

From the fishing boat or a pierside fish stall:

Buying direct from a boat may be an option in coastal areas. Small, inshore creel boats are often a good source of local shellfish and sometimes other fish too. Pierside, take-away shellfish stalls, with their immediate access to freshly landed, local fish and shellfish, are worth seeking out.

From the independent fishmonger:

Though the number of independent high street fishmongers has been greatly depleted, the service from those who remain has never been better. What they lack in quantity they make up for in quality and should be sought out. This is the place to find answers to fish-buying questions – some also like to give advice on cooking too and may even have a range of fish cookery books.

Many have also, helpfully, extended the range of their products on sale to include everything a seafood cook might need – from a floury tattie to a bottle of sesame oil. Others stock their shops with local food products, often artisanal, as well as local game.

From a travelling fish van:

Not every high street may have a fishmonger, but travelling fish vans are common in rural areas, sometimes run by previous high street fishmongers who know their fish. Travelling inland from the coastal fishing towns, they carry on the tradition of the creel-carrying fishwives who sold to the surrounding communities.

Usually they park at some convenient point in the town or village for a few hours at a set time every week. They will often take an order for the following week, depending on availability. They sometimes make house calls where the elderly are housebound, and in sparsely populated rural areas often provide this service to all residents.

Some operate an order-only service, taking orders by phone or email, then buying from their local market, thus eliminating left-over fish. They may advertise in local papers.

From market stalls:

Independent fishmongers also sell local fish at farmer's markets around the country. For details see *www.scottishfarmersmarkets.co.uk.*

From the internet:

Online buying means the time the fish spends in transit, if it comes direct from the boats, can be reduced. The online seller may be able to supply high quality fresh fish, though there are packaging and transport costs which have to be factored in as well.

From the supermarket:

Wet fish counters in major supermarkets sell a wide range of seafood from around the world. (Their market share of wet fish sold in the UK has increased from around 10% in 1982 to around 80% in the late 2010s.)

As with their buying policy for other fresh foods, they source extensively from the global marketplace to ensure year-round supplies of the most popular fish. Farmed fish, which has no season, fits in particularly well with this policy.

It follows that the supermarket wet fish counter is not the place to find local speciality seafood or to get much advice on UK seasons. The major supermarkets have varying policies on sourcing sustainable seafood. Their websites usually indicate those fish which have been sustainably sourced. Their labelling, however, has been proved in some cases to be unreliable.

It's also worth checking out whether the fish on the wet fish counter is fresh or has been previously frozen, which must be indicated on the label. Some recommend that even if the fish has been frozen 'it can be refrozen', which will not provide fish in the best condition. Others indicate on labels that no fish or shellfish sold has been frozen.

Knowing the seafood facts:

- That all finfish and shellfish have a life cycle, growing and maturing to a peak quality as eggs, or sperm, are created for the next generation. This creates an extra strain on them and uses up fat and proteins in their muscles. This means that just before and after spawning their muscles are wasted or 'spent', and do not make the best eating. In the cause of the conservation of stocks, it is also best to avoid buying fish or shellfish which is full of eggs or sperm just before spawning. For spawning seasons to avoid, see p. 231.

- That if possible shellfish should be bought live. If cooked, it should be bought from reliable sources. Dead, uncooked shellfish, even stored at 0 degrees C, will deteriorate very quickly, much faster than finfish.

- That though shellfish has no period of rigor mortis, finfish has a transient taste factor which occurs for a short time after rigor mortis when its savouriness increases, and this may last for 24-48 hours. Fish is stored in ice at 0 degrees C, immediately after it is caught at sea, which prolongs the period of rigor and therefore extends the time of increased savouriness. In countries where they prefer to eat fish either just after it has passed through rigor, or immediately after killing, fish are sold live from tanks. Some houses have kitchens with a built-in 'pond' for keeping live fish.

- That exposure of fish to oxygen in the air dulls its colours, turns its flavour stale and flat and softens its texture. Wrapping tightly in clingfilm limits the exposure to oxygen. Keeping it at a constant 0 degrees C will inhibit enzyme and bacterial activity. A domestic fridge, at 5-7 degrees C, is too warm for fish. It should be stored in the fridge in a single layer, covered tightly with clingfilm, and with ice or an ice pack.

- That freezing fish changes its proteins and this affects its quality, causing 'freeze denaturation', which may result in a tougher, spongy texture. Cod and its relatives are particularly susceptible to this. Storage life in the freezer for lean white fish and shrimp is around six months, oily fish and shellfish three to four months. All seafood to be frozen should be well wrapped to prevent freezer 'burn'.

How much to buy?

A portion of any protein food can vary in size from 75g (3oz) to 200g (7oz) depending on appetites and type of dish. An average portion is around 150g (5oz) to 175g (6oz) per person.

Fish

Flat fish on the bone – head on, gutted and fins removed (filleted yield 50%): 375–450g per person: x 4 = 1.5–1.8kg

Round fish on the bone – head on, gutted and fins removed (filleted yield 70%): 275–325g per person: x 4 = 1.1–1.3kg

Fish fillets or steaks: 150–175g per person: x 4 = 600–700g

Shellfish

Mussel, cockles in the shell: 750g–1kg per person main course

Razor clam in shell: 4-6 depending on size per person main course

Oyster in shell: 4-6 depending on size, per person starter

Scallop in shell: 2-4 depending on size, per person main course (half quantity starter)

Crab in shell: 1.25-1.5kg serves 2 main course, 4 starter

Lobster: 2 x 750-800g serves 2 main course, 4 starter

Langoustine: 16 large or 24 small serves 4 main course (half quantity starter)

Squat lobster: 2kg (yielding 175-225g meat) serves 4 starter

Shrimp unpeeled: 750g serves 4 starter

Prawn, in shell but headless: 550g serves 4 starter

Killing, Bleeding, Descaling, Gutting and Filleting

To kill a fish:
Hold it on a firm surface with one hand and give it a single blow on the head with a heavy piece of wood, or a stone, which will kill it instantly. Large fish might need a couple of blows, given in quick succession.

To bleed a fish:
This is done immediately after killing, while the blood is still circulating, by cutting through the gills on either side of the head with a sharp knife or a pair of scissors. This empties the blood from the veins and improves the appearance and taste of

the fish, essential if eating raw. Also, blood in the flesh attracts bacteria, so bleeding improves its shelf life. Another method, if gill-snipping is not possible, is to cut off the tail.

To descale a fish:
This is done to make the skin, with its valuable fats and minerals, edible. It should be done as soon after catching as possible and when the fish is whole and ungutted. Some fish, like mackerel, have no scales, while others, like bass and bream, have very coarse scales which should be thoroughly removed if the skin is to be eaten. Since scales lie in rows, overlapping from head to tail, they have to be scraped off in the opposite direction – from tail to head. A blunt knife or the back of a sharp one can be used. A running tap is useful to keep rinsing off the scales while scraping.

To gut fish:
Since bacteria and enzymes in the stomach will start attacking the fish muscles it should be gutted very soon (within a few hours) after catching. The exception to this is if the fish is being stored, immediately, in ice, reducing the temperature to 0 degrees C, which will inhibit the action of the bacteria and enzymes.

To gut a round fish:
Using a small sharp knife, cut from the anal vent along the length of the belly and through the head. Cut out the gills and pull them out with the innards. Wash the body cavity under a running tap, removing the membrane attached to the backbone which covers dark-looking congealed blood. This is the fish's kidney and should be thoroughly cleaned out with a stiff brush if necessary.

To gut a flat fish:
Using a small sharp knife make a cut below the head, slitting into the gut cavity. Pull out the innards and clean out the kidney (as above). The roe can be left in.

To skin and fillet fish:
First cut off all fins with scissors. Use a very sharp fish filleting knife with a long, thin, flexible blade. Aim to leave as little flesh on the bones as possible by sliding the blade edge over the bones.

FLAT FISH can be skinned before filleting.

- Make a cut in the skin across the tail end and loosen the skin to make a flap using the point of the knife. The flap should be large enough to grip. Take hold of it in one hand and hold the tail in the other and pull the skin off from tail to head. Repeat on the other side.

- To take off four fillets, cut from head to tail along the lateral (central) line of the fish. Slide the knife close to the bones starting at the head end and working from the centre outwards. Remove the fillet. Take off the other fillet the same way. Turn the fish over and repeat on the other side.

ROUND FISH

- Make a shallow cut along the back of the fish, starting at the head on one side of the fin bones. Feel for the backbones of the fish and slide the knife down one side keeping close to the bones. Repeat on the other side.

- Remove the skin by laying the fillet, skin side down, on a board. Loosen about two centimetres of skin from the tail end. Hold on to this while sliding the knife in a slow sawing action between the flesh and the skin, while keeping the fish flat on the board and the knife as close to the skin as possible.

HERRING

- Lay the cleaned and deheaded fish on the board skin side up with the belly flaps spread out. Press gently, but firmly, along the backbone till the fish flattens out. This releases all the fine bones from the flesh. Turn the fish over and catch the backbone at the head end, pulling it out of the flesh towards the tail. Cut off at the tail.

Cooking

The aim: to get the centre cooked before the outside is overcooked

How finfish cooks:
Compared with meat, the collagen sheath (connective tissue) between the muscle fibres in fish shrinks and ruptures at a much lower temperature (40C for fish, 60C for meat). As the collagen shrinks and ruptures, the muscle fibres begin to coagulate and the water in the muscle cells (the fish 'juices') begins to leak out.

The challenge for the fish cook is to control the cooking temperature so that the fish is removed from the heat immediately the fish muscle is coagulated when there will be a minimum loss of fish juices. Overcooked fish will be shrunken, dry, flaky, lacking flavour and not good to eat.

A check for doneness, visually, can be made by opening up the fish with the point of a sharp knife, at its thickest point, which will show the coagulation of the muscle fibres as they turn from translucent to opaque. If the fish is large, an internal thermometer can also be inserted into the thickest point.

Exact rules for cooking time related to the thickness of the fish (i.e. 10 minutes for every 2cm) can only be used as a rough guide, since the flesh of some fish is denser than others and will take longer to cook. More open-muscled fish like cod will take less time than denser fish like mackerel and tuna.

Fish in peak condition, with their muscles well-developed and high in protein, will absorb more heat before its temperature rises, so will also take longer to cook. Also, fish with a naturally fatty flesh will vary in the amount of fat in its flesh according to its spawning season. When it is low in fat after spawning, it will cook faster than when it is full of fat in peak condition.

Another consideration is that whole round fish are usually much thicker at the head end, and should be cut with two or three slashes (to about 5mm), through this part only, which will help the heat penetrate more rapidly. Thin tail-ends can be protected from over-cooking with a piece of foil.

Finally, whatever the cooking method, there is always latent heat in a cooked fish, so it will continue cooking after the source of heat has been removed.

How shellfish cooks:

Crustaceans – shrimps, lobsters, crabs, langoustines and relatives
Compared with finfish, there is more collagen between the muscle fibres of crustaceans, which is slower to shrink and rupture when heated, compared with finfish.

The challenge for the shellfish cook is that some shellfish have very active protein-breaking enzymes in the muscle fibres which, if not quickly destroyed, will turn the muscle mushy before the collagen has been dissolved. The enzymes work fastest at 55-60C so the shellfish should be cooked beyond this temperature quickly.

Molluscs: mussels, oysters, razor clams, cockles, whelks, scallops, squid and relatives
Molluscs with two shells have two types of muscle fibres. One is for closing and opening the shell and another 'catch muscle', with very strong muscle fibres and

high amounts of collagen, is to keep the shells tightly shut. While the opening and closing muscles, and the swimming muscle if they move about, are mostly quite tender when raw, overcooking will dry them out and make them chewy.

Squid, cuttlefish and octopus have the highest amount of muscle tissue with a high percentage of collagen and a complex fibre arrangement. When lightly cooked, before the collagen breaks down, they are slightly chewy. If they are cooked longer, as the collagen breaks down completely, they become very tough. To tenderise, once they reach this stage, they require longer cooking by a wet method. Spaniards beat octopus to break down the muscle fibres before cooking.

Oven Temperatures

The temperature in every oven will vary a little whether it's **gas, electric, fan-assisted** or **Aga**.

In a non-fan-assisted oven, the hottest part is at the top and the coolest at the bottom.

Keep baking tins in the middle of the shelf, away from the side, to prevent burning. If the heat is coming from the back it's a good idea to turn baking trays half way through the cooking.

Fan-assisted ovens: circulate the heat more evenly, making the whole oven hotter, which can reduce the baking time by 10 minutes in every hour.

Gas Mark	Fahrenheit	Celsius	Description
¼	225	110	Very cool
½	250	130	Cool
1	275	140	Very low
2	300	150	Very low
3	325	170	Very moderate
4	350	180	Moderate
5	375	190	Moderately hot
6	400	200	Hot
7	425	220	Hot
8	450	230	Very Hot
9	475	250	Very hot

Conversion – Metric to Imperial Scales

Spring-operated scales are less accurate compared with digital scales. The digital display will usually convert from metric to imperial. You can also put the mixing bowl or pot onto the scale and add ingredients directly. You can reset to zero once you have weighed an item, then weigh other ingredients on top. This is a great time-saver.

Other Measures

1 teaspoon = 5ml

1 tablespoon = 15ml

Measuring based on the American Cup

¼ cup = 2fl oz or 60ml

1/3 cup = 2½fl oz or 80ml

½ cup = 4fl oz or 125ml

1 cup = 8fl oz or 250ml

Conversion: use either Metric or Imperial

WEIGHT

15g (½oz)

25g (1oz)

40g (1½oz)

50g (2oz approx or 1¾oz exact)

75g (3oz approx or 2¾oz exact)

100g (4oz approx or 3½oz exact)

125g (4oz approx or 4½oz exact)

150g (5oz approx or 5½oz exact)

175g (6oz)

200g (7oz)

225g (8oz)

250g (8oz approx or 9oz exact)

275g (9oz approx or 9½oz exact)

300g (10oz approx or 10½oz exact)

325g (11oz approx or 11½oz exact)

350g (12oz)

375g (13oz)
400g (14oz)
425g (15oz)
450g (16oz)
500g (16oz approx or 1lb 2oz)
600g (1lb 5oz)
750g (1lb 10oz
1kg (2lb approx or 2lb 4oz exact)
2.25kg (5lb)

VOLUME

15ml (½fl oz)
25ml (1fl oz)
50ml (2fl oz)
75ml (3fl oz approx or 2½fl oz exact)
100ml (3fl oz approx or 3½fl oz exact)
125ml (4fl oz)
150ml (5fl oz – ¼pt)
175ml (6fl oz)
200ml (7fl oz)
250ml (8fl oz approx or 9fl oz exact)
300ml (10fl oz – ½pt)
325ml (11fl oz)
350ml (12fl oz)
400ml (14fl oz)
425ml (15fl oz – ¾pt)
450ml (16fl oz)
475ml (17fl oz)
500ml (20fl oz approx or 18fl oz exact)
600ml (20fl oz – 1pt)
1L (2 pt approx or 1¾pt exact)
1.2L (2pt)
2L (3½pt)
3L (5¼pt)

2 ... flavourings

Flavourings for Seafood: Making Taste and Flavour Compositions; Flavouring Butter with Herbs; A bundle of Herb Flavourings for Fish

Flavourings for Seafood

On the question of taste not everyone agrees. What's too sweet for one is not sweet enough for another. This largely depends on the number and position of taste-bud receptors – sweet, salty, sour, bitter and savoury – on the tongue. Likes and dislikes get much more complicated when the nose's smell receptors, designed to pick up more complex flavours, come into play, since they vary even more.

Flavours and tastes to go with seafood depend on whether the fish or shellfish is lacking in flavour and needs to be livened up with some exotic or robust notes. Or whether it's at its peak of freshness, and packed with its own unique tastes and flavours, when it needs nothing much added and certainly nothing taken away.

Fish and shellfish with most taste and flavour are those which breathe and swallow sea water. Most ocean creatures balance the saltiness of sea water by filling their cells with sweet and savoury-tasting protein compounds. Those richest in these flavourings are shellfish, members of the herring and mackerel family, sharks and rays. Most white fish have less, and therefore have a less strong taste and flavour. Some are almost tasteless, while others are delicately interesting. The other flavour factor is the amount of fat in the flesh, with fatty fish like herring, mackerel and salmon having more flavour.

Because the salt content of sea water varies, all fish and shellfish will be more, or less, tasty according to the saltiness of the sea water.

A transient taste factor in fish and shellfish occurs for a short time after it has passed through rigor mortis when its savouriness increases. Then it declines and disappears, which is why some countries make so much effort to make sure that they can eat their fish when it's very fresh.

Crustacean flavour
Unlike molluscs and finfish, the flavour of crab, lobster, langoustine, shrimp, prawn and crayfish – once boiled – has similarities to the flavour from the browning reaction when meats are roasted (i.e. when proteins and sugars react together at high temperatures). This sugar-protein reaction takes place at lower temperatures

in crustaceans. Some crustaceans also have an iodine-like flavour which they accumulate from algae and other foods which are then converted, in their gut, into these flavour compounds.

Oyster flavour

When an oyster is eaten fresh, unadorned by competing flavours, it's possible to note the natural flavours of the environment which have given it its character – or as the French would say, its *terroir*. Flavour notes to look for in oysters are salty-briny, sweet-creamy, meaty, buttery and nutty. There may also be notes of melon, cucumber or metallic tastes. Sour lemon balances the oyster's salty-briny notes and releases its sweet notes.

Seaweed flavours

One of the most distinctive savoury flavours in seaweeds comes from glutamic acid, from which monosodium glutamate (MSG) is made. Seaweeds, like shellfish, also contain the sulphurous notes (dimethyl sulphide) which are in sea coast air. Some seaweeds have iodine or astringent notes, while red seaweeds are more sulphurous and flowery. Some, like kelp, develop fishy notes if cooked too long. When dulse is fried, it smells of bacon. Pepper dulse is, as it implies, peppery.

Freshwater fish flavours

Freshwater fish, because they do not have to balance their body cells against a salty environment, do not develop tasty proteins in the same way as sea fish, so their flesh is milder by comparison. Wild brown trout and Arctic charr, from well-oxygenated Scottish freshwater lochs, fast-moving rivers and burns, will have a delicate but distinctive flavour from their feeding, much superior to the often 'muddy' tasting freshwater fish such as carp and pike from slow-moving rivers.

Making Taste and Flavour Compositions

In the spectrum of tastes and flavour aromas which are good partners for seafood and freshwater fish, there are some which are in the time-tested category. No need to guess if they will work, though it's still important to get the balance right.

To go with: ALL SEAFOOD

Citrus notes from lemon, and lime; aniseed notes from fennel, dill, tarragon, star anise and anise-flavoured alcoholic drinks such as Pernod; sulphurous notes from garlic; briny-salty notes from seaweeds; sweet-buttery notes from unsalted butter.

To go with: WHITE FISH AND SHELLFISH

Green-grassy notes from cucumber, parsley, coriander leaf and pea; briny-salty notes from olives and bacon; earthy notes from celery and mushrooms; fruity-creamy notes from mango and coconut.

To go with: WHITE FISH

Salty-briny notes from cured anchovies; mustardy notes from horseradish; earthy notes from paprika, potatoes (also with smoked white fish); fresh-fruity notes from tomatoes, grapes; cheesy notes from hard cheeses.

To go with: SHELLFISH

Meaty notes from lamb, chicken and black pudding; fresh-fruity notes from apple and almond; spicy notes from chilli pepper, black pepper and nutmeg.

To go with: OILY FISH

Mustardy notes; peppery notes from watercress; fresh-fruity notes from gooseberries, rhubarb or plums; earthy notes from beetroot and cumin; spicy notes from chilli pepper; allspice; black pepper and horseradish.

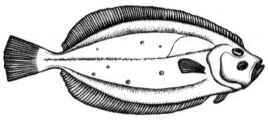

megrim

Flavouring Butter with Herbs

This is a hard butter which gives a flavour punch as it is sliced and placed on top of cooked fish or shellfish just before serving. While citrusy lemon and sulphurous garlic will work with most fish and shellfish, some herbs work better with seafood than others. It will keep for several weeks in the fridge, or longer in the freezer.

It is also useful to 'finish' vegetables and as the final flourish when splitting open a baked potato.

It can be added to seafood soups and sauces, or melted in a pan and cooked with some chopped tomatoes to make quick sauce for white fish.

Garlic Butter with Herbs

125g unsalted butter, softened
10-15g herbs,* finely chopped
2 cloves garlic, crushed with the edge of a sharp knife till smooth or in a garlic press
2 teaspoons lemon juice
Other flavourings**

MAKING BUTTER

Put the soft butter into a bowl and add all the other ingredients. Blend together evenly with a wooden spoon.

Or put the herbs, garlic and lemon juice and butter into a food processor. Blend together but not too finely. It should have a bit of texture.

Wrap in cling film and chill in the fridge till firm but not hard. Remove from the fridge. Roll, while still in the clingfilm, into a sausage shape. Serve in slices to put on hot fish.

Store in fridge. Will keep for up to two weeks, but will begin to lose flavour as it ages. It can be frozen.

*Herbs:

Fresh will have most flavour. **Dried** will have lost some of their essential oils as they dry. Very old dried herbs can develop an unpleasant hay-like flavour. Use a third to a half the amount if dried. Their aroma will be an indication of how much flavouring is left in them.

Parsley, fresh leaves: 10-15g
With its fresh grassy and earthy notes, it has the unusual ability to act as a foil for other flavours, linking them and giving them depth, while disappearing into the background itself. Both curly and flat varieties have hints of lemon and anise, but it's the flat variety which has the more complex flavour.

Dill, fresh leaves: 10-15g
Noted for its fresh, clean fragrant notes of anise and lemon. It is one of the most popular partners for seafood around the world, especially in Scandinavia.

Fennel, fresh young leaves only: 10g
It has more dominant anise-liquorice notes than dill, which makes it more suitable

for stronger flavoured oily fish. There are two types, green and bronze (milder than green) varieties. Fennel bulb (Florence fennel) is a different variety, eaten as a vegetable.

Tarragon, fresh leaves: 5-10g
Though the first wild varieties came from Siberia and western Asia (now known as Russian tarragon) this has less flavour compared with the French variety which has spicy-anise, pine and liquorice notes. It should be used discreetly with delicate seafood.

Sweet Cicely, fresh leaves: 10-15g
Sweet and musky, strongly aromatic when fresh, its anise notes fade when heated. It also has a hint of celery and brings out the sweetness in prawns and scallops.

Oregano and Marjoram, fresh leaves: 10g
Pungent and spicy, oregano is more robust and peppery, with some lemony notes, than marjoram, which has a sweeter, more subtle, spiciness. They both have some bitterish notes with a hint of camphor, so should be used cautiously with delicate fish.

Thyme, fresh leaves: 5-10g
Both common thyme and lemon thyme have a warm earthiness with peppery-spicy notes. The lemon variety is especially good with fish and shellfish.

Rosemary: 5-10g
A pungent, warm and peppery herb with resinous and slightly bitter notes of camphor and pine. There is also a woody, astringent aftertaste. It's best partnered with robust-flavoured fish like mackerel or red mullet. The Tuscan Blue variety is lemony-pine flavoured and less strident.

Wild Garlic, leaves and flowers: 5-10g
Flourishes in damp woods and shady lanes, making a dense carpet of vivid green. A truly wild plant, native to Britain, it has never been cultivated yet has all the taste and health advantages of cultivated garlic. As its flowers begin to open, the leaves lose their vitality, so switch to flowers, using them in the same way as leaves, either raw or mixed through hot food just before it's eaten, since they lose flavour when cooked.

**Other flavourings:

Anchovy and Caper Butter:

125g unsalted butter, softened; 20g anchovy fillets: 1 tablespoon capers; ground black pepper

Put softened butter into a food processor. Add anchovies and capers. Blend together not too finely. Taste and add pepper.

A Bundle of Herb Flavourings for Fish

This is an additional flavouring for slow-cooked dishes such as stocks, soups, stews and sauces, which adds depth of flavour.

Tie the bundle together with some white cotton thread and add at the beginning of the cooking.

Flavour combinations:

For all types of fish: *a few sprigs of parsley, tarragon, thyme and a few strips of lemon peel*

For more delicate fish: *a few sprigs of dill, parsley and lemon balm*

For oily fish: *a few sprigs of lemon thyme, fennel and bay leaf*

3 . . . in a liquid

Cooking slowly in a liquid, like poaching just below boiling point, allows more control than faster, hotter grilling or frying. There is also the latent heat in the liquid which can be used to finish cooking after the heat has been turned off. Herring, tuna, whiting, pollack, shrimp, lobster and crab are not suitable for this method, since they become mushy when cooked slowly.

BONES AND HEADS

Fish Broth

Every scrap of flavour is extracted from filleting debris (ask the fishmonger for this if buying fillets) to make a basic broth. Strained, it can be used to add more fish flavour to other fish soups, stews and sauces.

Turbot, brill, sole, John Dory, bream and bass bones and heads will add the best flavour and 'body', also a monkfish head.

Basic Broth to Make about Two Litres

2kg white fish bones and heads
4-5 tablespoons oil
2 onions, finely sliced
Water to cover
Bunch of parsley stalks and/or bunch of thyme
Bay leaf
1 tablespoon peppercorns
Equipment:
Large heavy pot

MAKING BROTH

Wash fish to remove any blood and cut out the gills from heads. Put a large pot over a medium heat and add the oil. Add the onion and cook gently without colouring for about 5 minutes, then add the bones and heads and continue cooking, stirring occasionally for another 5 minutes or so until the bones go opaque.

Cover with water and bring slowly up to a simmer. Skim off any scum which rises. Add peppercorns, bay leaf and parsley or thyme stalks. Simmer gently for 15-20 minutes (longer will bring out bitter tastes from the bones). Leave to cool a little. When still warm, strain. Reserve any fish pieces for other dishes.

To Finish as
A Simple Seafood Broth

Serves 4-6
2-3 tablespoons oil
300g onion, chopped finely
350g floury potatoes such as Desiree, Kerr's Pink, King Edward, Rooster
300g leek, finely chopped
1 litre strained Fish Broth or water
3 cloves garlic, crushed
Salt and ground black pepper
1-2 tablespoons chopped herbs (parsley, tarragon, lemon thyme)
150-200g unskinned fillet of white fish such as haddock, whiting, pollack or scallops, plus roe
OR cooked and shelled mussels, cockles, whelks or North Atlantic prawns

Garlic butter (see p. 158)
Crusty bread, toasted

PREPARING VEGETABLES

Preheat a large pot over a medium heat. Add the oil and when hot add the onion. Cook till soft but uncoloured, stirring occasionally. Add the potatoes and mix through the onions. Reduce the heat, cover and continue cooking, stirring occasionally until the potatoes begin to soften. Add the white of the leek, reserving the dark green top, and continue stirring for a few minutes until the leek begins to soften.

MAKING THE BROTH

Add the strained Fish Broth or water and bring up to a simmer. When the potatoes are soft, add the garlic and finely chopped dark green leek. Remove from the heat, stir through, cover and leave for a few minutes until the leek softens. Taste and season.

SERVING

While the broth is cooking, heat serving bowls. Slice the white fish fillets or the scallops and roe very thinly, on the diagonal like slicing smoked salmon. Just before you are ready to serve, put chopped herbs, sliced fish and/or cooked shellfish into heated bowls. Pour over hot soup. Serve with crusty bread, toasted and spread with garlic butter (see p. 158)

To Finish as
Saffron Cream Shellfish Soup

Serves 4-6
2 large pinches of saffron, *boiling water to cover*
4 large tomatoes, skinned and de-seeded
1 tablespoon light olive oil
2 cloves garlic, sliced
1.1 litres Fish Broth
2-3 sprigs tarragon
20g plain flour blended with 30g soft butter
250ml crème fraiche
250g cooked mussels, cockles, langoustines, North Atlantic prawns, or white meat from a cooked lobster claw
Salt and ground pepper

PREPARING FLAVOURINGS

Grind saffron in a pestle and mortar. Put into a cup and pour over a little boiling water, leave to infuse.

Heat a large pot over a medium heat and add oil. When hot add garlic and tomatoes. Cook for a few minutes to blend flavours, then add half the Fish Broth and the saffron infusion. Bring up to a simmer. Add the tarragon.

THICKENING AND FINISHING

Divide blended butter and flour into about ten small pieces. Scatter over the surface of simmering soup. Beat in with a balloon whisk. Leave to simmer until it thickens.

Use a hand-held blender in the pot, or blend in a food processor or liquidiser to a fine puree. Return to the pan and add the remaining Fish Broth. Whisk in the crème fraiche. Taste and season.

SERVING

Put the cooked shellfish into heated serving bowls. Pour over hot soup and serve with crusty bread.

*COOK'S NOTES

Saffron is an alluring aroma in food (and perfumes) which adds a deep fragrance to all seafood. It takes about three to four hundred hours to hand-pick a kilo of the dark orange stigmas of the autumn-flowering crocus. Top quality comes from Kashmir, Iran, Spain or Morocco. Packets of whole stigmas are better than ground, where there is always the chance of adulteration. Yet even buying whole stigmas is not without its pitfalls. It's graded for colour, taste, scent and the amount of non-stigma content. The packet may not always tell you the grade, or age. Colour and flavour fade with age so it's worth looking for a date.

'It's best to grind it in a pestle and mortar first and then soak it in a little boiling water,' says Sally Butcher, saffron supplier and author of *Persia in Peckham* (2007).

periwinkle

WHOLE FISH

Poached

Using trout, Arctic charr, salmon, sea bass, bream, gurnard, red mullet
or large mackerel

Served either hot with buttered new potatoes or cold with mayonnaise and salad,
the leftover cooking liquid is also useful fish stock for other fish soups, stews and
sauces.

Serves 4

1.4kg fish on the bone, cleaned and scaled: either 1 large, 2 x 700g or 4 x 350g or
a cut from a large fish, cleaned and scaled

Poaching liquid:

Water to cover
3–4 cloves garlic, crushed
1 medium carrot, thinly sliced
1 onion, finely chopped
Herbs: parsley, bay leaf, thyme, fennel, oregano, wild garlic (a good handful of
stalks, leaves, flowers, depending on season)
1 teaspoon salt
10–12 black peppercorns
500ml dry white wine (optional)

Equipment:

Large heavy pot (large fish can be cut in half to fit the pot)

PREPARING COOKING LIQUID

Fill the pot with the water. Bring to the boil and add the garlic, carrot, onion, herbs
and salt and peppercorns. Return to a gentle simmer. Cover and simmer for about
15 minutes. Add the white wine if using and simmer, covered, for another 15-20
minutes. Leave to cool a little.

POACHING FISH

Take the pot off the heat and put in the fish. Return to a very low heat and bring
back to almost simmering point. Cover.

Approx. cooking times: for one large fish (1.4kg) 10-15 minutes; for two medium
(700g) 6-8 minutes; for four small (350g) 3-4 minutes. Remove fish from liquid

and check it's cooked by opening up at the thickest part with a sharp pointed knife, when the translucent flesh should have changed to milky-opaque all the way through.

SERVING

Serve hot or cold.

Serve hot with boiled new potatoes and Mustardy Spinach (see p. 194). Strain over a little of the cooking liquid.

Or serve cold with mayonnaise (see p. 206) and salad leaves, or wild greens (see p. 176).

COOK'S NOTES

Potted Fish: Leftover poached fish can be used to make potted fish by reducing some of the poaching liquid to add flavour (see p. 212).

FISH FILLETS

Fennel and Mushroom Fish Stew

White fish fillets such as sole, plaice, whiting, cod, monkfish, saithe/coley, ling, hake, haddock or John Dory are lightly cooked on a bed of vegetables. It can be served, either as a basic stew, or thickened with cream and Pernod.

Serves 4

Basic stew
2 tablespoons olive oil
1 red onion, finely chopped
400g fennel bulb, finely sliced
200g button mushrooms
250ml fish stock/water or dry white wine
1-2 tablespoons chopped tarragon
Salt
4 x 150–175g white fish fillets
1 lemon

Creamy thickened stew
1-2 tablespoons Pernod (optional)
3 tablespoons crème fraîche (optional)

7g flour blended with 7g softened butter (optional)
Equipment:
Large sauté pan with lid or large frying pan with plate to cover

PREPARING VEGETABLES

Put sauté pan on a medium heat and when hot add the oil. Add the onion and cook over a medium heat till soft and translucent. Add the fennel and mushrooms. Toss in the pan occasionally to keep them moving for 3-4 minutes or so till they begin to soften. Add the liquid, 1 tablespoon tarragon and salt. Bring up to a slow simmer and cover. Cook until the vegetables are soft.

Creamy thickened stew: Add Pernod and crème fraiche. To thicken, divide the blended butter and flour into small pieces and scatter over stew. Stir through and simmer gently to thicken. Taste and adjust seasoning.

COOKING FISH

Place the fish on top and reduce the heat to a very slow simmer. Cover pan with lid. Check fish after a few minutes by opening up at the thickest part with a sharp pointed knife, when the translucent flesh should have changed to milky-opaque all the way through. Cooking time will depend on the thickness of the fish.

FINISHING

Sprinkle remaining chopped tarragon over the fish. Serve from the pan with boiled new potatoes tossed in butter.

Steamed Fillets with Lime and Olive Oil
(in microwave)
Using pollack, haddock, saithe/coley, cod, hake, ling, monkfish or wolf-fish/'catfish'

Serves 4
4 x 150–175g white fish fillets or thick steaks, skinned and boned
2 limes
3 tablespoons olive oil
Sea salt and ground black pepper
Flat leaf parsley, finely chopped

PREPARING FISH

Cut fish into portions. Mix the juice of one lime, olive oil and seasoning in a shallow non-metallic dish. Add the fish and turn to coat in the flavourings. Cover with clingfilm and leave in the fridge for an hour.

COOKING FISH

Turn once again in the marinade. Re-cover and make several holes with the point of a sharp knife in the clingfilm to allow the steam to escape. Microwave on High (700W) for about 4 minutes. Turn the fish once half way through the cooking. Check the fish by opening up at the thickest part with a sharp pointed knife, when the translucent flesh should have changed to milky-opaque all the way through. Cooking time will depend on the thickness of the fish.

SERVING

Remove clingfilm. Sprinkle over chopped parsley. Serve with wedges of lime and buttered new potatoes.

SHELLFISH

Shellfish Broth

Served in a deep Scottish soup plate – or a deep bowl – with nothing more complicated than the liquor it's cooked in.

Serves 4 as starter, 2 main course
2kg mussels or cockles in their shells
300 ml water
Garlic butter (see p. 158)
Crusty bread, toasted
2 tablespoons chopped parsley or finely sliced spring onions

PREPARING SHELLFISH

Scrub clean. Remove any 'beards' (the hairy bit that clings to the rock). Discard any that are open and stay open when tapped, since they are no longer alive.

COOKING

Put water into a pot over a high heat and bring to the boil. Add half the shellfish. Cover with lid. Boil for about 60 seconds. Remove lid and stir or shake. Put lid back and leave boiling for another 60 seconds. Check again. Remove from heat immediately they are all opened. Drain into a sieve or colander, catching the liquid in a large bowl. Cover and keep cooked mussels warm.

Return the liquid to the pot and bring back to boiling. Add remainder of shellfish and repeat cooking procedure. Drain and catch liquid in the bowl.

MAKE TOAST

Toast the bread and spread with butter while hot. Keep warm.

TO FINISH

Strain the liquid back into the pan. Taste for saltiness. Add more water if too salty. Heat up to just simmering. Put the hot mussels into heated deep soup plates or serving bowls. Ladle over enough liquid to half-fill the bowls and sprinkle with parsley or chopped spring onions.

Serve with garlic toast round the edges of the plates or bowls to soak up juices.

Spoot (Razor Clam) Broth

Most Scottish spoots are exported to Asia where they are cooked in a liquid – broth-style, as in the previous recipe – but including whatever mix of exotic flavourings takes the cook's fancy.

Serves 4 as starter, 2 main course
1.5kg spoots in their shells
2 tablespoons oil
3–4 cloves garlic, crushed
2 small hot red chillies
3 tablespoons root ginger or galangal, finely chopped
2 tablespoons finely chopped lemongrass
*1 level tablespoon tom yum paste**
500ml water
1–2 teaspoons fish sauce
Sugar, salt and pepper to taste
2 tablespoons chopped coriander
3–4 spring onions, finely chopped
Garlic butter (see p. 158)
Crusty bread, sliced

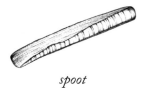

spoot

PREPARING SPOOTS

Scrub clean. Discard any that are open and stay open when tapped, since they are no longer alive. Soak in some salted water for half-an-hour or so, which will remove any remaining sand.

COOKING

Heat olive oil in a pan and add garlic, ginger, chillies and lemongrass. Stir-fry for a minute or two till they release their fragrance. Add the tom yum paste and mix with other ingredients. Add the spoots and toss over a high heat for a few minutes when the spoots will open. Add the water and fish sauce. Bring up to the boil and add sugar to taste. Simmer for a few minutes. Taste and season with salt and pepper. Remove from the heat. Cover and keep hot.

TO FINISH

Toast the bread and spread with butter while hot.

Put the spoots and their cooking liquid into heated deep soup plates or serving bowls. Sprinkle with parsley and chopped spring onions.

Serve with slices of garlic toast round the edge of the bowls or plates. Use to soak up juices.

*COOK'S NOTES

Commercial tom yum paste: this has distinctly hot and sour flavours and includes lemongrass, kaffir lime leaves, galangal, lime juice, garlic, dried shrimp and chilli.

Partan Bree

Bree is just another Scots word for 'broth' – simply the liquid something flavourful has been cooked in. Partans (brown crabs) make a very special bree with this method which extracts maximum flavour from the shells. Velvet crabs can also be used (see p. 209).

There is no quick way to do this.

Serves 4-6

To cook the crab:

100–150g (about 4 level tablespoons) salt to every 4.4 litres water

2 x 1kg live crabs

To make the bree:

Shells, after picking

2 tablespoon oil

25g butter

2 large carrots, finely chopped

2 stalks celery, finely chopped

1 leek, finely chopped

2 star anise

1 dessertspoon fennel seeds, ground

Fish stock or water to cover

Salt and pepper

Finishing bree:

Crème fraiche

PREPARING AND COOKING CRAB

Measure water into a large pot which will hold the crab and add the appropriate amount of salt. The water should be around the same saltiness as sea water, so the crab will not lose flavour into the cooking liquid.

The RSPCA (*www.rspca.org.uk*) recommends that crabs should be chilled to make them insensitive before killing. To do this, put them first into the fridge for a few hours to bring down their temperature gradually. Then they can be put in the freezer until they become insensible. Check for lack of movement every 15-20 minutes and remove. They can then be killed quickly by severing the nerve centres with a small sharp screwdriver or bradawl. Crabs have two main nerve centres.

The recommended method is to lift the abdominal flap (tail flap) in the centre of the underside and pierce into the hole over the hind nerve centre at the so-called vent all the way through the shell, followed by a repeat of the same process on the front nerve centre via the shallow depression at the top of the body, just above the movable plate closed over the mouth. This should be done quickly and take no longer than ten seconds. Lay the crab on the floor to give more downward pressure.

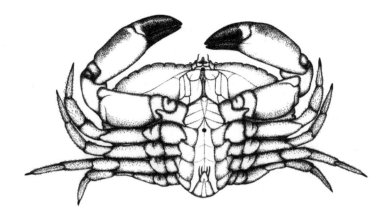

Drop the crab into the boiling salted water. Allow 15 minutes for a 1kg crab (add 5 minutes for every extra 500g). Remove, lay on its back and leave to cool. Repeat with second crab.

TO REMOVE THE CRAB MEAT

Twist off the claws and legs first. Using your thumbs together at the base of the underside of the body, push hard to release the central undercarriage from the top shell. Pull it all out and discard the small mouth with its grey stomach sac and discard the dull beige feathery 'dead man's fingers' which lie along the inside part of the body.

To extract the meat, crack the claws and legs with crab (or nut) crackers and remove the 'white' meat. Pick the rest of the white meat from the central undercarriage with a skewer or shellfish pick. Remove the soft 'brown' meat from inside the carapace (body shell). Keep the white meat from the claws separate.

PREPARING THE SHELLS

For extra flavour (optional) place the carapace on a roasting tray and put into a hot oven (220C/Gas 7) for 15–20 minutes, turning once.

MAKING THE BREE

Heat the oil in a large pot over a medium heat till hot. Add the tomato puree and all the broken shells and debris. Using a meat mallet, or the end of a rolling pin, break up the shells finely and stir for 5 to 10 minutes to release the flavour and colour from the shells. Add carrot, celery, leek, anise and fennel. Cover with fish stock or water. Bring to the boil and reduce to a very slow simmer for 1½–2 hours. Stir occasionally. Strain.

TO FINISH

This richly flavoured bree can be finished either as a rustic broth (thickened with rice) or as a rich cream soup (thickened with flour and butter) both garnished with the white claw meat.

Partan Bree Thickened with Rice

Serves 4
1 litre crab bree
40g long grain rice
70g brown meat
70g white meat
125ml crème fraiche
Salt and ground black pepper

Add the rice to the bree and cook till soft. Add the brown and white crab meat and crème fraiche. Heat through to simmering point, taste and season. Serve.

Partan Bree Thickened with Flour and Butter

Serves 4
1 litre crab bree
30g plain flour
30g butter, softened
125ml crème fraiche
150-200g white claw meat
Salt and ground pepper
Lemon juice
Brandy (optional)

Put bree into a pan and bring up to a simmer. Mix flour and butter together on a plate. Divide into about ten small pieces and drop them into the simmering bree. Using a balloon whisk, disperse them through the liquid. Bring up to the boil and simmer gently till the liquid thickens.

Stir in the crème fraiche. Taste and season with lemon juice and a splash of brandy. Serve with the claw meat as a garnish.

COOK'S NOTES

Unacceptable methods of killing crabs and lobsters (RSPCA advice):

- Cutting the lobster across the body and thus separating the head from the tail without first destroying the nerve centres
- Cutting crabs into sections without first destroying the front and rear nerve centres
- Boiling crabs/lobsters alive
- Leaving crabs/lobsters in freshwater to drown

SMOKED FISH

Boddam Skink (Soup-Stew)

An innovative version of Cullen Skink, served at the Boddam Inn near Peterhead, comes as a main course dish in a deep dinner plate with an 'island' of roasted monkfish wrapped in pancetta and some wilted greens, surrounded by the skink. This is a simpler version, using steamed chunks of white fish for the central island.

Serves 4

Finnan soup stew

2 tablespoons oil

2 onions, finely chopped

250ml fish stock or water

250ml milk or single cream

300g finnan haddock, undyed

500g new or waxy potatoes, cooked

1 teaspoon (5g) flour blended with 1 teaspoon (5g) soft butter

Salt and freshly ground black pepper

Steamed white fish – pollack, haddock, saithe/coley, cod, hake, ling, monkfish, wolf-fish/'catfish'

300–350g white fish fillets or thick steaks, skinned and boned

1–2 tablespoons fish stock, water, milk or cream

Sea salt and ground black pepper

COOKING THE SKINK

Heat the oil in a large pot over a medium heat till fairly hot. Add the onion and cook for 5-10 minutes till transparent and cooked through. Add fish stock and milk or cream. Skin and bone the finnan fillet and cut the flesh up into 1-2cm dice. Chop the potatoes into dice and add with the diced finnan to the pan. Bring up to a slow simmer. Scatter the blended butter in a few pieces over the soup. Stir in lightly and simmer till the fish is just cooked through and opaque and the flour has thickened the liquid slightly. Taste and season. Keep hot.

STEAMING WHITE FISH in a microwave

Cut fillets of white fish into bite-sized chunks. Place in one layer on a non-metallic dish. Season and add stock, water, milk or cream. Cover with clingfilm and make a few holes with a sharp knife to allow steam to escape. Microwave on high (700W) for 3 minutes. Leave for a minute to allow latent heat to finish cooking. Remove and test if cooked, when it should be opaque in the centre. Drain off liquid into a pan. Keep fish hot. Meanwhile boil up the cooking juices to reduce to a few tablespoons. Taste and season.

TO FINISH

Place a pile of white fish in centre of deep heated dinner plates, pour over reduced cooking liquid. Surround by skink. Serve with samphire (see p. 179) or other green vegetables.

*COOK'S NOTES:

Peterhead finnan smoker: John Milne, Peterhead. (See Directory p. 313)

Finnan Haddock and Poached Egg

A favourite 'Fish Tea' served with bread and butter and a pot of tea.

Serves 4
800g undyed, smoked finnan haddock, skinned or unskinned
250ml milk
Ground black or cayenne pepper
4 large fresh eggs
1 tablespoon vinegar

PREPARING AND COOKING THE FISH

Cut fish into portion sizes. Heat frying, or sauté pan, over a medium heat and add fish. Pour over milk or cream. Bring up to a slow simmer and cover with a lid or a large plate. Turn off the heat. Add pepper. Leave the flavours to infuse and the fish to continue cooking in the latent heat for 5 minutes. Check fish is cooked by opening up at the thickest part with a sharp pointed knife, when the translucent flesh should have changed to milky-opaque all the way through.

POACHING EGGS

Put a pan of water on a medium heat and bring to the boil. Add vinegar. Drop in eggs gently and simmer for 2-3 minutes till the whites are firm but the yolks still soft. Test by removing the egg in a skimming ladle and pressing the yolk lightly which should still feel soft. Remove and drain.

TO FINISH

Put the fish on heated deep soup plates. Boil up the cooking liquor and reduce slightly, taste and season. Place eggs on top of fish. Pour over milk or cream. Serve with bread and butter and a pot of tea.

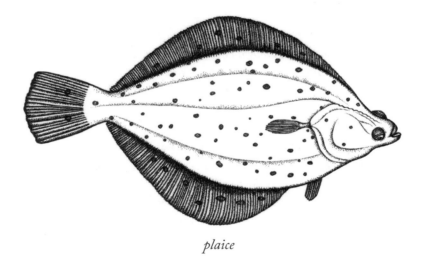

plaice

4 . . . grilled under or over heat

Intense heat, whether under a kitchen grill or over an open fire, browns the surface, adding both colour and flavour quickly. It works best with relatively thin whole fish, fillets or steaks, still with their skin attached to hold the flesh together, and with some shellfish.

WHOLE FLAT FISH

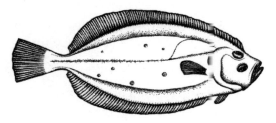

megrim

Grilled with Mixed Wild Greens Salad

Using Dover sole, plaice, lemon sole, dab, megrim, flounder, brill or bream (flat-shaped)

The best flat fish for grilling whole are those with firm meaty fillets which come away easily from a strong bone structure.

Serves 4
4 x 375–450g fish per person (1.5–1.8kg)
2 tablespoons flour, seasoned with salt
50g melted butter or 3-4 tablespoon oil
Salt
1 lemon
Garlic and Herb Butter (see p. 158)
Mixed Wild Greens Salad:
Handfuls of young tender leaves or flowers of wild garlic, or young tender leaves of sweet cicely; garlic mustard; chickweed; common sorrel; water-cress Alexanders or young tips of marsh samphire*
Salad Dressing:
2 teaspoons Dijon mustard; 100ml favourite vinegar; 300ml olive oil
or
Olive oil and lemon juice, to taste
Equipment:
Large shallow-sided roasting tray

PREPARING FISH

Clean and wash, drain. Trim off fins and bony edges (optional) and trim tail. The dark, top-side skin can also be removed (the fishmonger will do this if asked). Coat lightly with seasoned flour. Shake off excess. Grease a roasting tray which will hold the fish with either butter or oil.

GRILLING FISH

Small fish: Lay fish in tray, presentation side (top skin side) down. Brush with butter or drizzle over some oil. Pre-heat the grill to a high heat. Grill the fish for about 4-5 minutes. Turn, brush with more butter or oil and grill the top side for another 4-5 minutes or until cooked through.

Check if cooked by opening up at the thickest part with a sharp pointed knife, when the translucent flesh should have changed to milky-opaque all the way through.

Large fish: Lay prepared fish in tray, presentation side (top skin side) up. Brush with butter or drizzle over some oil. Salt lightly. Pre-heat the grill to a high heat. Grill the fish for about 6-7 minutes. Finish cooking in the oven (200C/Gas 6). Check after 5 minutes. Brush top surface with some melted butter to prevent drying out. Time will depend on the thickness, size and type of fish.

SERVING

Serve fish with its juices, garnished with lemon wedges and some slices of Garlic Butter on top of the hot fish.

To make dressing for salad, put mustard into a bottle and add vinegar, shake together till emulsified. Add oil and shake to mix thoroughly. Taste and season. Serve with Wild Greens Salad. Or simply drizzle some oil and lemon juice over the salad.

Can also be served with Stir-Fried Dulse and Kale (see p. 229) Mustardy Spinach (see p. 194) or Marsh Samphire (see p. 194).

*COOK'S NOTES

For identification of edible wild greens see:

Field Guides: Richard Mabey, *Food for Free* (2007); Fiona Houston and Xa Milne, *Seaweed, and Eat It: A Family Foraging and Cooking Adventure* (2008); Vivien Weise, *Cooking Weeds* (2007).

Reference Guides: Miles Irving, *The Forager Handbook* (2009); Keble Martin, *The Concise British Flora in Colour* (1979); Ray Mears, *Wild Food* (2007); Pamela Michael, *Edible Wild Plants and Herbs* (2007); Roger Phillips, *Wild Food* (1983).

Grilled with Marsh Samphire

Using trout, red and grey mullet, sea bass, bream or gurnard

Serves 4

4 x 275–325g fish per person (1.1-1.3kg)

50g butter, melted or 3-4 tablespoons oil

Salt

1 lemon

For the samphire:*

500g samphire, washed and trimmed

Water to cover

1 small hot red chilli, very thinly sliced

1 lemon

Olive oil

Sea salt

Equipment:

Large, shallow-sided roasting tray

PREPARING FISH

Clean fish and remove fins. Make two or three slashes with a sharp knife on both sides of the fish through its thickest part at the back of the head. This allows faster heat penetration. Salt the body cavity. Oil or butter a roasting tray which will hold the fish. Put in fish. Brush the fish with butter or drizzle over some oil. Salt skin lightly.

GRILLING FISH

Preheat the grill to a high heat. Grill fish for 4-5 minutes. If fish is large, finish cooking in the oven or turn fish and grill on other side for another 4-5 minutes or until cooked.

Check if cooked by opening up at the thickest part with a sharp pointed knife, when the translucent flesh should have changed to milky-opaque all the way through.

To finish in the oven: heat to 200C/Gas 6. Check after about 5-6 minutes. The time will depend on the thickness of the fish.

COOKING SAMPHIRE

Put the samphire into a pot and cover with boiling water. Bring up to the boil and simmer for about a minute. Drain and put into heated serving dish. Add chilli and a few tablespoons of olive oil. Toss together. Sprinkle over some sea salt.

SERVING

Serve fish with its juices, wedges of lemon and samphire. Can also be served with Stir-Fried Dulse and Kale (see p. 229), Mustardy Spinach (see p. 194) or Wild Greens Salad (see p. 176).

*COOK'S NOTES

To identify marsh samphire see Identification Guide p. 296.

Grilled on a Cast Iron, Ridged Grill Pan
Using mackerel, trout or thick, unskinned salmon steak

This method works best with oily fish.

Serves 4
4 x 275–325g fish per person (1.1-1.3kg)
Sea salt
150g wild rocket

TO GRILL

Lightly sprinkle the ridged grill pan with sea salt. Heat the pan over a medium heat. Hand test the heat by holding the flat of the hand about 4cm from the surface, when it should feel hot but not too hot.

Clean fish and remove fins. Dry thoroughly inside, and especially its skin.

Place fish on the grill pan (steaks: skin side down) and leave for about seven minutes without moving, when the oil in the fish will have released its skin from the pan and a good brown crust should have formed so it turns easily.

Turn. Cook on second side for another 5-7 minutes depending on thickness. Turn down heat if cooking too quickly. It should not smoke or burn.

Check if cooked by opening up at the thickest part with a sharp pointed knife, when the translucent flesh should have changed to milky-opaque all the way through.

TO SERVE

Serve with chips or mashed potatoes. For oily mackerel, serve with mustard or a sharp fruit sauce such as gooseberry or rhubarb. Serve a peppery rocket salad with salmon or trout.

Can also be served with Stir-Fried Dulse and Kale (see p. 229) Mustardy Spinach (see p. 194) Wild Greens Salad (see p. 176) or Marsh Samphire (see p. 178).

FISH FILLETS

Grilled Thin Fillets

Using whiting, haddock, saithe/coley, wolf-fish/catfish, pollack, ling, sole, plaice, flounder, dab, brill or John Dory

Serves 4

150–175g fish fillets per person (600–700g)
Salt
2 tablespoons flour, seasoned with salt
50g melted butter or 3-4 tablespoons oil
1 lemon
Garlic and herb butter (see p. 158)

Equipment:

Large, shallow-sided roasting tray

PREPARING FISH

Brush a roasting tray which will hold the fillets lightly with butter or oil. Coat fillets lightly with flour, shake off excess. Place fillets in tray presentation side (flesh side) down. Brush with butter or oil.

GRILLING FISH

Preheat the grill to a high heat. Grill for about 2-3 minutes, depending on thickness. Turn, brush surface with more butter and grill for another 2-3 minutes. Check if cooked by opening up at the thickest part with a sharp pointed knife, when the translucent flesh should have changed to milky-opaque all the way through.

FINISHING

Place slices of flavoured butter on top and serve immediately with lemon wedges.

Can also be served with Stir-Fried Dulse and Kale (see p. 229) or Wild Greens (see p. 176) or Mustardy Spinach (see p. 194) or Marsh Samphire (see p. 178).

Grilled Thick Fillets with Puy Lentils

Using pollack, haddock, saithe/coley, cod, hake, ling, wolf-fish/'catfish'

Served on a bed of spicy puy lentils with grilled cherry tomatoes.

Serves 4

Lentils:

125g puy lentils

1 tablespoon oil

1 red onion, finely chopped

8g medium hot chilli peppers, deseeded and finely chopped

250ml fish or chicken stock (if not available use water and other flavouring*)

Salt

Fish and Tomatoes:

4 x 175g steaks of (about 3cm thick) skinned or unskinned fillet

50g butter, melted or 3–4 tablespoons oil

Pinch or two of cayenne pepper or paprika to taste

Salt

200g cherry tomatoes, on the vine

Equipment:

Large, shallow-sided roasting tray

COOKING LENTILS

Wash the lentils and leave to soak for a few hours. Heat a pan over a medium heat and add the oil. When hot, add onion and cook till soft and transparent. Add chilli and cook for a few minutes.

Drain lentils and add to the onions. Stir over a low heat for a minute to blend flavours and then add the water or stock and salt. Simmer gently, uncovered, for about 10 minutes, stirring occasionally till the lentils have just softened and most of the liquid has evaporated. They should still be moist. Check seasoning. Keep warm.

PREPARING FISH

Place fish in a greased roasting tray presentation side down. For skin-on fish this should be skin side down, for unskinned fish, flesh side down. Add cayenne pepper or paprika to oil or butter and use to brush top and sides of fish. Season lightly with salt.

GRILLING FISH AND TOMATOES

Pre-heat the grill to high and grill the fish for about 5-6 minutes. Turn and brush other side with more oil or butter and grill for another 5-6 minutes. If skin-on it should be cooked till brown and crisp, which may take longer.

Add the cherry tomatoes still on the vine, brush with butter or drizzle over some oil and grill for the last 2-3 minutes cooking time.

Check if fish is cooked by opening up gently at the thickest part with a sharp pointed knife, when the translucent flesh should have changed to milky-opaque all the way through.

SERVING

Place a heap of lentils in the centre of heated serving dishes and place fish on top. Pour over any remaining oil or melted butter and serve with cherry tomatoes.

*COOK'S NOTES

If stock is not available to flavour the lentils, instead use anchovies and capers: blend in food processor 5-6 fillets of tinned anchovies in oil; 1 tablespoon capers; and 1-2 cloves garlic, crushed. Add to onions and lentils and stir over the heat for a few minutes, then add water and cook as above.

Grilled Fillets in Oatmeal
Using herring, mackerel or trout

A popular Fish Tea.

Serves 4
Oil for greasing roasting tray
50g coarse or pinhead oatmeal, seasoned with salt
4 x 150–175g fish fillets unskinned per person (600-700g)
Coarse or smooth mustard

Equipment:
Large, shallow-sided roasting tray

PREPARING FISH

Brush a roasting tray which will hold the fillets with oil. Put oatmeal on a large plate and season with salt. Press fish into the oatmeal on both sides. Place in roasting tray, flesh side down.

GRILLING FISH

Preheat the grill to a high heat. Grill skin side of fillets for about 3-4 minutes till lightly browned. Turn and grill flesh side. Add more oatmeal if some has fallen off. Grill for another 3-4 minutes depending on thickness. Check if cooked by opening up at the thickest part with a sharp pointed knife, when the translucent flesh should have changed to milky-opaque all the way through.

TO FINISH

Serve with coarse or smooth mustard, bread and butter and a pot of tea.

Grilled Kippers or Arbroath Smokies

Another popular Fish Tea. Whole, bone-in, undyed kippers will have the best flavour. Smokies are already cooked, so only need heating through.

Serves 4

4 kippers or 4 smokies
25g butter, melted
Ground black pepper

Equipment:
Large, shallow-sided roasting tray

PREPARING KIPPER

Cut off the head and remove the fins. Trim the tail. Line a roasting tray with foil and place the kippers in it, skin side down. Brush lightly with melted butter.

PREPARING SMOKIE

Slide a small sharp knife into the base of the belly cavity and loosen the fillet from one side of the backbone. Move the knife downwards towards the tail, then up towards the head end. Open up the fish and lie flat with the boned fillet on the right. Hold the tail and slide the knife under the backbone, releasing it from the other fillet. Lift the backbone out. Tidy up the area round the top flaps and remove any fine bones. Place in a roasting tray and brush the two open fillets liberally with butter.

GRILLING KIPPER OR SMOKIE

Preheat the grill to a high heat. Grill smokie for about 2-3 minutes to heat through only and lightly brown the butter.

Grill kippers for 5-6 minutes, depending on size. Remove from grill. Check if cooked by opening up at the thickest part with a sharp pointed knife, when the translucent flesh should have changed to milky-opaque all the way through.

TO SERVE

Remove the backbone from the kipper. Serve the smokie with grinding of black pepper. Serve both with bread and butter and a pot of tea.

SHELLFISH

Grilled (Uncooked) Langoustine
in the shell with garlic butter

All the flavours from the head and tail can be enjoyed in this simple grilled method.

Serves 4 starter, 2 main course
8 large (around 100g) live langoustine
Garlic butter (see p. 158) softened
1 lemon

PREPARING LANGOUSTINE

To kill quickly and humanely, place on chopping board, belly side down, and cut in half through the head, lengthways with a heavy, very sharp chef's chopping knife. Open them up. Put in a roasting tray. Make the garlic butter a spreading consistency and spread the cut sides.

GRILLING LANGOUSTINES

Preheat the grill to high. Grill for 2-3 minutes. Remove and check if cooked through. Serve immediately with lemon wedges and crusty bread.

Grilled (Cooked) Langoustines
with dipping sauce

All the special flavour from the soft head end is blended with other flavours in a dipping sauce.

Serves 4 starter, 2 main course
50g unsalted butter
8 large (around 100g) live langoustine
Water to cover
2-3 teaspoons salt
Dipping Sauce:
1 small shallot, finely chopped
1 dessertspoon flat-leaf parsley, finely chopped
85ml light olive oil
Lemon juice, to taste
Salt and ground black pepper

COOKING LANGOUSTINES

Put langoustines in a large pot, cover with boiling water and add salt. Bring to the boil and simmer for 2 minutes. Remove and drain. Leave to cool.

MAKING SAUCE

Melt butter. Cut langoustines in half lengthwise and, with a teaspoon, scoop out the soft creamy contents of the heads. Put this into a bowl and stir in the shallots, parsley, oil, lemon juice, salt and pepper to taste.

GRILLING LANGOUSTINES

Preheat the grill to high. Place the halved langoustines on a shallow roasting tray, cut side up, and brush with melted butter. Grill for 1-2 minutes to heat through the shells and meat.

SERVING

Place langoustines on the plates and spoon over a little of the dipping sauce. Put the remainder in a bowl and serve with sliced crusty bread.

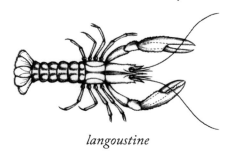

langoustine

Grilled Spoots (Razor Clams)
in the shell with garlic and chilli

Serves 4 starter, 2 main course
12 spoots
2 hot red chillies, de-seeded and sliced thinly
3-4 cloves of garlic, finely crushed
3-4 tablespoons light olive oil
2 tablespoons coriander, roughly chopped
1 lemon, halved and de-seeded

CLEANING SPOOTS

Check that all the spoots are live. The shells should shut when tapped. Wash them to remove any sand from outside of the shells. If they still seem sandy they can be soaked in salted water for 15-20 minutes to remove any remaining sand.

GRILLING

Preheat the grill to medium. Place the spoots in one layer on a baking tray and place under the grill for 1-2 minutes, turning once, till they open. Discard any that remain shut.*

Leave to cool. When cool enough to handle, remove spoot muscle (though all the spoot is edible, if preferred the digger end can be removed, also the dark sac). Cut each muscle diagonally into 2-3cm pieces and return to the shell.

Sprinkle the garlic and chillies evenly over all the spoots. Drizzle over olive oil so all are well covered. Put back under a hot grill for another 1-2 minutes to heat through.

SERVING

Remove from the grill, sprinkle with coriander and squeeze over some lemon juice. Serve immediately with crusty bread.

*COOK'S NOTES

They can also be opened by steaming. Put spoots into a wide pan, in a single layer, with about half an inch of water. Cover with a tight-fitting lid and bring to the boil, simmer until the shells open. Discard any that don't.

5 . . . on an open fire

Cooking seafood on an open fire in the wild is one of the best methods for those hard-shelled shellfish which only require a wire grid to hold them. Whole fish work well too, especially if held in a hinged fish basket.

COOKING TOOLS

Grid for open fire cooking: Use wire racks from old ovens or grill pans. The larger the better, since some space at the cooler edges of the fire is useful for keeping the food hot, yet away from the intense heat in the centre.

Rub the bars with some oil if the grid is not already seasoned. Grilling bacon will also leave a layer of burnt fat which will prevent food sticking. Fish which have been oiled will also season the grid.

Fish basket: A metal holder for whole fish removes the problem of turning large fish on the grid. A fish basket also makes it easier to keep turning the fish to ensure more even grilling and it can be propped up at the side of the fire to finish cooking while something else is on the grid.

Wooden plank: A plank of wood can be used to grill an unskinned fillet of a large fish. Place the fish skin side down on the plank and nail the tail end firmly onto the wood to hold it in place. Nail down the belly flaps at the head end to keep them from curling. Season fish with salt and drizzle with some oil and set against one of the hearth stones.

Metal Skewers: Useful for threading fish and shellfish together to cook on the grid.

Fish tongs are better at turning whole fish over an open fire than a fish slice.

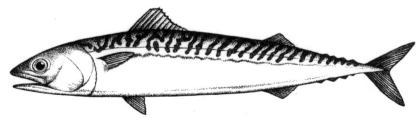

mackerel

WHOLE FISH

Mackerel, Herring, Trout, Arctic Charr, Red or Grey Mullet, Sea Bass, Bream

Oil and salt

Herbs: parsley, bay leaf, thyme, fennel, oregano, wild garlic (a good handful of stalks, leaves, flowers, depending on season)

Lemons

PREPARING THE FISH

Make a few slashes at the thickest part of the fish to allow the heat to penetrate faster. Rub the fish all over with oil. Season skin and body cavity with salt. Put some herbs and a bay leaf into the body cavity.

COOKING

Small to medium-sized fish on grid: When the fire is very hot and all the flames have died down, put the grid over the fire. Leave for a few minutes till it heats up. Put fish on the grid and leave for about five minutes. Turn and cook on the other side. Keep turning.

Test for readiness by opening up at the thickest part with a sharp pointed knife; the flesh should have turned from translucent to milky-opaque and come away easily from the bone.

COOKING

Medium to large-sized fish in a fish basket: Once the fire is ready for cooking, put the prepared fish in the fish basket and place over the hottest part to start the cooking and crisp and brown the skin. Turn over after five minutes to crisp the other side. Turn again twice, by which time the skin should be nicely crisp. Move away from the centre of the fire and prop up at the side to finish the cooking at a lower temperature. Continue turning so both sides get cooked through. Test for readiness (see above).

SERVING

Drizzle fish with lemon juice. Eat with bread and butter.

COOK'S NOTES

Potatoes and other root vegetables can be baked in the embers of an open fire. Rub vegetables with oil and season with salt. Wrap up in foil and bury at the edges of the fire before it gets going. Turn them occasionally to ensure even cooking and check after half an hour to see how they are cooking, since some will cook faster than others.

SHELLFISH

Large Mussels, Clabbies (Horse Mussels), Cockles, Oysters, Razor Clams

Garlic butter:
½ pack unsalted butter, softened
2 large cloves garlic, crushed to a paste with a knife or in a garlic press
1 heaped tablespoon chopped dill or parsley
1-2 teaspoons lemon juice

Or

Herb dressing with oil:
1 lemon, juice
1 heaped tablespoon chopped parsley
1 heaped tablespoon young thyme leaves
Extra virgin olive oil
Ground black pepper

MAKE GARLIC BUTTER

Beat the butter in a bowl and add all the other ingredients. Mix well.

MAKE OIL DRESSING

Mix all ingredients together.

PREPARING SHELLFISH

Wash off all sand and dirt and remove 'beards'.

COOKING SHELLFISH

Place mussels, clabbies, cockles and razor clams on their sides, oysters on their curved side, on a heated grid. Cook shells which are roughly the same size together. Medium to small sized shells should be ready just after they open. Clabbies and large oysters and razor clams will take longer.

If the cooking has been planned so all the shellfish are ready at the same time, the whole grid can be removed. Otherwise the shellfish can be removed individually with tongs. Preserve as much of the shellfish liquor as possible.

SERVING

Once they have cooled a little either:

Remove the top shells and put a little garlic butter on top of each shellfish. This is a better method for large shellfish like razor clams or clabbies. Eat while still warm.

Or:

Put them all into a bowl – better for smaller shellfish like mussels or cockles – catching all the cooking liquid in the shells, adding the dressing and mixing through. Eat while still warm with bread and butter

COOK'S NOTES

Seafood Kebabs: Thread metal skewers with fish and shellfish, such as scallops, of about the same size, brush with oil or melted butter and grill over the fire, turning frequently. Finish with flavoured butter or oil dressing.

Scallops
grilled in their curved shells

4–8 scallops, in the shell
Walnut-sized piece of butter per scallop
Garlic butter: see previous recipe
Salt and pepper

PREPARING

Slide sharp knife into the join along the flat shell to sever the muscle. Open and cut muscle and roe from the curved shell. Remove frill. Wash shell, muscle and roe.

COOKING

Put curved shells onto the grid over a very hot fire. Leave for a few minutes to heat up. Add some butter and leave for another few minutes till it heats up. When the butter is fairly hot, drop in the scallops and cook, turning occasionally till cooked through. Since the corals will cook faster than the scallops, once they are almost cooked and firm, add the corals and continue cooking until they are firm.

When all are cooked, put some garlic butter on top of each scallop while still hot, and eat with bread and butter.

6 . . . in the oven

Dry, convection heat in a moderate oven is easier to control than the high fast radiant heat of a grill. As in poaching, there is always some latent heat which can be used to finish the cooking.

Another oven method is to wrap fish and flavourings in a parcel which is opened at the table, releasing a sudden burst of enticing flavours. Shellfish does not cook well with this method.

WHOLE FISH

Roast with Aromatic Vegetables and Herbs
Using whole trout, Arctic charr, red mullet, sea bass, mackerel or salmon tail cut

Serves 4

Vegetables:
1.5kg new potatoes, suitable for salads or roasting, such as Charolotte
2 medium courgettes, sliced
1 lemon, cut in thin wedges
3-4 tablespoons olive oil
1-2 tablespoons lemon thyme leaves
Salt and ground black pepper

Fish:
4 x 225-275g fish
Salt

Herbs:
parsley, thyme, bay leaf, fennel, dill, oregano, wild garlic (a good handful of leaves, flowers, depending on season)
1 lemon, sliced
3-4 tablespoons oil
150ml water or dry white wine

Equipment:
Ceramic dish or large roasting tray, greased, approx 23 x 28cm

Preheat oven to 220C/Gas 7.

PAR-COOKING AND SEASONING POTATOES

Wash potatoes and cut roughly into 4-5cm chunks. Put into a pan of boiling salted water and parboil for about five minutes. Drain. Return to the pan and add sliced courgettes, lemon wedges, lemon thyme and 3-4 tablespoons olive oil. Toss together while the potatoes are still hot. Put into a roasting tray and spread evenly. Put into the oven and roast for 10 minutes till just soft, turning once.

PREPARING FISH

Clean and de-scale fish. Wash well. Salt body cavity and skin surface. If the fish are very thick at the head end, make 2-3 slashes at the thickest part on both sides. Fill body cavity with a bunch of herbs and a slice of lemon.

ROASTING FISH

Remove vegetables from the oven, shake and toss them. Lay fish on top and drizzle oil over the fish and salt lightly, then put into the oven. Add water/wine. Roast for about 20 minutes. Turn the fish and continue cooking until the fish is cooked. The time will depend on the size and thickness of the fish. Add more water/wine if vegetables look as though they are drying out. Check if fish is cooked by opening up at the thickest part with a sharp pointed knife, when the translucent flesh should have changed to milky-opaque all the way through.

Serve.

Baked Fish in a Package
whole or fillets

Any whole fish can be sealed with its flavourings. The bone will give the flesh added flavour as it cooks, but fillets can also be used.

Serves 4
4 x 225–275g or 2 x 500g or 1 x 1.1kg whole fish, cleaned
Or 4 x 150–175g fillets per person (600–700g)
Olive oil
Herbs: parsley, bay leaf, thyme, fennel, dill, oregano, tarragon, wild garlic (a good

handful of stalks, leaves, flowers, depending on season)
1 lemon, sliced
Salt and freshly ground black pepper
300-400g courgette, grated
4-6 tablespoons wine or fish stock

Pre-heat oven to 220C/Gas 7.

Foil: For both large and small fish allow plenty of foil, since there should be a space above the fish to allow the steam to circulate. For a single fish 25-30cm in length, use a 50cm square piece of foil. For larger fish overlap the foil and fold the edges together to make an airtight join.

PREPARING FISH

Measure thickness of fish: Timing in the oven is approx 10 minutes for every 2cm measured at the thickest part of the fish, plus another 10 minutes. Dense, oily fish like salmon and mackerel will take longer to cook than delicate white fish like sole.

Trim the tail and trim off all the fins. Season the body cavity with salt. Put the sheet of foil on the baking tray and drizzle some oil where the fish will lie. Scatter over the courgette to make a bed for the fish. Place the fish on top. Put the herbs into the body cavity with slices of lemon. Scatter more herbs on top. Season with salt and pepper. Drizzle over some more oil. Add wine/fish stock. Seal two edges of foil together, folding over and crimping tightly together to make it airtight, leaving space inside for the steam to circulate and cook the fish. Leave in a cool place for several hours or overnight for flavours to mingle.

For fillets: follow the above, omitting the herbs and seasoning in the body cavity.

BAKING FISH

Put in the preheated oven. Bake for the estimated time, and then remove one package to test for readiness. Check by opening up fish at its thickest part, when the translucent flesh should have changed to milky-opaque all the way through.

TO FINISH

Transfer to heated serving plates. For one large fish, transfer to a large ashet and open up at the table, taking off the fillets in individual portions, spooning the sauce, courgette and lemon slices over the fish. Serve with a bowl of chips (see p. 202).

FISH FILLETS

Baked with Gratin Potatoes
Using sole, haddock, whiting, saithe/coley, hake, monkfish or wolf-fish/'catfish'

Serves 4
Gratin potatoes in the oven:
1kg potatoes (such as Maris Piper or Desiree) peeled
600ml milk
2-3 cloves garlic, crushed with salt using a sharp knife or in garlic press
Salt
50g butter, chilled
Nutmeg, about ¼ grated
Fish:
25g melted butter or 2 tablespoons oil for greasing dish and foil
600-700g fish fillets
Lemon juice
2-3 tablespoons fish stock, water, dry cider or dry white wine
1 tablespoon chopped dill, marjoram or parsley
Mustardy Spinach:
400g washed spinach
25g butter
2 teaspoons Dijon mustard
1 tablespoon crème fraiche
Equipment:
2 ceramic dishes or roasting trays approx 23 x 28cm

Pre-heat oven to 190C/Gas 5.

MAKING POTATOES

Slice the potatoes thinly (about 5mm thick) with a sharp knife or on a mandolin slicer. Dry in a tea towel, removing excess moisture. Put a large pot on a medium heat and add the milk. Heat till almost boiling and add the potatoes. Stir the potatoes and simmer gently for 3-4 minutes. They should not soften. Remove from the heat and add the garlic and salt. Pour into the earthenware dish. Spread potatoes evenly. Grate shavings of chilled butter all over the top and then some nutmeg. Put into the oven and bake for 40-50 minutes, or until the surface is well browned and the potatoes are soft.

BAKING THE FISH

Butter the other dish or roasting tray. Cut fillets into portion sizes, season with salt, and either lay flat if thick, or roll up or fold over, if thin. Squeeze over some lemon juice and drizzle over some white wine or dry cider or fish stock or water. Cover with a layer of foil, greased with butter. Bake below the gratin for the last 20-30 minutes. The time will depend on the thickness of the fish. Check by opening up at the thickest part, when the translucent flesh should have changed to milky-opaque all the way through.

MAKING THE SPINACH

Melt the butter in a pan and add the spinach. Stir over a medium heat till the spinach wilts. Put into the food processor with mustard and blend for a few seconds – it should not be pureed. Stir in the crème fraiche. Taste and season.

TO FINISH

Remove the foil from the fish and sprinkle over the chopped herbs. Place each portion on a bed of spinach. Serve with the gratin and fish juices.

Baked Fish with Spicy Peppers
Using cod, saithe or coley, haddock, pollack, whiting, ling or wolf-fish/'catfish'

This is layered – Greek moussaka-style – with spicy peppers in the base, then cheese, fish and a lightly set custard dusted with paprika and browned in the oven.

Serves 4-6
Peppers:
2 tablespoons olive oil
50g butter
2 onions, finely chopped
1-2 teaspoons each: ground cumin, ground coriander
750g red and yellow peppers, cut in thin strips
1 rounded teaspoon flour
Salt to taste

Fish and Custard:
100g mature cheddar, grated or thinly sliced
350g thick fish fillet, cut in 2cm chunks or lightly-salted fish (see p. 215)
4 large eggs
375ml half sour cream, half plain yogurt
1 teaspoon smoked paprika

Equipment:
Ceramic dish 23cm square x 6cm deep (or any dish approx. 2 litres capacity)

Pre-heat oven to 180C/Gas 4.

COOKING THE VEGETABLES

Heat the butter and oil in a frying pan and cook the onions till translucent and lightly brown. Add spices and stir for a few minutes. Add the peppers and cook until they begin to soften. Stir in flour. Put into the base of an earthenware dish and spread evenly. Season with salt.

ADDING CHEESE, FISH AND SAUCE

Scatter half the cheese over the peppers. Cover with the fish, season with salt and pepper and scatter the remainder of the cheese over the fish. Beat eggs together in a bowl and then beat in the sour cream/yogurt. Pour on top of fish and cheese and sprinkle paprika generously over the top.

BAKING

Bake for 40-45 minutes till the custard is set and the top browned. Serve with crusty bread and green salad.

Fish Pie

Using haddock (smoked or fresh), whiting, saithe or coley, ling, pollack, wolf-fish/'catfish', hake, salmon or trout

This can be made with either fresh fish or leftover cooked fish, adding any cooking juices to the sauce.

Serves 4

Potato topping:
1kg medium-floury potatoes (Maris Piper, Rooster, Desiree)
200ml milk or single cream

50g butter
Salt and pepper
Filling:
3 hardboiled eggs
100g baby spinach leaves, washed
75g North Atlantic peeled prawns, cooked
300g fish fillet, smoked or fresh (or cooked)
500ml milk
40g butter
40g plain flour
1 tablespoon dill or parsley, chopped
Salt and pepper
Equipment:
Ceramic dish 23cm square x 6cm deep (or any dish 6cm deep round or
rectangular, approx. 2 litres capacity)

Preheat oven to 200C/Gas 6.

MAKING POTATO TOPPING

Boil potatoes till soft. Drain, peel and mash with milk and 50g butter. Taste and season. Beat to a creamy texture.

MAKING FILLING

Boil eggs for 5 minutes. Run under cold tap to cool. Cut in quarters. Put a layer of spinach in the base of the dish and scatter eggs and prawns evenly on top.

Put the fish in a pan with milk over a medium heat. Heat gently till the fish is cooked through. Drain off milk and reserve. Flake the fish flesh from the skin and remove any bones. Spread evenly on top of prawns.

Melt the 40g of butter and add flour. Cook for a few minutes without browning and then gradually add the reserved milk, stirring all the time. Simmer to thicken, when it should coat the back of a wooden spoon thinly. Finally add dill or parsley. Taste and season.

FINISHING AND BAKING PIE

Pour sauce evenly over filling. Spread potatoes on top. Draw a large fork across the surface, making deep, rugged furrows. Bake till well browned and crusty on top, about 30-40 minutes.

7 . . . in fat or oil

Fragile fish flesh needs some sort of protection from the high heat of frying which browns and adds flavour. At its simplest, this can be the fish skin, left on a whole fish, or a deskinned fillet lightly coated in flour, which crisps and browns when shallow fried.

Dipping fish in an insulating layer of wet batter is another ploy, since the coating takes the full force of the high frying heat, while the delicate fish inside steams and retains its fish juices as it cooks at a lower temperature.

FISH AND SHELLFISH, WHOLE OR FILLETS

Shallow-fried with Nut-brown Butter, Lemon and Fried Potatoes

Using a whole or a cut of a whole fish such as lemon sole, plaice, dab, megrim, trout, turbot, brill, salmon, haddock, whiting, bream, OR fillets of salmon, hake, saithe/coley, haddock, lemon sole, Dover sole, ling, pollack, monkfish, wolf-fish/catfish, halibut, turbot, herring, mackerel, scallops

Serves 4
To fry potatoes:
1.2kg medium floury potatoes such as Maris Piper, Desiree or Rooster
Groundnut or sunflower oil
Salt

To fry fish:
Flat fish on the bone: 375–450g per person: x 4 = 1.5–1.8kg
Round fish on the bone : 275–325g per person: x 4 = 1.1–1.3kg
Fish fillet: 150–175g per person: x 4 = 600–700g
Scallops: 2-4 depending on size, per person main course (half quantity starter)*
2-3 tablespoons plain white flour (4 tablespoons coarse oatmeal for herring and mackerel)
Salt
2 tablespoons oil for frying
1 lemon, halved and de-pipped
60-70g unsalted butter
1-2 tablespoons parsley, finely chopped

Many fish, either whole or filleted, can be cooked by this method. The exception is a very thin fillet of delicate textured fish which will break up too easily during cooking. Very thick fish cuts and steaks (over about 3cm) can be finished in a hot oven.

TO MAKE FRIED POTATOES

Parboil potatoes. Drain and leave to cool. Peel and cut into slices about 5-10mm thick. Pour enough oil into the frying pan to just cover the surface. Heat over a medium heat till hot but not smoking hot. Fry potatoes on both sides till crisp and evenly golden brown. Drain on kitchen paper and sprinkle with salt. Keep hot till fish is cooked.

PREPARING THE FISH

Clean, wash and drain the fish. Large flat fish can be cut to fit the pan. Put the flour on a plate, season with salt and coat the fish on both sides. Shake off excess.

SHALLOW FRYING

Heat a non-stick, heavy based frying pan over a moderately high heat till hot. Add the oil. When hot add the fish, presentation side down (top side for flat fish, flesh side for fillets). Fry on one side for about 3-4 minutes depending on thickness, turn onto other side and cook for another 3-4 minutes. Check if cooked by opening up at the thickest part with a sharp pointed knife, when the translucent flesh should have changed to milky-opaque all the way through to the bone. Remove fish to heated serving dish and keep warm. Or finish cooking in the oven if fish is not quite cooked through (see under Grilling, p. 177).

MAKING BROWNED BUTTER

Clean out pan if there is a lot of burnt debris. Add butter and heat over a moderate heat until it sizzles and starts to brown slightly. To stop the browning (it should not darken and burn) quickly squeeze the juice of a de-pipped lemon into the pan. Continue shaking and stirring while it sizzles and steams. Remove from the heat and throw in chopped parsley, mix through. Pour immediately over the fish and serve with fried potatoes.

*COOK'S NOTES

Scallop fisherman's breakfast onboard: a pile of soft scrambled eggs with crisp fried salty bacon and some sweet scallops fried in the bacon fat.

An option is a scatter of finely chopped spring onions over the eggs.

Deep-fried Thin Fillets

Using whiting, haddock, saithe/coley, pollack, ling, cod, hake, monkfish,
wolf-fish/catfish, pouting, bass, John Dory, bream, squid or cuttlefish
and North Atlantic prawns

Method 1: Tempura with Vegetables and Dipping Sauces

A very light Japanese tempura batter is used to fry small quantities – to order – of
fish and vegetables. They are served in napkin-lined bowls with dipping sauces and
eaten with chopsticks.

Serves 2

300–350g fish fillets, skinned (squid or cuttlefish cut in rings), peeled prawns

Vegetables:

mushrooms (sliced) red or yellow peppers and onions (cut into rings), small florets
of broccoli or cauliflower, asparagus spears

Batter:

1 egg yolk
250ml bottled, carbonated Scottish water, chilled
75g fine plain flour (with a very low gluten content such as Italian '00')
Large pinch of bicarbonate of soda

Dipping sauce:

Soya sauce or Mirin
1 lemon

Oil for frying:

Use 2-3 litres groundnut or sunflower oil

Or for more flavour use a blend of oils (favoured by Japanese tempura chefs)
see Cook's Notes:*

750ml groundnut or other light-tasting vegetable oil such as sunflower
200ml sesame seed oil (not roasted)
50ml refined olive oil, for cooking

PREPARING FISH

Cut fish into bite-sized pieces. Dry thoroughly.

PREPARE DEEP-FAT FRYER

Either use a large pan with a fish basket or a free-standing deep-fat fryer (Tempura chefs use a very large wok on a gas burner). If using a pan with a fish basket have the oil only a third of the way up the pan, since it rises as it cooks. Also have a fire blanket or fire extinguisher in the kitchen.

Put oils into the pan or fryer and heat to 190C. This is usually the top heat in a fish fryer. If using a pan and thermometer, it can be heated to 200-220C, which will cook the batter and fish faster.

MAKING BATTER

Put egg into a bowl and add about three-quarters of the chilled fizzy water. Sift the flour and soda on top and whisk in. The consistency should just coat the back of the spoon. Add more water if too thick.

DEEP FRYING FISH AND VEGETABLES

Put onto a fork or skewer and dip into the batter, coating all sides. Lift out and hold it over the batter to let the excess batter drip off. Lower into the deep-fat fryer.

Repeat with more fish but do not fill the fish basket too full or the temperature will drop and the batter will not crisp and puff up. Cook vegetables in the same way.

Drain and serve immediately in a bowl lined with a small paper napkin. Have dipping sauces: a bowl each of soy sauce and mirin. Eat with chopsticks. Serve with a bowl of warm sake.

COOK'S NOTES

Though some seed oils have a low smoke point (the temperature at which a fat or oil begins to break down) light sesame oil's smoke point is high, making it suitable for deep-frying.

The oil from roasted sesame seeds (dark oil), however, has a slightly lower smoke point and is not suitable for deep-frying though it can be used for stir-frying.

Extra virgin olive oil is unsuitable since it has a low smoke point, but more refined olive oils have a higher smoking point so can be used. Using sesame and olive oil adds extra flavour to the batter.

Method 2: Egg White Batter for Fish and Vegetables, with Chips

This uses the air bubbles in beaten egg whites to lighten the end result. Fry in small quantities to order.

To make chips:

Serves 2

600g floury or medium floury potatoes such as Maris Piper, Arran Victory, King Edward, Kerr's pink, Rooster, Desiree, Romano, Sante and Carlingford

2 litres groundnut or sunflower oil

Salt

TO MAKE CHIPS

A floury potato will make a dry chip, waxy varieties a soggy chip.

PREPARING POTATOES

Wash and peel potatoes. Cut into chips, thin or thick. Dry thoroughly in a tea towel.

PREPARING DEEP-FAT FRYER

Either use a large pan with a chip basket or a free-standing deep-fat fryer. If using a pan with a chip basket, have the oil only a third of the way up the pan, since it rises as it cooks. Also have a fire blanket or fire extinguisher in the kitchen. Put oil into pan or fryer and heat to 130C.

FIRST SLOW FRYING to just cook through

Fill the chip basket half-full and lower into the fat. Fry slowly till the chips are just cooked through but not browned. Time will depend on the size of chips. Remove and drain on kitchen paper. They can be stored in the fridge uncovered for a day like this or they can be finished as soon as the fryer heats up again.

To fry fish and vegetables:

Serves 2

300-350g fish fillets, skinned (squid or cuttlefish cut in rings)

Salt

Vegetables:

mushrooms (sliced) red or yellow peppers and onions (cut into rings), small florets broccoli or cauliflower, asparagus

Egg-white batter:

100g fine plain flour (with very low gluten content such as Italian '00')

Pinch of salt

2 tablespoons groundnut, olive oil

100–125ml water
2 egg-whites

MAKING EGG-WHITE BATTER

Sift the flour and salt into a bowl. Make a well in the centre and add the oil and half the water. Beat together with a wooden spoon, or whisk, till smooth. Thin out with the rest of the water. It should coat the back of a wooden spoon, but not too thickly. Add more water if necessary. Leave to rest for at least half an hour or longer. When ready to use, beat the egg-whites until they just hold their shape. Fold in carefully, aiming to retain as much of the air as possible.

PREPARE DEEP-FAT FRYER

Either use a large pan with a fish basket or a free-standing deep-fat fryer. If using a pan with a fish basket, have the oil only a third of the way up the pan since it rises as it cooks. Also have a fire blanket or fire extinguisher in the kitchen. Put oils into the pan or fryer and heat to 190C. This is usually the top heat in a fish fryer.

FRYING THE FISH AND VEGETABLES

Put onto a fork or skewer and dip into the batter, coating all sides. Lift out and hold it over the batter to let the excess batter drip off. Lower into the deep-fat fryer.

At 190C, thin fillets of sole will be cooked in about 2 minutes. If too many pieces of food are added at once the temperature will be reduced, the crust will become soggy and the fish will take longer to cook. When cooked, remove from the fryer. Shake basket over oil to drain. Turn onto kitchen paper to drain thoroughly. Reheat oil and fry the remainder of fish and vegetables in the same way. Season with salt. Serve immediately.

CHIPS: SECOND FAST FRYING

Heat up oil to 190C. Lower in the chips and fry till a light golden brown. This should only take a few minutes. Drain again on kitchen paper. Serve immediately.

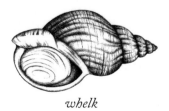

whelk

ROE

Fried Cod Roe
Served with bacon and fried or scrambled eggs on toast

Serves 4
3–4 tablespoons oil
300g dry-cured smoked bacon
600g cooked cod's roe, cut in 1–2cm thick slices
4 tablespoons milk
2 tablespoons white flour
Salt
Worcestershire Sauce
Ground black pepper

FRYING BACON

Put a large frying pan on a medium heat and add 1 tablespoon of oil. When hot, add the bacon and fry on both sides till crisp. Remove and keep hot.

FRYING COD'S ROE

Reheat pan. Add another tablespoon of oil. Put the milk in a deep soup plate and the flour on another plate. Season the flour with salt. Dip the rounds of roe into the milk first, then into the flour. Shake off excess flour. Put slices of the roe into the pan and fry over a fairly hot heat till lightly browned on both sides. Remove when cooked. Keep hot with the bacon.

TO FINISH

Make fried or scrambled eggs on toast and arrange on heated plates with the bacon and cod roe. Serve Worcestershire Sauce for the roe and black pepper and chopped spring onions for the scrambled eggs and bacon.

8 . . . to serve cold

Shellfish like oysters and sea urchins have complex, mouth-filling tastes, textures and flavours, some of which are lost when heated.

Other seafood which can be served cold are rich oily fish, like salmon, which have been poached (see p. 164) or richly flavoured crustaceans like lobster, crab and langoustines which involve some picking of shells.

Potted fish or shellfish are always served cold.

SHELLFISH

Oysters on Ice

On the tables of those who import Scottish shellfish in quantity, it is often served on a large platter of heaped crushed ice, raised up on a metal stand, and set in the middle of the table. The crushed ice and the large platter are essential. Raising it up on a stand makes an eye-catching statement that this seafood is something worth celebrating in style.

Serves 4 as a starter
20-24 Pacific oysters or 16-20 native oysters, chilled
Seaweed, if available
Ice, crushed in food processor
2 lemons, halved
Hot chilli sauce

Equipment:
A folded tea towel or oyster 'holder' and a bevel-edged, short-bladed, pointed 'oyster' knife
Large ashet or platter

TO OPEN OYSTERS

Hold the oyster, cupped shell down and flat surface facing up, in the tea towel or 'holder' in one hand. Position the oyster with the pointed 'hinge' end towards you. Insert the point of the knife where the two shells join at the hinge end. If the join is hard to find, just keep digging with the point of the knife, it *has* to be there.

When you find it, push the point in very firmly and scrape the knife against the inside surface of the top shell where the 'heel' of the oyster is attached to the shell. Cutting through this loosens the top shell.

Always keep the shell level to avoid any of the oyster liquor spilling out. Remove and discard the top shell and any chips of shell which have fallen into the oyster.

The oyster muscle, still attached to the cupped shell, can be cut and the oyster flipped over, or this final preparation can be left for the eaters.

SERVING

Serve on a large ashet on a layer of crushed ice mixed with some fresh seaweed if available. Add flavouring immediately before eating. A few drops of acidic lemon juice balances the sweet-salty sea flavours of the oyster. The 'hot' flavouring option is a chilli sauce, a counterbalance to cold oyster, provided it does not numb the taste buds to the nuances of the oyster's natural flavours.

Half-Lobster and Scottish Asparagus*

Serves 4 starter, 2 main course
2 live lobsters 750-800g
Enough water to cover
125-150g salt (about 4 level tablespoons) per 4.5 litres water
450-500g Scottish asparagus
Mayonnaise:
3 large egg yolks
1 dessertspoon Dijon mustard
500-600ml olive oil
Lemon juice to taste

A special springtime treat.

COOKING LOBSTER

Live lobster claws should be bound with heavy duty rubber bands. The RSPCA (*www.rspca.org.uk*) recommends that lobsters should be chilled to make them insensitive before killing. To do this, put them first into the fridge for a few hours to bring down their temperature gradually. Then they can be put in the freezer until they become insensible. Check every 15-20 minutes for lack of movement. They can then be killed quickly by severing the nerve centres with a heavy sharp pointed knife.

Lobsters have a chain of nerve centres which run along the central length of their body. These nerve centres must be destroyed by rapidly (within 10 seconds), cutting through the midline, lengthways, with a large, heavy sharp knife.

The lobster should be held on a flat surface, on its back. Hold it around the top of its head with a firm pressure. Note the midline on the lobster's under-surface. Keeping the midline direction, place the knife on the head beneath the mouth parts. Cut through the head via this point to pierce and destroy the brain. Take care not to push the knife all the way through the head. Then cut through the under-surface midline to pierce and destroy the rest of the nerve chain in two stages. Starting at the midline near the junction of the tail and the thorax, the first cut is directed forwards toward the head and the second backwards down the midline towards the tail.

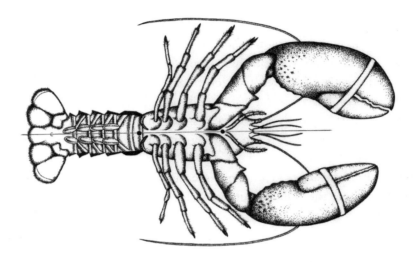

Prepare a large pot with boiling water, add salt. Put in lobsters and bring back to the boil. Cook a 750-800g lobster for 15 minutes, then add 5 minutes for every extra 500g. Remove from pot and drain.

PREPARING LOBSTER

When cold, cut the lobster in half. Place on a chopping board belly-side down with legs and claws splayed out. Hold the lobster body with one hand with the head towards you. With a very heavy, sharp chopping knife stab the tip into the head at the central point about 2cm behind the eyes, and with the blade facing away from your hand cut firmly all the way through. Press with your palm on the upper edge of the knife if necessary to cut through.

Remove the knife and turn the lobster round to cut through the rest of the body to the end of the tail, making two halves of lobster.

Discard the black intestinal tract which runs the length of the tail, also the small gritty stomach sac behind the mouth.

Everything else is edible. Besides the 'white' meat there is the soft-smooth liver meat, known as the tomalley, which is a special flavour and not to be missed.

COOKING ASPARAGUS

Break off woody ends. Bring a pan of water large enough to hold them to the boil. Add salt and the asparagus. Simmer till just soft. Test with a sharp knife. Drain and leave to cool.

MAKING MAYONNAISE

Put the egg yolks and mustard in a food processor. Turn on to a medium speed and begin adding the oil very, very slowly to begin, so the mixture emulsifies as the egg and oil blend together. If it becomes too thick, add a few teaspoons lemon juice. Once the emulsion has formed, the oil can be added faster. Keep on adding the oil till it reaches a soft 'coating' consistency, it should not be too solid. If too stiff, add a few teaspoons warm water. It can also be made in a bowl with an electric beater. Taste and add lemon juice.

If the emulsion separates (splits), put another yolk of egg into a clean bowl and begin again, adding the split mixture very slowly to begin with, and it will come thick and creamy again.

SERVING

To serve lobster in the shell: Loosen the tail meat. Crack the claws and serve with shellfish picks for removing the body meat and the meat from the smaller legs. Serve a side-bowl of mayonnaise. Serve asparagus in a bundle on the plate for dipping into the mayonnaise.

*COOK'S NOTES

Around the end of April, the first asparagus of a season ending about mid-June has been delivered to the packing shed. This is not asparagus from the English heartland in the Vale of Evesham, but grown in the fertile Vale of Strathmore at Eassie Farm. Local women are sorting and grading it. There's a large basket of bargain rejects, either bent, too thick or too thin, as well as bundles of perfect specimens.

Sandy Pattullo, the farmer, began growing Scottish asparagus twenty years ago and now has fifteen acres. Such are the favourable growing conditions here, that his crop is only a few days behind Evesham.

Crab, Brown or Velvet
in the shell or in a sandwich*

Brown Crab

Serve with soft, 'coating' consistency mayonnaise and a rocket salad

Serves 4
2 x 1kg brown crab
125–150g salt (about 4 level tablespoons) to 4.5 litres water
1 lemon
Half cucumber
100g salad leaves
Salt and black or cayenne pepper
Mayonnaise: see lobster recipe, p. 206

KILLING, COOKING AND EXTRACTING CRAB MEAT

See p. 170.

SERVING

Break off the protruding edge from the underside of the carapace along the joining line which opens up the shell. Wash out the shells and scrub clean. Mix the brown meat together in a bowl and season with salt and black or cayenne pepper and a little lemon juice. Divide in half and put back into the shell at either side. Pile the white meat up in the centre. Garnish with some lemon and cucumber and serve with some salad leaves and a bowl of mayonnaise.

Velvet Crab

Caught in Scottish waters, and mostly exported, this crab is similar in structure to a brown crab but with swimming legs and a more intense seafood flavour.

Serves 4
16 x 100g live velvet crab
Water to cover
1 tablespoon salt

COOKING

Put crabs in a large pot, cover with boiling water, add salt, and simmer for 3-5 minutes. Drain and leave to cool.

EATING

Turn crab onto its back, pull off the apron flap and push body away from shell. Remove and eat the soft brown meat from inside the shell. Remove and discard the dead men's fingers (as in brown crab, see p. 171). Break body in half, leaving legs attached. Begin with the swimming legs, twist off one by one and eat their attached morsels of white meat. Break large claws at a joint and crush the shell to open, pick out white meat. Crush the remaining body shell and legs for any remaining morsels of white meat.

Shell debris and saved white and brown meat can be used to make Partan Bree, using equivalent weight of velvet crabs (see p. 169).

COOK'S NOTES

Make a **Crab Sandwich** with leftovers. Spread one side of a large crusty baguette with mayonnaise. Cover the other side with a layer of brown and white crab meat. Season with a sprinkling of hot cayenne pepper and a squeeze of lemon. Cover with some sliced cucumber and a handful of salad leaves. Press two halves together. Wrap up very tightly in foil and leave in cool place for a few hours for the flavours to mingle. It can also be put under a weight.

Irish culinary wisdom advises that this kind of sandwich really only reaches perfection after it has been sat on for some time by the eater.

Langoustines in the Shell
Served with soft, 'coating' mayonnaise and green salad

Serves 4 main course, or 8 starter
16 large or 24 small langoustines in the shell
Water to cover
1 tablespoon sea salt
2 lemons
Fresh bread
Unsalted butter

Mayonnaise: see Lobster recipe p. 206

COOKING

Wash shellfish. Fill a large pan with water, add salt and bring to the boil. When the salt has dissolved, add the shellfish and cook for about 2 minutes for small, and up to 5 minutes for large shellfish. Drain and leave to cool.

SERVING

Make the mayonnaise. Serve the shellfish in bowls with mayonnaise for dipping and wedges of crusty bread and butter.

EATING

Twist off the head and suck out the rich flavours from inside the head. Hold the tail, shell side down, and break open about 1-2cm at the top with your thumbs. It's not necessary to break open the whole length of the tail since it should now pull easily out of the shell. If the shell is too hard, it can be cut with sharp scissors, taking care not to cut the tail meat. Finally pick the meat from the legs and claws. It can be picked out with shellfish picks or sucked out. Large claws may be crushed with a heavy knife or shellfish crackers.

Sea Urchins with Bread and Olive Oil

On Greek beaches, where sea urchin roe is a popular seafood treat, it's spooned from the shell onto slices of rustic bread which has been drizzled first with extra virgin olive oil. A squeeze of lemon adds just the right acid balance to rich roe.

Serves 4
4 sea urchins (approx 1kg)
Bread
Extra virgin olive oil
2 lemons
Equipment:
Tea towel, scissors

PREPARING THE SEA URCHIN

Wrap the sea urchin, mouth upwards, in a folded tea towel and hold in one hand. With a pair of kitchen scissors, put one blade into the open end and cut a circle from the top about 7.5cm diameter. Pull out all the black parts from inside the shell, leaving behind the small clusters of roe which look a bit like cooked couscous.

SERVING

Put the urchin on a serving plate with a wedge of lemon. Serve with slices of bread. Drizzle oil over bread. Spoon roe out of shell with a long spoon and spread on bread. Add a squeeze of lemon juice and some more oil.

COOK'S NOTES

Sea urchins in Orkney are known as *scarrimans heid* (meaning a street child with unruly, spiky hair) and are much larger than their Mediterranean or South Pacific relatives. They are about the size of a grapefruit with short white spines. Only the sweet, fragrant, orange-coloured roe (known as coral) is eaten.

Sea urchin roe is a Japanese sushi delicacy, on a par with mullet roe. It's served flavoured with soy sauce and wasabi. It can also be sautéed lightly in butter and used to thicken a sauce, or folded into hot pasta. Sea urchin is sometimes available from local food supplier, Orkney Rose (*www.orkneyrose.com*) who also provide recipes for linguine with sea urchin roe; also basil, lemon and chilli and sea urchin bruschetta.

POTTED FISH – FRESH AND SMOKED – AND SHELLFISH

Potted Fresh

Using salmon, trout, Arctic charr or mackerel

Antique ceramic pots for potted charr (a Lake District speciality), 14cm in diameter and 4cm deep, are now collector's items, but reproductions are also available.

400g leftover poached fish, skinned and boned (see Poached Fish recipe p. 164)
500ml poaching liquid
½ teaspoon each of ginger and mace, ground
200g unsalted butter
Salt and pepper
1 lemon, juice

Clarified butter:
200g unsalted butter

REDUCING COOKING LIQUID

Strain 500ml from the poached cooking liquid and put into a shallow frying pan. Boil to reduce to a quarter. Remove from the heat and gradually beat in the butter.

BLENDING FISH

Flake the fish, removing bones, put into the food processor. Add ginger and mace. Pour over buttery reduced liquid. Add 2 teaspoons lemon juice. Process to a coarse paste. Taste and adjust seasoning and lemon juice. Spread into a shallow round pot, approximately 14 x 4cm deep. Cover with clingfilm and put into the fridge to chill. Serve with hot toast for lunch or with salad for supper.

MAKING CLARIFIED BUTTER TO STORE POTTED FISH

If keeping for longer than a few days, the potted fish can be preserved by covering with a very thin airtight layer of melted butter.

Put butter in a pan and bring to the boil. Leave to cool for about 10 minutes. It will have separated into three layers: foam on top; the middle clear yellow butter; sediment at the bottom. Lift off the foam with a wide, flat skimming spoon. Decant the clear butter into a bowl. Use the liquid sediment left in the pan and the removed foam for flavouring soups or sauces.

TO FINISH

Cover paste with a thin layer of clarified butter. Cover the whole pot with clingfilm and foil, or a lid, to prevent the butter drying out and shrinking from the edges, when the airtight seal will be lost. Store in the fridge. It will keep for several weeks with its airtight seal. Use within a week once the seal is broken.

Potted Smoked
Using mackerel or hot smoked salmon, Arbroath smokie or crab

Smoky-salty flavours from the cured fish, and special shellfish flavours from crab, all make their own richly flavoured spreading pastes.

Serves 4-6
300g hot smoked fish, skinned and boned, or crab meat (brown and white)
200g full fat soft cheese
1 clove garlic, crushed (omit with crab)
1 lemon, zest and juice
Hot cayenne or ground black pepper, to taste
Salt (may not be necessary if fish is salty)
Good-flavoured oil to drizzle
Warmed crusty loaf
Watercress or rocket salad

BLENDING FISH

Flake fish into a food processor while making a final check for bones or shell. Add soft cheese, garlic, grated lemon zest and lemon juice. Blend to a coarse or fine paste according to taste. Taste and adjust seasonings. Add more lemon juice, salt, ground black or cayenne pepper and garlic to taste.

SERVING

Pile into a shallow earthenware pot. Drizzle over a little good flavoured oil. Put into the fridge to firm up if necessary. Serve with a warmed crusty loaf and a peppery watercress or rocket salad, or Pickled Cucumber (see p. 219).

9 . . . to preserve fish by salting, drying, pickling or sousing

Not, as it might seem, an inferior taste-relic of history, but a useful method of lengthening the shelf life of highly perishable fish while developing new flavours and textures.

Lean white fish of little flavour are transformed into such desirable items as salt cod, which has been popular since Roman times. Saithe, ling and pollack, also have a history of salt treatment, certainly in Scotland, and taste as good if not better than cod.

When fish dries out during salting, its cell structure is disrupted and flavour molecules begin to react with one another, producing new layers of flavour. The length of time salting and drying will determine its shelf life. A short salting and drying can keep otherwise highly perishable fish for a week. But if saturated in salt, dried till hard, excluded from the air and kept in a cool place, it will keep useable for years.

Oily fish are not suitable for drying and instead are immersed in brine (salt-pickle) which gives them a long shelf life. For a shorter shelf life, they can be immersed in a sweet-spiced vinegar pickle which 'cooks' the fish (i.e. coagulates the fish protein by the action of acid, as in South American *ceviche*). Or they can be cooked, with heat, in a vinegar pickle (soused) which will also lengthen the shelf life.

In the past, to keep oily fish from turning rancid, it was also wrapped up tightly and buried in the ground to exclude air. Now known as Scandinavian *gravlax*, (*grav* meaning 'grave' and *lax*, salmon) the modern method wraps salmon up tightly in a package with salt, sugar and dill, keeping it in a cool place for a few days.

In Shetland, there is an ancient, Norse-inherited fish preservation method known as *Kiossed Heid*s, when fish heads were wrapped up and stuffed into the crevice of a stone wall till they became gamey. Then they were roasted and eaten with butter and potatoes.

LIGHTLY-SALTED

Lightly-salted White Fish
Using whiting, saithe (coley), haddock, pollack, wolf-fish or 'catfish', cod, hake,
ling or bass

This adds flavour and firms up the texture of white fish, while increasing its shelf life. The aim is to introduce a very light salty flavour.

500-750g fillets, large or small
Sea salt*

SALTING

Lightly salt the base of a ceramic dish, or plastic container which will hold the fish. Place the fish fillets skin side down on top. Sprinkle the flesh side of the fish lightly with salt.

Leave small thin fillets, such as whiting, for up to 5 minutes. Large thick fillets of saithe can be left for 30-35 minutes.**

RINSING AND DRYING

Remove and wash off salt. Dry well. Place on a rack in the fridge where air can circulate, or put in a cool airy place which is not damp for 24 hours.

Wrap tightly in clingfilm and it will keep for 3-4 days.

COOK'S NOTES

***Salt** varies in flavour and texture, and the type will affect the taste of the fish being salted. It is either mined where it has formed salt rocks millions of years old (rock salt), or is evaporated from seawater (sea salt). Both types contain 'impurities', which will mostly be removed by refining.

Fine Table Salt: contains additives which prevent it absorbing moisture from the atmosphere so it remains free-flowing. Though it is the cheapest form of salt, the additives can produce undesirable tastes if used in salting or pickling. Also, because of its fine texture it penetrates the fish much faster, which professional curers believe does not produce the best cure.

Flake Salt: produced by surface evaporation of seawater or brine. Expensive, but suitable for curing.

Natural Sea Salt: made from the slow evaporation of sea water, a coarse or medium coarse rather than a fine granule is regarded the best for curing. Unrefined salt has a more interesting taste, but it may add unwanted flavours to the curing process.

**When the salt begins to penetrate it draws out the moisture in the fish and starts to 'run'. If this happens with a light salting, the fish may have become too salty and will need to be soaked in cold water for an hour or two before use. Taste test by slicing off a thin sliver of the fish.

Spicy Tomato Stew with Beans and Lightly Salted Fillets

Lightly salted fillets add a robust fishy contrast to this rustic tomato stew made, as in Italy, to provide more than one meal.

Serves 8

250g streaky bacon, chopped
75ml sunflower oil
750g onions, finely chopped
1–2 tablespoon tomato puree
8 cloves garlic, crushed
4 tins chopped tomatoes
2 tablespoons wine vinegar
2 tablespoons thyme leaves
4g hot cayenne pepper, or to taste
Demerara sugar to taste
1 x 400g tin haricot beans
500–750g lightly-salted large fillets

TO MAKE STEW

Put a large pot on a medium heat and add the bacon. Cook till crisped and lightly browned. Remove. Add oil and onions and cook slowly for about 15 minutes, stirring occasionally till they have reduced by half and are very soft but not browned.

Return the bacon to the pan. Add the tomato puree, stir in and cook for a few minutes over a high heat. Add the garlic, tinned tomatoes, vinegar, thyme and cayenne. Stir well and simmer gently for 10-15 minutes. Taste and add sugar to balance the acid flavours of tomatoes and vinegar. There should be approximately 2litres. Ladle about half the stew into a 1 litre container and store in the fridge (it will keep for 4-5 days) or freeze for use later.

TO FINISH

Add beans to the remaining stew. Remove skin from fish. Cut up into 2cm chunks and add to the stew. Stir in. Cover with lid and reheat to a gentle simmer. Turn off the heat, cover and leave for 5 minutes when the fish will be cooked. Taste and season.

Serve with mashed potatoes and chopped spring onions or baked potatoes and butter.

COOK'S NOTES

Remaining stew: Can also be used with any thick fillets of fresh white fish. It can also be used with squid or cuttlefish, but this should be cooked till tender. Or it can be made into a shellfish stew with cooked and shelled mussels, cockles, razor clams and langoustines. Cook the shellfish in their shells (see p. 167) remove meat and add approx 500g to the stew with some of their cooking liquor just before serving.

Lightly-salted Salmon Fillets – Gravlax*
With Gravlaxsas and Pickled Cucumber

Gravlax:
1.5kg middle cut of salmon, unskinned and cut in half lengthwise with bone removed
50g coarse sea salt
50g granulated sugar
2 tablespoons white or black peppercorns, crushed
50g bunch of dill

Gravlaxsas (mustard dill sauce for cold seafood):
4 tablespoons Dijon mustard
1 rounded teaspoon powdered mustard
2 tablespoons white wine or cider vinegar

65g caster sugar
100g sunflower oil
12g dill, stalks removed, finely chopped

MAKING GRAVLAX IN A PACKAGE

Mix the salt, sugar and peppercorns in a bowl. Put dill into a plastic bag and crush to release its flavour, or chop. Place a double sheet of clingfilm, large enough to wrap up the fish, in a ceramic dish or plastic tub which will hold the fish.

Lay one half of the fish skin side down. Cover the flesh side with half the salt mixture. Cover with the dill. Sprinkle over the remaining salt mixture. Place the other fillet of salmon on top, flesh side down. Fold over clingfilm tightly to make a parcel. Wrap in foil. Mark side 1 and side 2 with a pen or sticker and put in the fridge. Put a small chopping board or plate with 3 or 4 tins of food on top as weights.

MARINATING

After 12 hours turn onto side 2. Continue to turn every 12 hours for 2-3 days when the gravlax will be ready. Wrapping in a package has the advantage of self-basting and is also easier to turn.

MAKING GRAVLAXSAS – MUSTARD DILL SAUCE

In a small deep bowl, mix the two mustards, sugar and vinegar to a paste. With a balloon whisk, slowly beat in the oil until it forms a thick mayonnaise-like emulsion (this can also be done with an electric beater). Stir in the chopped dill. Pour into a glass jar, cover with lid and store in the fridge.

TO SERVE GRAVLAX

Remove the gravlax from its wrappings and scrape off the dill. Pat dry with paper towels. Place skin side down on a carving board. Slice the salmon thinly, on the diagonal.

As an appetiser: Serve very thin slices chilled, on plates which have been chilled in the freezer, with buttered rye bread or crispbread and gravlaxsas. To drink: vodka and glasses which have both been chilled in the freezer.

As a main course: Serve not-so-thin slices with gravlaxas and wedges of lemon with boiled new potatoes tossed in dill and melted butter and Pickled Cucumber Salad (see below).

Leftovers: can be cooked through scrambled eggs, or used in a fish pie.

Pickled Cucumber Salad
lightly-salted

This transforms the texture of the cucumber and adds a sweet, sour tang which works well with all oily fish. As in lightly salting fish, the salt extracts moisture and adds flavour.

2 medium sized cucumbers (600-700g each)
2 level teaspoons salt
125ml white wine vinegar
15g caster sugar
2 tablespoons dill, chopped

MAKING CUCUMBER SALAD

Wash the cucumbers. Score lengthways with a fork. Remove ends and slice thinly using the slicing blade of a food processor, a mandolin slicer or slice by hand. Put into a large ceramic dish or plastic tub and sprinkle with salt. Turn occasionally and leave for 2-3 hours, or overnight, till the excess water has run out. Drain off. Pat dry in a tea towel. Return to the dish.

Mix the vinegar and sugar till dissolved. Pour over the cucumber. Leave in a cool place for 2-3 hours. Just before serving, drain off most of the excess liquid. Sprinkle with dill. Chill. This keeps in the fridge for a week or two.

*COOK'S NOTES

Finnish fishmongers add decorative bunches of feathery dill to their fish displays when the *gravlax* season begins in June. While customers wait in the queue, the fishmonger makes up bespoke packages for them to take home and put in the fridge, which they turn every twelve hours waiting till it's ready to eat. Middle cut is the most popular. A whole salmon will be prepared for a party.

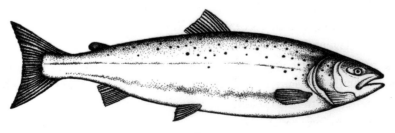

salmon

HEAVILY-SALTED

Heavily-salted White Fish
Using saithe, ling, pollack or cod

This method adds flavour to large white fish while increasing its shelf life.

2 x 750g unskinned fillets saithe, ling, pollack, cod
Medium or coarse sea salt (see Cook's Notes for Lightly-Salting, p. 215)

LONG SALTING FOR 10–14 DAYS

Use a large earthenware dish, or plastic tub, which will hold the fish lying flat. Put a thick layer of salt in the base and lay the fish on top, skin side down. Press down into the salt. Cover with another layer of salt about the same thickness. Cover and leave in a cool place for 24 hours.

Place a wooden board or large plate with a weight on top of the fish. This will press more liquid out of the fish. Keep in a cool place. Check after a few days and drain off any liquid. Cover the fish with more salt if necessary. Keep checking every couple of days and keep draining off the liquid and adding more salt when required. In a week to 10 days, the fish should be fairly well dried out. It can be kept, covered in a cool place in the salt, for up to a year.

Depending on the size of the container, several layers of fish can be salted together.

TO DRY OUT (OPTIONAL) TILL HARD

Remove fish from the salt. Tie a piece of string through the tail. Hang up in a cool, dry, airy place free from flies or lay on a wire rack in the fridge so the air can circulate.

TO RECONSTITUTE

Rinse fish. Cover with cold water and leave to soak for 12-24 hours. The length of time will depend on the saltiness of the fish. The aim is to restore the water content but still retain flavour.

To test: remove the fish after 12 hours. Take a thin sliver of the fish and taste for salt content. If still very salty, change the water and soak for longer. Keep checking with the taste test until it is no longer overpowering.

Soaking for too long or changing the water too often may remove all the salt and make the fish tasteless.

Hairy Tatties with Milk and Butter

This can be made with either the traditional flavourings of milk and butter, or with garlic and olive oil. They both end up looking like a 'hairy tattie'.

Serves 4

500g heavily-salted fillets, reconstituted (see previous recipe)
500g floury potatoes
150ml milk
150g butter
Pepper
4 large free-range eggs, poached or boiled
Hot buttered toast

COOKING SALT FISH

Put fish into a large pot, just cover with water and bring to the boil. Cover and turn off the heat. Leave for 15-20 minutes. The remaining heat should cook the fish. Leave till cold. Strain the fish. Remove any bones. It is not necessary to remove the skin, which will add extra flavour and food value.

COOKING POTATOES

Wash potatoes and boil till soft, skin and mash.

TO FINISH

Heat the potatoes in the pan. Remove from the heat and add the milk and butter. Beat well with a wooden spoon, whisk or electric beater till light, creamy. Add the salt fish and beat till 'hairy'. Taste and season. Serve with boiled or poached eggs and hot toast.

Hairy Tatties with Garlic and Olive Oil

500g heavily-salted fillets, reconstituted (see previous recipe)
500g floury potatoes
300ml extra virgin olive oil
4–6 cloves garlic
50ml hot milk
1 tablespoon parsley, chopped
4 large free-range eggs, poached or boiled
Hot buttered toast

COOKING SALT FISH AND POTATOES

As for traditional hairy tatties.

MAKING WITH OIL AND GARLIC

Put the fish into a food processor and add the garlic. Warm the oil a little in a pan which will help it blend with the fish. Add a few spoonfuls to the fish in the food processor and blend together for a few seconds. Continue adding the oil gradually, whizzing between each addition. When the oil is all added, add parsley and whizz till smooth.

Scrape into a large bowl. Beat in the mashed potatoes. Add the hot milk and beat with a whisk or electric beater till light and 'hairy'. Taste and season.

SERVING

Serve with hot toast and poached or boiled eggs.

COOK'S NOTES

Hairy Tattie Fish Cakes: Either of these mixtures can be used to make fish cakes.

Add two or three sliced spring onions and two or three rashers of grilled bacon, finely chopped.

Mix through and shape into round cakes. Coat in flour and fry in oil or butter till lightly browned.

Serve with a fried or poached egg and a bowl of green salad.

MARINATED, PICKLED OR SOUSED

Marinated Herring or Mackerel

The fillets are covered with a light Japanese sweet-spiced pickle, using the acid to 'cook' the fish flesh by coagulating the protein.

4 x 150–175g fresh mackerel or herring fillets
4 tablespoons sea salt
1 tablespoon allspice berries, crushed
1 tablespoon black peppercorns, crushed
700ml rice vinegar
3 tablespoons Japanese mirin, or sugar to taste
1 small red onion, finely sliced

TO SALT LIGHTLY

Lay the fillets skin side down in a ceramic dish and cover the flesh side evenly with salt. Rub the salt into the flesh and leave for 2–3 minutes. Rinse off the salt and dry the fillets with kitchen paper. Wash out dish.

TO MARINATE

Crush the allspice and peppercorns in a pestle and mortar. Put into a pan with vinegar, mirin and onion and simmer for a few minutes to infuse. Cover with a lid and leave till cold. Pour into the earthenware dish. Add the fillets flesh side down and leave to marinate for at least 2-3 hours, when the flesh will have changed from translucent to firm milky-opaque. Can be left, well-covered to prevent drying out, in the fridge for at least a week.

SERVING

Skin fillets: work from the tail end, separate a cm or so of skin with a knife first to get enough skin to grip. Then turn the fish flesh side down and pull off the skin cleanly. Slice the fish into bite-sized pieces. Garnish with spring onion. Strain marinade and pour some over the fish to serve.

Serve as a starter with rye bread and Gravlaxas (mustard dill sauce p. 217) and a Pickled Cucumber Salad (see p. 219).

TO STORE

The skinned fillets can be stored in the fridge in a sterilised jar with a tight-fitting lid. Fill up with pickling liquid to cover the fish completely. Will keep for at least a month.

Pickled Herring

A spicy herring cure which can be used for traditional tatties and herring.

6 fresh whole herring, gutted and scaled
600ml malt vinegar
100ml water
110g coarse sea salt
50g sugar
1 tablespoon black peppercorns
1 teaspoon all-spice berries

SOAKING IN VINEGAR

Put the herring into a large ceramic dish which will hold them in two layers and cover with vinegar and water. Leave to soak for 12 hours. Drain.

SALTING

Crush the allspice and peppercorns in a pestle and mortar. Mix the salt, sugar, peppercorns and allspice together and put a layer in the base of the dish. Put herrings on top, heads to tails. Cover with remaining salt mixture. Put a weight on top to help extract moisture from the fish. Cover and keep in a cold place until the herring are covered in liquid brine. They can be used within a few days or kept for longer, provided they are kept covered with brine in a cool place.

COOKING

Can be used to make Tatties and Herrin'.

Tatties and Herrin'

Serves 4-6

4-6 x 125-150g salt herring* (or pickled herring, see above)
1.5kg floury potatoes such as Golden Wonder or Rooster, whole unpeeled

SOAKING HERRING

Cover herring with cold water. Change the water after about 12 hours. Add fresh water and leave for around another 12 hours. Drain.

COOKING HERRING AND POTATOES

Put potatoes in a pot which will hold both them and the herring. Put herring on top of potatoes. Fill up pot with boiling water. Bring up to a slow simmer. Cover and simmer until the potatoes are cooked. Drain.

SERVING AND EATING

Put potatoes and herring into a large shallow dish, such as an ashet, which will hold them all. Put in centre of the table. Eat with fingers (traditional) or knives and forks. The herring comes easily off the bone and is used to flavour the potatoes. Serve with glasses of milk.

ALTERNATIVE METHOD

Some prefer to cook the herring and potatoes separately, but provided the herring has been well soaked and the potatoes are left whole and unpeeled, they should not become too salty.

*Salt, as for Heavily-Salted white fish (see p. 220), but do not pour off the liquid brine from the salting and store in an airtight container in the fridge.

Soused Mackerel

This method cooks and preserves the fish in a sweet and sour vinegar pickle.

Serves 4
4 summer mackerel fillets
Flavouring ingredients:
14g fresh ginger root, peeled and sliced thinly
1 tablespoon black peppercorns, crushed
1 tablespoon whole allspice, crushed
120ml vinegar, cider or wine
250ml cider or apple juice to cover
1-2 tablespoons dark soy sauce
Pre-heat oven to 130C/Gas ½
Equipment:
Shallow ceramic dish to fit fish in one layer approx 23 x 28cm

PREPARING THE FLAVOURING LIQUID

Put the ginger, peppercorns, allspice, vinegar, soy sauce and 250ml cider or apple juice into a pan and bring to the boil. Leave to infuse for half an hour.

BAKING THE FISH

Put the fish into the dish to fit fairly tightly, skin side down. Pour over the hot flavouring liquid. Bake 1½–2 hours.

SERVING

HOT: Strain off cooking liquid into a pan and bring to a simmer. Reduce, if necessary, to concentrate the flavour. Taste and adjust seasoning so there is a balance of sweet, salty and sour. Strain. Serve with boiled new potatoes and butter.

COLD: Leave the fish in its cooking liquid till cold. Serve the fish with a little of the cooking liquid and a Pickled Cucumber Salad (see p. 219).

Can be kept covered, in a cool place, for at least two weeks.

10 . . . with sea vegetables

Sea vegetables, or seaweeds, have a savoury taste and fresh sea-beach aroma. A few are thin and tender enough, like sea lettuce, to be eaten raw, but most are tougher and have to be cooked.

Some, like kelp, can develop strong fishy flavours if cooked for too long. Dulse, also known as 'sea parsley', is the most traditional Scottish seaweed flavouring, used in soups, with potatoes and in breads.

They can also be lightly toasted to make a seaweed condiment.

Another asset is the jelly-like substance which gives them strength and flexibility in the sea and prevents them drying out when exposed to air. When some are cooked in water, they release this substance which sets to a gel when cold. Sea-moss (Carrageen or Irish Moss) is the most common seaweed found around the Scottish coast with this function.

SEAWEED CONDIMENT

Total Dry-out to Crisp-crumbly

Suitable seaweeds already dried:*
Toothed Wrack, Fucus serratus; *Bladder Wrack,* Fucus vesiculosus; *Thongweed/ Sea Spaghetti,* Himanthalia elongate; *Dulse,* Palmaria palmate; *Sloke/Laver/ Nori,* Porphyra umbilicalis

Preheat oven to 180C/Gas 4.

Dry out each type separately since they are not all the same thickness. Place dried seaweed in a baking tray in a single layer. Put into the oven and leave thin seaweeds for 3-4 minutes, thicker types for 5 minutes. Remove and check for crispness. Return if still soft and check every two or three minutes.

TO CRUMBLE

Thin seaweeds can be crumbled by hand. Thicker seaweeds can be ground with a pestle and mortar if necessary. Store in an airtight jar.

*COOK'S NOTES

To Dry Seaweed: This is best done in a dry, warm atmosphere, preferably with a warm draught. The best natural conditions are a sunny summer's day, with a light wind. The seaweed can be hung up on a washing line or laid out on rocks or wooden boards, when it should be turned every day. It is also possible to dry out in a warm airing cupboard or in a very cool convection oven or in the coolest part of an Aga.

Using Fresh Seaweed: Depending on the type, seaweed dries out to between a quarter and a fifth of its original weight. All recipes are for dried weight, so if using fresh seaweed, multiply the quantity by 5 for thin seaweeds and 4 for thick.

SEAWEED SOUPS

Kelp Clear Broth

Serves 4-6

1.5 litre water
15g dried kelp, washed
80g white miso
1 spring onion very finely sliced
100g skinned fresh fillet of fine-textured fish, such as sole
8-12 cooked North Atlantic prawns

MAKING THE CLEAR BROTH

Put the water into a pot over a high heat and bring to the boil. Drop in the kelp. Bring it back up to the boil and remove kelp. Remove from the heat and leave to cool a little. Rub the miso through a sieve with the back of a wooden spoon, moistening it with some of the hot liquid to help it through. Put the sieved miso into the kelp stock. Bring up to simmering, stir well. Taste and dilute if too strong. Add more miso if necessary.

TO FINISH

Cut the fish in thin slices at an angle, as if slicing smoked salmon. Divide into 4 or 6 portions and put in the base of serving bowls. Add prawns and spring onions.* Ladle over the boiling broth and serve.

*COOK'S NOTES

*Alternative ingredients to put into the bowl: sprigs of watercress; dried and reconstituted or fresh dabberlocks (*alaria*) or laver, or dulse or sea lettuce, sliced thinly.

dulse

Dulse Broth

This is a mutton broth flavoured with dulse. In the Hebrides there is also a Dulse and Potato Brose, without meat. *

Serves 6-8

1.5kg neck or shoulder lamb or mutton, or 500g Shetland reestit mutton
3 litres cold water
1 whole onion, stuck with 3 or 4 whole cloves
*Herbs: Sprigs of parsley stalks, thyme, bay leaves, celery stalk and leek green tied
in a bundle with cotton thread*
3 onions, finely chopped
8 medium floury potatoes, peeled and thinly sliced
4 carrots, grated
4 celery stalks, diced finely
50g dried dulse, cut up finely with scissors
4 tablespoons kale, blended finely in a food processor
Salt and pepper

MAKING THE BROTH

Put the meat into a large pot and add the water. Bring slowly to the boil and skim. Turn down the heat and add the onion and herbs. Cook at a gentle simmer till the meat is tender and falling off the bones. Leave to cool. Remove the top layer of solid fat and save. Remove meat and strain.

COOKING THE VEGETABLES

Heat 4 tablespoons of the saved fat in the pot and when hot, add the onions. Cook over a medium heat till they are translucent and soft. Add the other vegetables except the kale and cook for about 5 minutes, stirring all the time. Add the dulse. Pour over the broth. Simmer till the vegetables are tender.

TO FINISH

Cut all the edible meat from the lamb or mutton and add to the broth. Add finely blended kale. Taste and season. Serve in heated bowls or deep soup plates with bannocks or oatcakes and seaweed condiment (see p. 226).

*COOK'S NOTES

Dulse and Potato Brose: Use 500g cooked potatoes, peeled, drained, mashed and beaten with butter and milk to a cream. Chop 10g dulse, cover with boiling water and simmer in a pan for about 10 minutes. Beat the dulse into the creamed potatoes to make a thick-soup-cum-brose consistency. Season and serve in heated bowls with a knob of butter in each bowl.

SEAWEED AND VEGETABLES

Stir-fried Dulse and Kale

Peppery dulse and kale with sweet raisins is a lively combination to serve with grilled or fried fish dishes.

Serves 4
15g dried dulse
250g kale
1 tablespoon oil
2 tablespoon raisins, soaked in water
Seaweed condiment (see p. 226)

PREPARING DULSE

Chop up the dulse finely. Put into a bowl and cover with cold water. Leave for 5 minutes till it softens and drain.

COOKING KALE

Wash kale. Remove any thick stalks and whizz in food processor till fairly fine. Heat oil in a wok and stir-fry with the dulse for a few minutes till soft. Drain raisins and stir through the kale.

TO FINISH

Put in a heated serving dish and sprinkle crumbled seaweed condiment on top.

SEAWEED JELLY

Sea Moss (Carrageen) Jelly

Served with thick cream (sweet or sour) and fruity jam or jelly.

Serves 4
10g dried sea moss
1 litre milk
Sugar to taste
300ml fresh cream
Jar of fruity jam or jelly

COOKING SEA MOSS

Put sea moss into a pan with the milk and bring to the boil. Simmer gently for about 10-15 minutes until it expands and the liquid starts to thicken. Add sugar to taste. Stir to dissolve the sugar. Strain through a fine sieve into a wetted glass serving dish, pressing all the jelly from the seaweed through the sieve with the back of a wooden spoon.

SETTING AND SERVING

Leave to cool and set. Add sugar to fresh cream and beat till stiff. Turn out the jelly onto a plate and serve with a bowl of fresh cream whipped and a pot of fruity jam or jelly. The Irish like it with a sprinkling of soft brown sugar.

COOK'S NOTES

To add an egg: Beat the egg in a bowl and sieve the cooked mixture onto it. Return to the pan and cook over a very low heat to thicken, stirring all the time. Remove, and pour into the glass serving dish. The egg can be separated and the white beaten till stiff and folded through once it's cooled a little to make a lighter jelly.

SEAFOOD IDENTIFICATION
buying advice and conservation status

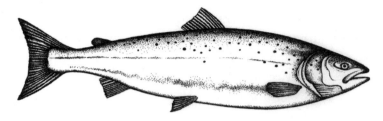

salmon

SALMON AND TROUT
Salmon, Atlantic; trout, brown or sea/salmon; trout, rainbow; Arctic charr (freshwater)

Salmon, Atlantic
Salmo salar

Profile, Wild: Hatched in Scotland's purest fresh-water rivers, after two years or so they migrate to the sea, grow fat over several years, then return to their native waters, fight their way back upstream to where they were hatched and then spawn. The female lays her eggs on the riverbed and the male fertilises them. By this time, both fish are badly run down and most die while the remainder go back to sea to return another year. (For their life-cycle, see *www.atlanticsalmontrust.org.*)

Around 5% return to spawn, coming back after two, three or four years. The best quality are caught when still fat and flavoursome from the rich sea feeding grounds. They are likely to weigh from 4kg upwards. They usually spend two to three winters in the sea, though there is a record of a salmon, caught on Loch Maree in Wester Ross, which was thirteen years old and had spawned four times. Compared with Pacific salmon, it is paler and has more subtle flavours. Also, its finer, more satiny texture allows it to be sliced to translucent thinness when smoked. To test if wild or farmed: clasp the whole fish just below its tail-fin and hold it up. A farmed fish tail will slip through your fingers, since its tail is flabby, a wild fish will not.

Profile, Farmed: There are concerns about farming with open net pens which can cause pollution from both nutrients and organic matter, leading to environmental changes in the seas. There are also concerns about escaped farmed fish; disease transfer between farmed and wild species; widespread use of chemicals; and some remaining concerns surrounding enforcement and regulatory controls. They are carnivorous fish that require more fish in their diet than they actually produce, causing a loss of marine proteins and oils. Also, the fish used to make their feed cannot be assumed to have come from a sustainable supply.

Buying Advice: Stocks of wild Atlantic salmon are severely depleted. There may be several reasons for this, not least overfishing. Other factors may include: pollution, environmental changes, aquaculture, freshwater habitat deterioration and impediments to migration routes. In 2001 the International Atlantic Salmon Research Board was set up to investigate salmon mortality. There are several individual salmon stocks throughout the UK, some of which may be more abundant than others. Scientific advice has called for reducing exploitation of as many stocks as possible to allow the species to reach conservation limits. Avoid wild caught Atlantic salmon unless from a known and sustainable source.

Trout, Brown or Sea/Salmon
Salmo trutta

Profile, Wild: The migratory sea/salmon trout, with a natural range from North Africa to Norway and Iceland, has a similar life cycle to Atlantic salmon; it also eats the same kind of food (among other things, pink crustaceans) and therefore has a similar pink flesh. It is different in size – smaller than salmon and with a more delicate flavour which is preferred by many. Non-migratory freshwater brown trout are smaller, and their flavour is entirely dependent on the richness of their feeding grounds.

Size: Can grow up to 15kg.

Spawning Habits: Sea/salmon trout, November to March; Brown trout, October to January.

Buying Advice: Only eat wild trout if it is line-caught from a well-managed fishery. Avoid eating fresh sea or salmon trout caught during the breeding or spawning season from November to March – brown trout from October to January. The current status of some of the wild sea trout stocks in the Gulf of Bothnia and the Gulf of Finland is considered critical by ICES. Avoid eating fish from these stocks.

Trout, rainbow
Oncorhynchus mykiss

Profile, Farmed: They may not be wild and native, like brown trout, but this native North American species has adapted well to Scottish freshwater rivers and lochs. They first arrived in British waters in the 1850s, around the time colonials were also transporting native brown trout eggs around the globe. More plentiful, and more available now than the slower-growing brown trout, they are also easier to catch.

Though they do not breed naturally in cold Scottish waters, they are still wild in the sense that they take their character from their native environment. In a well-oxygenated Scottish loch or river, with good native feeding, they will be firm-fleshed and sweet-tasting. The quality of rainbow from an overstocked trout farm, where the feeding is not native and the water too muddy, will be in doubt.

Size: Can grow up to 10kg.

Buying advice: Trout are carnivorous fish whose feed relies on wild fisheries. Buying organic farmed trout is the best choice, as fish stocking densities are generally lower in comparison to non-organic farms, feed is sourced sustainably and welfare is of a high standard.

Arctic Charr (Freshwater)
Salvelinus alpinus

Profile, Wild: Charr migrated south from its native Arctic waters around Iceland and got trapped as the seas froze during the last ice age. Scottish Highland freshwater lochs were a welcome refuge and became a stronghold for them as they morphed into freshwater fish. Now there are around two hundred populations in the Highlands, though their numbers are not large. They now look quite different from sea water charr, with highly variable colouration depending on their environment, from bright red to pale pink flesh depending on feeding. They have smaller scales than trout, brighter colouring and sometimes pinkish spots on back and sides. While Arctic charr have a long history as part of the Eskimo's diet, they have now graduated from the igloo to the dining tables of the world's top restaurants, as their fine quality and flavour has become more widely appreciated.

Profile, Farmed Freshwater: Unsustainable supplies of other more popular salmon and trout have revived interest in freshwater fish such as the Arctic charr which have a low-risk conservation status. This has encouraged some farmed ventures.

Size: Maximum Length 1m sea-run fish, 40cm freshwater landlocked populations. Maximum size sea-run around 9kg. From freshwater lochs up to 2kg, usually smaller.

Spawning Habits: In the autumn from September to December.

Buying Advice: Mostly an angler's fish, but supplies may be available from a farmed source. (see Directory, p. 311)

HERRING AND ITS RELATIONS
Herring; sardine and pilchard; sprat; anchovy

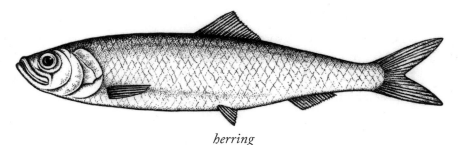

herring

Herring
Clupea harengus

Profile, Wild: The word 'herring' comes from the Teutonic word 'heer', meaning an army, which is a good description of the shoals of herring numbering many thousands which swim together for protection. The back is dark blue, shading to silvery white below, sometimes with golden or reddish tints. Herring are available all year round from different sources, but the heavier, fatter summer fish have more flavour than the lean winter ones. The amount of fat in the flesh varies throughout the annual reproductive cycle. After a period of starvation following spawning there is a time of intensive feeding while the new milts and roes begin to develop. The fat is in the flesh of the fish, so this determines its flavour. Fat content can vary from as little as 2% to as high as 20%.

Herring are sexually mature at between 3-9 years (depending on stock) and have an important role in the marine ecosystem as a transformer of plankton at the bottom of the food chain to higher feeding species when they are eaten by cod, seabirds and marine mammals.

The largest single fishery is for Atlantic herring which is fished throughout much of the North Atlantic. In European waters, herring is managed by a system of Total Allowable Catches and quotas. The North Sea stock has recovered from a depleted state, however it is not yet above the precautionary limits recommended by scientists. The main reason for this is a prolonged period of poor recruitment which is yet to be explained, however scientists consider fishing efforts to be a minor factor, and it is likely due to environmental conditions.

There are a variety of sub-species, distinct breeding stocks or 'races', such as the Baltic herring which is smaller than the Atlantic herring and has a lower fat content.

Size: Most herring landed are around 25cm. Can grow to 40cm. Size varies among breeding stocks.

Spawning Habits: Populations include both spring and autumn spawners. At least one population in UK waters spawns in any one month of the year.

Buying Advice: Only available in summer from June-September. Stocks in the southern part of the Firth of Clyde off Scotland's west coast are depleted and fish from this stock should be avoided.

Marine Stewardship Council Certified Sustainable Fishery: Drift net fisheries in the Thames Blackwater and the Eastern English Channel are certified as environmentally sustainable fisheries. A number of pelagic trawl and purse seine fisheries (the two main methods used in the North East Atlantic) are also certified as sustainable.

Look for the MSC sustainable label (blue label with white tick). Visit *www. msc.org/track-a-fishery* for up-to-date information.

Sardine and Pilchard
Sardina pilchardus

Profile, Wild: A pelagic shoaling fish, like herring and mackerel, the sardine is the young of the pilchard. The pilchard has a green back, yellowish sides and a silver belly and is widely distributed in European seas, reaching its northern limit around southern British seas. Pilchards migrate northwards after spawning in spring and summer to their feeding grounds when they are found inshore in coastal waters, mostly in South West England. Scottish waters are too cold for them. In winter they migrate southwards again. Maximum reported age is 15 years. Fat content is in the flesh which determines flavour.

Size: The maximum length of a pilchard is 25cm.

Spawning Habits: During spring and summer in the open sea.

Buying Advice: The best choice is pilchard – sometimes sold as Cornish sardines – caught in coastal waters off Cornwall in the South West of England using traditional drift or ring nets.

Sprat
Sprattus sprattus

Profile, Wild: Small, coastal, pelagic shoaling species which can survive in waters of low salinity. Their range is from the north of Norway to the Mediterranean. Their back is blue or bluish green and underneath is silvery. They move to the surface at night. Sprat fisheries for canning in Norway produce 'brisling'. In Sweden they are canned as 'Swedish anchovies'. Fat content is in the flesh which determines flavour.

Size: Maximum length is 14-16cm.

Spawning Habits: They migrate between winter feeding and summer spawning grounds

Buying Advice: Sprat are mostly caught for reduction, or industrial fisheries, and are used almost entirely for fish meal and fish oil. Small artisanal fisheries may be found locally which are at such low levels they are unlikely to affect the sprat population. Sprat is a short-lived species, and stock biomass is subject to large natural fluctuations. The wider ecosystem effects of taking large volumes of fish from the base of the food chain is poorly understood, however sprat is a main prey species for cod. The state of the stocks in the North East Atlantic is generally unknown.

Anchovy, European
Engraulis encrasicolus

Profile, Wild: It is a short-lived, schooling fish feeding on plankton at the base of the food chain. The back is green, sometimes with a blue tinge, while the sides and underneath are bright silver. It is mostly to be found in the warmer waters of the Mediterranean, the Iberian Peninsula and the Bay of Biscay, though it also comes into the English Channel and sometimes reaches Danish waters. It is prey for other fish and marine mammals. Fat content is in the flesh which determines flavour.

Size: Maximum length 20cm.

Spawning Habits: In summer it moves inshore to spawn between June and August in the southern North Sea and the Channel, and April to September in the Mediterranean.

Buying Advice: Anchovy stocks in the Bay of Biscay have recovered following the closure of the fishery in 2005 and the fishery has now reopened. However, there are management concerns, so eat with caution. The state of the stock off the Portuguese coast is unknown. MCS does not have enough information on other stocks to give a rating. A fast growing species like anchovy should be resistant to fishing pressure, however they are also an important part of the ecosystem and the effects of removing large numbers is not properly understood. Eat with caution.

Mackerel
Scomber scombrus

Profile, Wild: Svelte and iridescent, it has a greeny blue back, marked with dark curving lines and metallic sides. Shoals of mackerel hibernate in winter deep in northern waters, where its nutritious oils protect it from intense cold. It has an extensive ocean range from the Mediterranean to Iceland and the north of Norway, and from Cape Hatteras to Labrador on the American side. Fat content is in the

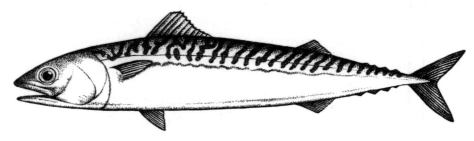

mackerel

flesh which determines flavour. Compared with herring, its texture is 'meatier' and it does not have the herring's small fine bones.

Size: By 3 years old most are mature. Juveniles grow quickly and can reach 22 cm after one year and 30 cm after 2 years. It can reach a maximum length of about 70cm and a weight of 3kg. It may live for more than 20 years.

Spawning Habits: They spawn mainly from March to June. Females shed their eggs in about 20 separate batches over the course of the spawning season.

Buying Advice: Available early summer (June) through to November with some variable availability. Also available in January and February. This is Scotland's most abundant species, high in omega 3.

Marine Stewardship Council Certified Sustainable Fishery: Much of the commercial mackerel fisheries in the Northeast Atlantic have been certified as sustainable by the Marine Stewardship Council.

Look for the MSC sustainable label (blue label with white tick). Visit *www. msc.org/track-a-fishery* for up-to-date information.

COD AND ITS RELATIONS
Cod; saithe or coley; haddock; hake; ling, common; pollack; pouting; whiting

Cod
Gadus morhua

Profile, Wild: A cold-water fish, there are various 'races' of cod such as Icelandic, Arcto-Norwegian and Baltic, which have minor variations and also grow at different rates. Fishermen also distinguish more categories according to the time of year the fish appear and the fishing 'grounds' where they are caught.

The skin colour also varies but its back is mostly a marbled, greenish-sandy colour with brown mottling, while the lateral line and belly are white.

Its very white flesh and firm 'meaty' texture, rather than its distinctive flavour, have made its reputation as the prime fish of this family, particularly for salting and drying. It is one of the world's 'too much loved' fish with subsequent overfishing and an endangered profile for many stocks.

Size: North Sea cod mature at 4-5 years, at a length of about 50cm, and can live up to 60 years. Maximum length 150cm, weighing 40kg.

Spawning Habits: They spawn in winter and spring from February to April.

Buying Advice: Prime season August-November. Avoid during spawning February-April. Available all year. Cod stocks have increased in recent years. MCS advice is that stocks in the North-east Atlantic are either overfished or at an unknown level except for stocks in the North-east Arctic, Baltic, Iceland and the Faroes Plateau, and the most depleted stocks are in the Irish Sea, North Sea, and West of Scotland. Icelandic fisheries are being overfished as quotas are being set above scientific recommendations, but the North-east Arctic stock is healthy and is fished at a sustainable level.

Choose line-caught cod where available to help reduce the impact of trawler fishing on fish stocks. Longlines, however, can result in seabird by-catch. Buy fish caught using seabird-friendly methods.

Marine Stewardship Council Certified Sustainable Fishery: Part of the Norwegian long line fishery for cod, in the North-east Arctic, has been certified as sustainable by the MSC and is available in the UK.

Look for the MSC sustainable label (blue with a white tick). Visit *www.msc. org/track-a-fishery* for up to date information.

Saithe: coley, coalfish, cuithe, sillock
Pollachius virens

Profile, Wild: A cold-water fish, living on the sea bed, its ocean range covers all the northern waters of the Atlantic to a southern limit of the English Channel in the east, and in the west to the US coast of New Jersey. The colour of its back varies from greenish charcoal to black (hence the name from *col*, coal). In the last fifty years or so it has been less highly rated than cod, possibly because of its less than white flesh. Its darker flesh, however, has more flavour than cod. Evidence of its previous popularity in Britain can be found in the high number of vernacular British names for it – at one count fifty-seven. Its more traditional name in Scotland is saithe, in England, coley. Both its interesting flavour, and under-fished status, makes it ready now for a revival.

Size: It is mature when between 4-10 years old and 60-70cm long. Can grow up to 130cm and reach ages of more than 25 years.

Spawning Habits: Spawns from January to March at about 200m depth along the Northern Shelf edge and the western edge of the Norwegian deeps. Usually enters coastal waters in spring and returns to deeper water in winter.

Buying Advice: Available all year, but avoid during its spawning period from January-March, and immature saithe below about 50cm. The North-east Arctic (Barents and Norwegian Sea) saithe stock and the combined saithe stock in the North Sea, Skagerrak, West of Scotland and Rockall, are currently healthy and above the minimum level scientifically recommended and are harvested sustainably.

To help reduce impact of trawler fishing where fishing effort is too high (Iceland and Faroes) on fish stocks and the marine environment, choose line-caught fish where available. When buying long line-caught saithe, look for fish caught using 'seabird-friendly' methods.

Marine Stewardship Council Certified Sustainable Fishery: Two Norwegian fisheries for saithe, and the German North Sea fishery, are assessed as environmentally sustainable fisheries by the MSC.

Look for the MSC sustainable label (blue with a white tick). Visit *www.msc. org/track-a-fishery* for up to date information.

Haddock
Melanogrammus aeglefinus

Profile, Wild: A cold-water fish living on the sea bed, it migrates from coastal waters in summer to deeper waters in winter. It spans the North Atlantic, travelling as far south as the Bay of Biscay on the east and the US coast of New England on the west. Its back is dark greyish with a black lateral line and a charcoal coloured 'thumb-print' on either side just behind its head.

Its flesh is very white, like cod's. Some claim it is better flavoured than cod, and it is certainly popular with Scottish fishermen who often rate it their favourite fish. It is also the favourite choice in Scots chippies and has made its name worldwide in a variety of smoked cures. In France 'haddock' on the menu means a smoked Finnan haddock. All of which has put it into the 'too much loved' and endangered status in some areas, though not in the North Sea area fished by Scottish boats which now have MSC status (see p. 116).

Size: Smaller than cod, it can attain a length of 70-100cms and can live for more than 20 years. Adult length for market 40-60cm.

Spawning Habits: It spawns sometime between February and June, but usually in March and April. North Sea haddock become sexually mature at 3-4 years at a length of 30-40 cm. Maturity occurs later and it grows to greater lengths in more northern areas of its range.

Buying Advice: Prime season from September-January. Avoid from March-May when spawning. Available all year. To help reduce the impact of fishing on fish stocks which are depleted or being heavily fished, choose line-caught fish where available. Avoid eating haddock from West of Scotland stocks which are overfished. Marine scientists recommend a closure of the fishery.

Marine Stewardship Council Certified Sustainable Fishery: The Scottish component of the North Sea fishery, and part of the Norwegian fishery for haddock in the Northeast Arctic, are certified as sustainable by the MSC and offer the best option for haddock.

Stocks in North-east Arctic (Barents and Norwegian Sea) and in the combined areas of North Sea, Kattegat and Skagerrak are at healthy or at sustainable levels and being fished sustainably. Haddock, however, occur in mixed fisheries with other fish such as cod, which are depleted in some areas such as the North and Irish Sea and waters west of Scotland.

Look for the MSC sustainable label (blue with a white tick). Visit *www.msc. org/track-a-fishery* for up to date information.

Hake, European
Merluccius merluccius

Profile, Wild: This is the only species of hake found in European seas. It has two mains stocks, northern and southern. Its back is a slate grey and it has a large mouth, grey-black inside with dangerous-looking teeth. As it approaches maturity, it moves into deeper offshore waters. Its soft, tender white flesh is dense and full of flavour, and 'too much loved' by fish eaters in Spain and Portugal, so that stocks are depleted round their shores (see p. 132).

Size: Usual market length is from 30-70cm, though it can attain a length of 100-180cm, with a weight of 11-15kg. Females which are mature at 5-6 years are about 50cm.

Spawning Habits: It is a late maturing fish, spawning from February to July in northern waters.

Buying Advice: The northern stock is classified as healthy and harvested sustainably, having recovered from unsustainable levels. The southern stock is depleted, however, and should be avoided. Avoid immature fish below about 50cm and during their breeding season, February to July.

Marine Stewardship Council Certified Sustainable Fishery: The only hake fishery with an MSC certification is South African, Cape hake (*Merluccius capensis*) and the deep water Cape hake (*Merluccius paradoxus*) which is similar but slightly smaller. They breed throughout the year with peaks of reproductive activity in August and September and can reach a size of 140cm

Look for the MSC sustainable label (blue with a white tick). Visit *www.msc.org/track-a-fishery* for up to date information.

Ling, Common
Molva molva

Profile, Wild: The largest member of the cod family, it has a marbled bronze-green back with a dark spot at the rear of the first dorsal fin. The dorsal and anal fins have white edges. It is a deep-water fish which frequents the sea bed. It can also be found nearer the coast. It is mainly fished around Iceland, in the Norwegian

Sea and on the west coast of Britain. It is considered a fine fish, on a par with cod, and with an especially firm liver, the preferred choice in Shetland fish liver recipes (see p. 104).

Size: Males are mature at about 80 cm and females from 90-100cm when 5 to 8 years old. The species can grow to 200cm long, 45 kg in weight, and live for at least 25 years.

Spawning Habits: Spawn between March and August.

Buying Advice: Deepwater stocks appear to be overfished and current management measures are not deemed sufficient to restore abundance. Scientific advice recommends that catches be limited or reduced in all commercial fisheries to allow stocks to recover. Avoid eating fish from deepwater stocks. Line caught from inshore fisheries is a more sustainable option.

Pollack, Lythe
Pollachius pollachius

Profile, Wild: It has an extensive range from Iceland and Norway down to the Iberian Peninsula. Its colour varies with its habitat, but compared with cod, its back is usually a darker, greeny-brown colour and its sides a bright bronze or gold colour. Young fish in their first year are particularly common close inshore. Larger fish frequent rocky coastal waters and like to feed on small cod, sand eels and small herring. Its flesh is perhaps not as pure white as cod, but it is equally good to eat and should be more widely used instead of the 'too much loved' cod. Also a good substitute for haddock in the chip shop.

Size: Market length is 40-50cm, but the species can reach a length of 120-130cm and an age of more than 8 years.

Spawning Habits: Between January and April.

Buying Advice: It is taken as by-catch in trawl fisheries for cod and saithe and is also line-caught. The best choice to make in terms of selectivity and sustainability is line-caught pollack. Avoid eating immature fish (below 40cm) and during its breeding season (January to April).

Pouting, Bib
Trisopterus luscus

Profile, Wild: A short-lived species common in British inshore waters, it is not commercially fished and therefore not assessed, and no information is available on its stock status. Large schools form around wrecks and reefs.

Size: Usually between about 20-32cm. Can grow to 40cm. The maximum reported age reached is 4 years.

Spawning Habits: March and April.

Buying Advice: When buying, choose mature (over 20cm) locally caught fish. Avoid eating fresh fish caught during their spawning season.

Whiting
Merlangius merlangus

Profile, Wild: Ranges from Iceland and Norway to the Mediterranean. It likes shallow, sandy waters and is often caught close inshore. It is slender-bodied; the back may be dark blue or green or sandy, but the sides are always silvery or white. It is a junior member of the cod family with a nice white flesh but not a lot of flavour. Since it is currently not an A-list fish a large amount is turned into fishmeal, though it was much more highly valued in Scotland's fish-eating past.

Size: Mature fish (2-4 years old) are about 30cm. The average landed length is usually around 30-40cm, however it can grow up to 70cm and weigh up to 3kg. The maximum reported age is 20 years.

Spawning Habits: Between January and July, but mostly in spring between April and June in northern waters.

Buying Advice: Prime season August-January. Avoid fresh fish during peak spawning April-June. North-east Atlantic whiting stocks are overfished and scientific advice is to reduce catches to the lowest possible level. Avoid eating immature fish less than 30cm.

OTHER ROUND FISH
white or part oily

Bream, black; bream, gilthead; eel, European; eel, conger; garfish; gurnard, grey; gurnard, red; John Dory; monkfish; mullet, grey; mullet, red; pangasis, basa, panga, tra, Vietnamese catfish or river cobbler; scad; redfish; sea bass; wolf-fish, 'catfish'

Bream, Black
Spondliosoma cantharus

Profile, Wild: Ranges from southern Norway and Orkney to the Mediterranean and the Canary Islands, but is more prolific in warmer waters southwards from the English Channel. When freshly caught it has a steel-blue head and a silver-purple sheen on its sides which is interspersed with black stripes. When it has been dead for an hour or two its back darkens to a greyish charcoal. Its eating quality is highly rated, firm meaty flesh with a good flavour. Keeping this fish whole is also a good move, since the bone gives the flesh more flavour as it cooks.

Profile, Farmed: See Gilthead Bream.

Size: All fish mature as females at 20cm, but when they reach 30cm some change into males. All fish over 40cm are males.

Spawning Habits: Lay eggs in hollows in seabed gravel in April and May. Since large males over 40cm guard the nests, over-fishing of this size of fish may affect the sustainability of the stocks.

Buying Advice: Avoid fish under 23cm.

Bream, Gilthead
Sparus auratus

Profile, Wild: Most of the wild species which belong to this family come from tropical or near tropical seas and are only occasionally found in the colder waters of the North Atlantic.

Profile, Farmed: In Greece, fish farming has emerged as one of the fastest growing industries and now accounts for around 50% of the European Union's production of gilthead sea bream (also sea bass). Spa n, France and Italy are also key producers.

Size: Farmed, around 250-300gm.

Spawning Habits: Spawning occurs between November and December.

Buying Advice: There are concerns about farming wi-h open net pens, which can cause pollution from both nutrients and organic matter, leading to environmental changes. There are also concerns about escaped farmed fish; disease transfer between farmed and wild species; widespread use of chemicals; and some remaining concerns surrounding enforcement and regulatory controls. They are carnivorous fish that require more fish in their diet than they actually produce, causing a loss of marine proteins and oils. Also, the fish used to make their feed cannot be assumed to have come from a sustainable supply.

Eel, European
Anguilla Anguilla

Profile, Wild: In an opposite breeding cycle to Atlan_ic salmon, the eel is born in the Sargasso Sea between the Bermudas and the Bahamas, and returns to freshwater rivers and lakes to live. The eggs hatch into larvae, and during their first year they develop into tiny transparent elvers, or glass eels, while travelling to Europe carried in the surface waters of the Gulf Stream. Here they move up rivers, arriving in the UK early in the year. The freshwater stage is a growing phase when they feed on other fish, hunting at night and hiding under stones or roots during the day. Immature eels have a dark brown back and yellow sides. As they mature their back turns black and their sides silvery, when they are known as silver eels. As they mature sexually they migrate to the sea. If silver eels are prevented from returning to the sea, they start to feed again and can live up to 50 years. It's possible that they use the earth's magnetic field to find their way to the Sargasso Sea to spawn.

Profile, Farmed: Rely on juveniles from wild stocks.

Size: When they are about ten years old they are about 70-80cm, though they can grow to 135cm and weigh about 9kg.

Buying Advice: Avoid eating. European eel stock s severely depleted and at a historical minimum which continues to decline. Eels are exploited in all life stages and those that are fished do not have the chance to breed. Eels spawn only once in their lifetime and it is almost certain they die after spawning. Fishing for juvenile eels (elvers) was banned in English waters until February 2011.

Eel, Conger
Conger conger

Profile, Wild: A much larger fish than the European eel, it has a grey or black body, creamy brown belly, and colour varies according to habitat. It has a snake-like body with an extended fin along most of its length. Young eels live along rocky coasts in the east Atlantic from Iceland to the Mediterranean, where they are usually found in deep pools. When mature, they migrate to the open sea and spawn deep in the eastern Atlantic between the 30th and 40th latitudes. They are sexually mature at 5-15 years and die after spawning.

Size: Can reach a length of 3m and 110kg weight, although females are lighter and smaller at 1m maximum.

Buying Advice: Because they take such a long time to mature and spawn only once, after which they die, they have a very low resilience to fishing. Avoid eating.

Garfish
Belone belone

Profile, Wild: It ranges from Iceland and Norway to the Baltic and the Mediterranean. It is an ocean fish which comes into coastal waters to spawn. It has a long pointed nose and streamlined shape, which makes it one of the fastest moving fish in British waters. It's also extremely agile and leaps over low rocks. Its back is a brilliant green or dark blue and its sides silver with a yellow tinge on the belly. Its other distinguishing feature is its green bones, though this does not affect the eating quality of its flesh, which is firm, moist and as flavourful as the freshest mackerel.

Size: Market length 40-60cm, weight 500g. Maximum length 75cm.

Spawning Habits: In coastal waters between May and June.

Buying Advice: Since they grow fast and mature young, they can be considered a safe choice.

Gurnard, Grey

Eutrigla gurnardus

Profile, Wild: Ranging from Iceland and Norway to the Mediterranean, it is the most common gurnard in British waters. Its back is greyish-green or brown marbled with pale spots, and its belly whitish. Although an offshore species, grey gurnard is also found in shallow water. Gurnards are able to grunt or growl by use of muscles associated with the swim bladder, and this is thought to be an aid to keeping schools together. Their flesh is firm and white and rated highly. Cooking this fish whole is also a good move since the bone gives the flesh more flavour as it cooks.

Size: Market length is around 30cm. Females are sexually mature at 4 years (24cm), males at 3 years (18cm). Though market length is about 30cm they can grow to 45cm. The maximum life span rarely exceeds 6 years.

Spawning Habits: Intermittently throughout the early spring and summer – April to August.

Buying Advice: Grey gurnard are taken as by-catch in trawl fisheries in deeper offshore waters. Avoid eating immature fish (less than 24cm) and fresh fish caught during the spawning season (April-August).

Gurnard, Red

Aspitrigla cuculus

Profile, Wild: Ranges from the Mediterranean to British waters but is not common in the North Sea. Dark red on its head, back and sides with a lighter pinkish grey belly. It is an exotic-looking fish which at one time UK fishmongers had such difficulty selling that they used them as visual 'bait', hanging them outside their shops or decorating market stalls with them. Cooking this fish whole is a good move since the bone gives the flesh more flavour as it cooks.

Size: Mature at 20cm, it can reach 40cm and a weight of about 900g.

Spawning Habits: In summer.

Buying Advice: Taken as by-catch in trawl fisheries, it is a fast-growing fish which matures early at a large size. Avoid eating immature fish (less than 20cm) and fresh fish caught during the spawning season (summer).

John Dory
Zeus faber

Profile, Wild: Range is in the Atlantic along European coasts from southern Norway to the Cape of Good Hope. It is also in the Mediterranean and sometimes in the Black Sea. It mostly lives a solitary life or is found in small schools in inshore water. It is a yellowish-brown or greyish colour with characteristic 'thumbprints' on its sides. It has a very flat body and is sometimes classed along with other flat fish. Cooking this fish whole is a good move since the bone gives the flesh more flavour as it cooks.

Size: Becomes sexually mature at 3-4 years and a length of 25-35cm. It reaches lengths of 40-70cm at about 12 years.

Spawning Habits: Spawns in June-August off the coasts of southern England, earlier in the Mediterranean.

Buying Advice: Avoid eating immature fish (less than 25-35cm) and during their breeding season, June-August. It is generally taken as by-catch in trawls, and because it is an unregulated species immature fish may be landed.

Monkfish or Anglerfish
Lophius piscatorius

Profile, Wild: Ranges from Iceland to the Mediterranean and is found in both deep and shallow waters on both sides of the Atlantic. It is a long-lived species which has been over-fished by trawlers. It is camouflaged by its muddy sea-bed colouring as it burrows to hide from unsuspecting fish, opening its huge jaws when the antennae projecting from its head tells it there are fish around. Its tail is a firm, succulent chunk of bone-free flesh which is highly rated.

Size: Maximum length is 2m – minimum recommended size 70cm.

Spawning Habits: Spring and early summer.

Buying Advice: Prime season is October-December. Not at its best when spawning from March to June. Variable availability from July to September. Though it became overfished in the late 1990s, stocks have been recovering in the 2000s. Because it is a long-lived species, it has a low resilience to fishing and is therefore always under some threat. Recent EU marketing standards fixed a minimum weight of 500g for anglerfish.

Mullet, Thick-lipped, Grey
Chelon labrosus

Profile, Wild: Common on many North European coastlines, the thick-lipped grey mullet belongs to a large family of about eighty species, many of them belonging to warmer waters. It is more plentiful and popular in the Mediterranean and on the Iberian Peninsula. It is more common in southern than northern UK waters. Unlike most other ocean fish, it does not eat other fish but survives on a diet of worms, maggots, seaweed, algae and mud which it hoovers up with its wide mouth. Not an A-list fish, yet with a well flavoured, slightly oily flesh. It has some troublesome bones which are difficult to fillet out, so leaving whole is a better option when they will come away with the backbone.

Size: Grey mullet become sexually mature at a length of 30-35cm and an age of 3-4 years. Maximum length 75cm, weight 4.5kg and a reported age of up to 25 years.

Spawning Habits: It spawns in the Channel and in Irish waters in July-August, earlier in southern parts.

Buying Advice: Avoid fish under 35cm and during spawning in July-August. Little information is available on abundance due to lack of scientific data.

Mullet, Red
Mullus surmuletus

Profile, Wild: Ranges throughout the world in tropical and warm temperate seas, it is also found as far north as Britain and Ireland in summer. Not a member of the mullet family, but one of the species known as goatfish from its distinctive barbels – sensory organs – which are used to detect food on the sea bed. It has developed a particularly long gut which may be left in the fish and eaten, or just the liver may be left in, giving it the title 'the woodcock of the sea' and imparting a slightly gamey flavour around the belly area when cooked. The flesh, with or without the gut, has an outstanding flavour, well-balanced between curdy white and rich oily. It should be cooked whole to appreciate its full flavour, colour and natural juices.

Size: Grows quickly and matures young at 2 years to about 22cm length. It can attain a length of 45cm and is reported to live up to 10 years.

Spawning Habits: May-July in the Channel area.

Buying Advice: Avoid eating immature fish (less than 22cm) and fresh fish caught during the summer spawning season (May-July). Red mullet is subject to high fishing pressure in Mediterranean fisheries. Taken as by-catch and in mixed trawl fisheries.

Pangasius, Basa, Panga, Tra, Vietnamese Catfish, River Cobbler
Pangasius bocourti and Pangasius hypophthalmus

Profile, Wild: Not native to northern waters, the natural habitat of this farmed species is medium to large rivers in Asian countries such as Vietnam, where they can grow up to 44kg. They are omnivores, feeding on a diet of other fish, vegetable matter and crustaceans.

Profile, Farmed: Pangasius bocourti is one of the most important farmed species in Vietnam. UK imports of farmed Vietnamese catfish, block frozen at low prices ,are on the increase. Sometimes used in fish and chip shops, where there have been prosecutions for selling it – and charging for it – as more expensive cod. When deep-fried in batter it is difficult to taste the difference since, like cod, catfish is almost tasteless, though its texture is less firm. It could also appear in ready-made, fish-based meals or on supermarket fish counters described as pangasius or panga or basa or grey sole or Vietnamese catfish or river cobbler.

Buying Advice: Avoid fish of the above names which does not give origins on the label. Pangasius, farmed to GlobalGap certified production standards, addresses a number of issues of environmental concern associated with production. These include: habitat alteration; disease outbreak and parasite transfer; nutrient and organic pollution; escapes; interactions with local wildlife and problems of enforcement of regulations. Because Pangasius is an omnivore it is not heavily reliant on marine proteins and oils to form part of its diet, however the fish used to produce the feed is currently not certified as being responsibly managed or sustainable. Its all-year-round availability makes it popular with supermarkets.

Redfish or Ocean Perch
Sebastes marinus and Sebastes mentella

Profile, Wild: A deepwater fish, mostly found in the North Atlantic, its back is a deep red colour which fades to yellowish red on the belly. The two main species of Redfish (*S. marinus* and *S. mentella*) which are exploited commercially in the Northeast Atlantic are extremely slow growing and long lived. *S. mentella* frequents the subarctic waters of the northern Atlantic. A very meaty, white-fleshed fish with large flakes. Their flesh is highly rated and also their skin, which has a lot of flavour if fried or grilled till crisp.

Size: Market length is 25-30cm. *S. marinus* is the larger species, reaching a maximum size of 100cm and 15kg, while *S. mentella* grows to 55cm. They both reach maturity at 10 to 13 years old and have maximum reported ages from 60 to 75 years old.

Spawning Habits: Mating occurs in late summer or autumn, females then carry the sperm and eggs, and later larvae, that hatch in winter.

Buying Advice: Redfish stocks have been subject to intensive fishing pressure over the last 10 years. The slow growth, high age at maturity and low rates of reproduction make them highly vulnerable to over-exploitation. Most stocks are now at historical lows and are considered depleted. Avoid unless from a known sustainable source.

Scad or Horse Mackerel
Trachurus trachurus

Profile, Wild: Not a member of the mackerel family, it is found off the European coast where it forms large shoals. In summer it migrates northwards as far as Norway, the Baltic and the UK in search of food, returning south when the temperature drops. It has a grey-blue back with greenish tints, silvery sides and a white belly. It is not an A-list fish but does not deserve to be used – as it is in the UK – for cat food or pellets for farmed fish. Southern Europe and Japan make better use of its oily, omega-3 rich flesh. Not as obviously oily as mackerel, it is sometimes described as 'chickeny'.

Size: Sexual maturity is reached at about 3-4 years at a length of about 25cm; however, the legal minimum landing size is 15cm. Can reach 50cm in length.

Spawning Habits: In summer in the North Sea, and earlier to the south of Biscay.

Buying Advice: The status of horse mackerel stocks is unknown and scientists recommend no further expansion in these fisheries. Avoid eating immature fish under 25cm.

Sea Bass
Dicentrarchus labrax

Profile, Wild: Range in the region of the continental shelf, generally in open water but also near the bottom. They mostly form small shoals which hunt together for food, usually pilchards, migrating northwards in summer as they search. The back is dark grey or olive and the main colour of the body silver. The flesh is a cross between white curdy texture and rich oily flavour, highly rated and much sought after. Cooking this fish whole is also a good move since the bone gives the flesh more flavour as it cooks.

Profile, Farmed: Using sea-located cages around the eastern Mediterranean from Greece to Turkey and Cyprus to Malta, they are also being farmed off the coast of Wales. Farming is able to supply the demand for a whole fish per portion which is smaller than the minimum 40cm allowed for wild fish. The downside to farming is possible environmental contamination. They are carnivorous fish that require more fish in their diet than they actually produce, causing a loss of marine proteins and oils. Also, the fish used to make their feed cannot be assumed to have come from a sustainable supply. Texture of farmed stock is less firm and the flavour has less character.

Size: Male bass mature at 31-35cm (aged 3-6 years) and females mature at 40-45cm (aged 5-8 years). It is a long-lived species, which may exceed 25 years of age, and can achieve a length of up to 1m with a weight of 12kg.

Spawning Habits: Breed from March to mid-June, mostly in April, in British coastal and offshore waters.

Buying Advice: Avoid eating sea bass captured by pelagic trawls. Avoid fish below 40cm. Choose line or net-caught fish. Ensure nets are 'dolphin friendly'. For more information on line-caught and tagged sea bass from Cornwall, see *www.linecaught.org.uk*.

Marine Stewardship Council Certified Sustainable Fishery: A gill-net fishery off the Holderness Coast (NE England), between Flamborough Head Lighthouse and Spurn Point and managed by the North Eastern Sea Fisheries Committee (NESFC), has been certified.

Look for the MSC sustainable label (blue with a white tick). Visit *www.msc.org/track-a-fishery* for up-to-date information.

Sea Wolf or Wolf-fish or 'Catfish'
Anarhichas lupus

Profile, Wild: Not a true catfish, it ranges from Greenland and Spitzbergen as far as Cape Cod to the west and France to the east. It is a dark, blue-grey or greenish colour, one of three species found in northern European seas. They are sometimes referred to as 'catfish', although true catfish are a freshwater fish. They are solitary fish living in 'lairs' close to the seabed. Voracious-looking, they have a set of pointed teeth at the front and another set of crushing teeth for eating sea urchins, crabs and molluscs. They do not eat other fish. Their shellfish diet gives the flesh a distinctive flavour.

Size: They are a slow growing fish that can grow to 125-150cm, although the majority landed are less than 100cm.

Spawning Habits: Become sexually mature at an age of 8-10 years and at a length of 50-60 cm, weight 1-3 kg. Spawning takes place in winter (October–January).

Buying Advice: May be caught on longlines or as a by-catch in mixed trawl fisheries. Because it is a slow-growing fish that would be quickly affected by heavy fishing, avoid unless from a known sustainable method. There is no information available on stock status in European waters. Iceland does manage its sea wolf fishery but catches are over the set quota, which in turn is set beyond scientific advice.

FLAT FISH WITH BOTH EYES ON THE SAME SIDE – WHITE-FLESHED

Brill; dab; flounder; halibut; megrim; plaice; sole, Dover; sole, lemon; sole, witch; turbot.

Brill or Kite
Scophthalmus rhombus

Profile, Wild: Ranges off the European shores of the Atlantic from Norway, southwards as far as the coast of Morocco; also in the Baltic, the Mediterranean and the Black Sea. It has a greenish or greyish brown upper surface, mottled with large dark and small white spots. This colour changes according to habitat. The blind side is creamy white. The flesh may be less meaty than turbot, its close relative, but it is on a par with the A-list Dover sole. Compared with the bony bumps on the turbot, brill has scales and is more oval than the round-shaped turbot. Best roasted whole to preserve the natural flavour and fish juices.

Size: Females are fully mature at about 4 years and 40cms. Both sexes grow to about 50cm. Usual weight 1.5-2kg. Maximum weight 3.6kg.

Spawning Habits: May to August

Buying Advice: Brill is mainly taken as by-catch in beam trawl fisheries in the North Sea. A considerable proportion of the catch is immature and the stock over-exploited. The state of the stock in the Baltic Sea is unknown. Avoid eating immature fish (less than 40cm) as these will not have had a chance to spawn.

Dab
Limanda limanda

Profile, Wild: Dab live on the sandy beds of coastal waters throughout the north-east Atlantic, from Iceland and Norway to the Bay of Biscay, also in the White and Baltic seas. Dab is a right-eyed flatfish (both eyes are on the right side of the body); it has a pronounced arc in the lateral line above its pectoral fin. Its upper surface is brown or greyish brown, marked with irregular darker spots. The blind side is white. It has a good flavour and delicate texture on a par with other flat fish, which are more sought after and less plentiful.

Size: In the North Sea the males become sexually mature at 2-3 years when 10-20cm long, the females at 3-5 years when 20-25cm. It can reach a length of about 40cm and an age of 10-12 years.

Spawning Habits: Southern England and the North Sea (April to June).

Buying Advice: Dab is mostly taken as by-catch in trawl fisheries and often discarded, so by choosing to eat this under-utilised fish you are helping to reduce this wasteful practice. Avoid eating immature fish below about 20cm, and fresh fish caught during or prior to the breeding season (April-June).

Flounder or Flukie
Platichthys flesus

Profile, Wild: It is the only flat fish found in freshwater estuaries living in the sandy or clayey seabed from the intertidal zone to a depth of 60m. It moves to deeper water in winter to spawn in the spring. It ranges along the coasts of Europe from the Barents Sea to Gibraltar, in the Mediterranean, the Black Sea and the Sea of Azov. The upper side is a dull brown, grayish or dull green, and may have light orange speckles. The blind side is white. Like the dab, its flesh is underrated and can often be as good, if not better, than plaice.

Size: Males become sexually mature when 2-3 years old (20-25cm) and females when 3-4 years old (25-30cm), but in the northern part of the range some mature 1-2 years later. They grow to 50-60cm and can live up to 15 years.

Spawning Habits: In the southern North Sea from February to May

Buying Advice: There are no targeted fisheries for flounder and they are taken as by-catch in trawl nets. Avoid eating immature fish (less than 25cm) and fresh fish caught during the spawning season (February-May in the North Sea).

Halibut, Atlantic
Hippoglossus hippoglossus

Profile, Wild: It is the largest flat fish and lives in deep, cold waters ranging from the North Atlantic and adjoining areas of the Arctic Ocean. Its back varies in colour from greenish brown to dark brown or black. The blind side is pearly white. Now a highly esteemed flat fish with a high market value.

Profile, Farmed: Some farmed fish available but they are carnivorous fish that require more fish in their diet than they actually produce, causing a loss of marine proteins and oils. Also, the fish used to make their feed cannot be assumed to have come from a sustainable supply. The best choice is organic.

Size: Can attain a length of 2.5m and 300kg. Atlantic halibut become sexually mature at 10-14 years and can live over 50 years.

Spawning Habits: During winter and early spring.

Buying Advice: Atlantic halibut is heavily overfished, which means it is caught in such high numbers that a sustainable fishery cannot be maintained by the current population size. Assessed as 'Endangered'. Avoid unless from a known sustainable source.

Marine Stewardship Council Certified Sustainable Fishery: Pacific halibut is less vulnerable to overfishing and fisheries are generally much better managed. Longline fisheries for Pacific halibut in US waters off Alaska, Washington and Oregon are certified as environmentally responsible fisheries by the Marine Stewardship Council (MSC). The longline fisheries for Pacific halibut in Pacific waters of British Columbia, Canada, are currently undergoing assessment by the MSC.

Look for the MSC sustainable label (blue with a white tick). Visit *www.msc.org/track-a-fishery* for up to date information.

Megrim
Lepidorhombus whiffiagonis

Profile, Wild: Ranges the Atlantic coasts of Europe and Africa from Iceland and northern Norway to Morocco. It is a deep water fish found in shelf seas throughout this area. It has a light yellowish upper surface with some dark markings. The blind side is white. Its flesh may be a little dry and not quite up there among the most flavourful flat fish. Yet it should not be ignored, as it has been, when most of the UK's catches are shipped to Spain and Portugal.

Size: Mature at about 20cms at 2.5 years old. Males reach maturity first at a lower length and age than females. It can attain a length of about 60cm, although more usually 35-45cm and a maximum age of 14-15 years.

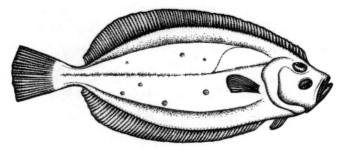

megrim

Spawning Habits: Between January and April along the edge of the continental shelf to the southwest and west of the British Isles. Also spring spawning in Iceland waters.

Buying Advice: Prime season May-June. Not at its best during peak spawning, February-March. The state of stocks is generally unknown, but indications are that they are stable. It is a more sustainable option to plaice and sole which are overfished. Avoid eating immature fish less than 20-25cm.

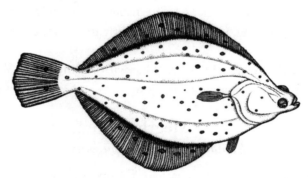

plaice

Plaice
Pleuronectes platessa

Profile, Wild: Ranges in the Atlantic from Iceland and off the south coast of Greenland to Gibraltar. Also in the Mediterranean and the Baltic Sea. Its upper surface is a rich brown or greenish brown, marked irregularly with bright red or orange spots. Its flesh is exceptionally fine and delicate. It is very popular in Denmark and Sweden.

Size: Reaches sexual maturity between 3-7 years (female), 2-6 years (male). They are between 35cm and 45cm in their sixth year. Minimum landing size is 30cm.

Spawning Habits: January to March.

Buying Advice: Prime season June-July. Not at their best when spawning, February-March. Variable availability from January-April. Stocks have been subject to intense fishing pressure in many areas where they are now scarce. Avoid sizes below 30cm.

Sole, Dover, Common, Black or True
Solea solea

Profile, Wild: Live mostly on sandy seabeds round the Atlantic coasts of Europe and Africa, the Mediterranean Sea, the southern parts of the North Sea and the western parts of the Baltic Sea. The upper surface is brown with irregular light and dark spots, with a black spot at the end of the pectoral fin. The underside is creamy white. Its outstanding flavour and meaty texture have made it overfished in certain places. Flavour develops 24 hours after catching. It is best grilled whole.

Size: Become sexually mature at 3-5 years, when 25-35cm long; the males are smaller than the females. It can grow to 60-70cm and weigh 3kg.

Spawning Habits: In shallow coastal waters from April to June in the southern North Sea; from May-June off the coast of Ireland and southern England; and as early as February in the Mediterranean.

Buying Advice: Stocks in the Irish Sea are depleted and a closure of the fishery is recommended. Avoid immature sole (less than 28cm) and fresh fish caught during the breeding season (April-June). Stocks in the Celtic Sea, North Sea, Skagerrak and Kattegat and Bay of Biscay are classified as healthy and harvested sustainably. The Eastern English Channel population is healthy but the fishing effort is too high and stock levels in the Western Channel are unknown. The state of the stocks in the seas of SW and W Ireland are unknown.

Marine Stewardship Council Certified Sustainable Fishery: Dover sole from the Hastings Fleet trammel net, gill net and otter trawl fisheries in the Eastern English Channel are certified as environmentally sustainable fisheries by the Marine Stewardship Council.

Look for the MSC sustainable label (blue with a white tick). Visit *www.msc. org/track-a-fishery* for up to date information.

Sole, Lemon
Microstomus kitt

Profile, Wild: Ranges in the Atlantic Ocean from the White Sea to the Bay of Biscay, including the North Sea and Iceland. It has a relatively thick, fleshy body and small head. Its upper surface is usually brown or reddish brown with dark irregular spots. It prefers sandy or stony seabeds of 30-200m depth. It has a fine, delicate flesh rated above plaice and flounder but below Dover sole.

Size: Sexual maturity occurs in males at 3-4 years and at 4-6 years in females around 25cm length. It can live for up to 17 years, reaching a length of over 60cm.

Spawning Habits: Spring and summer with a peak in March-May.

Buying Advice: Prime season July-August. Not at their best from March-May during peak spawning. Does not have a designated fishery but is a trawl by-catch. Avoid immature fish under 25cm.

Turbot
Psetta maxima

Profile, Wild: Ranges in the Atlantic from the middle of Norway southwards to Gibraltar, also in the Baltic, the Mediterranean and the Black Sea. It is a round shape and its colour varies depending on its habitat. Its upper side is usually dark greyish or olive brown with dark spots all over, even on the fins. The blind side is white. The flesh is firm and succulent with a highly desirable flavour, a luxury fish for special occasions. It should be left for 24-48 hours after catching for the flavour and texture to mature.

Profile, Farmed: In Norway, Portugal, Spain, France and the UK. They are carnivorous fish that require more fish in their diet than they actually produce, causing a loss of marine proteins and oils. Also, the fish used to make their feed cannot be assumed to have come from a sustainable supply.

Size: Becomes sexually mature at an age of 3-5 years and females each produce up to 10-15 million eggs. In the North Sea it reaches a length of 30cm (males) and

35cm (females) in about 3 years. In the Baltic Sea growth is slower, and the males become sexually mature at a length of 15cm, the females at 20cm. For some reason males are generally more abundant than females. Turbot can attain a length of 1m and a weight of 25kg. Females are larger than males at any given age. Maximum reported age is 25 years.

Spawning Habits: In most parts of its range, spawns in April to August.

Buying Advice: Not at their best June-August. There is no specific management of the turbot fishery except for a minimum landing size of 30cm in Cornwall. Stock levels are unknown and the limited information available suggests that they are overfished. Avoid unless from a known sustainable source.

Witch Flounder (or Torbay Sole)
Glyptocephalus cynoglossus

Profile, Wild: Ranges the Atlantic from northern Norway south to northern Spain. It is a moderately deep-water fish which lives on the lower continental shelf. Its upper side varies in colour according to the habitat, while its blind side is white. Its flesh is similar to Megrim, not as flavoured or meaty as Dover sole, but deserves to be better appreciated.

Size: Has a slow growth rate, and reaches sexual maturity in 3-4 years. Witch on average live for about 14 years, but the maximum reported age is 25 years.

Spawning Habits: From March to September.

Buying Advice: Avoid eating immature fish (less than 28cm) and fresh fish caught during the breeding season (March-September). Witch sole fisheries in EU waters outside the 6 mile limit are unregulated, i.e. there is no Minimum Landing Size (MLS) or other measures specified, and so they are generally taken as by-catch in trawls targeting whitefish.

In some coastal areas of England and Wales MLSs are enforced, e.g. Cornwall Sea Fisheries District and North Western and North Wales SFC prohibit the landing of witch below 28cm.

SHARK, SWORDFISH AND RAY FAMILIES
Shark; Dogfish or Catshark; Swordfish; Marlin; Ray; Skate

Shark (Various Species)

Profile, Wild: There are between 380-480 species of shark found world-wide. Depending on species, sharks are thought to live for between 25 and 200 years. They are slow-growing and have a low reproductive capacity.

Spawning Habits: Internal fertilisation of eggs.

Buying Advice: Worldwide it is estimated that 100 million sharks are killed each year, directly threatening their long-term survival. 16 of 21 oceanic pelagic shark and ray species have been classified as threatened or near threatened. Many are killed for their fins, which are used to make the high status 'Shark-fin Soup' popular in the Far East. Shark meat is also sold skinned and cut into steaks. It may also be sold deep-fried in fish and chip shops as 'flake'. Sharks are vulnerable to exploitation because they are slow-growing, long-lived, and have low reproductive capacity.

Dogfish or Catshark
Scyliorhinus canicula

Profile, Wild: A small shark which lives in sandy, muddy sea beds and is common in European Atlantic waters from the middle of Norway to below the equator: also occurs in the Mediterranean and Black Sea. It is a yellowish brown to grayish red colour with small dark spots and a few larger spots on its back and fins. Its belly is light and unspotted.

Size: Females and males mature from 54 to 60cm in length at around 5 years of age. Can grow up to 1m in length, maximum age is unknown.

Spawning Habits: Mating occurs from late summer to November, after which females move to spawning grounds in shallower water. The shark embryos are enclosed in cases (called mermaids' purses) whilst they develop and mature (usually around June/July).

Buying Advice: Due to landings being recorded as mixed-shark in many cases, it is difficult to be certain of stock patterns for any species. The fisheries for all shark species and particularly those for dogfishes (catshark, huss and spiny dogfish) would benefit from species specific recording of landings/catches.

Swordfish
Xiphias gladius

Profile, Wild: Ranges all the world's oceans. It is a highly migratory species, moving towards temperate or cold waters in summer to feed and returning to warmer waters to spawn. Its back is a deep blue-black and the upper part of its sides have a metallic blue sheen, while the lower half is lighter in colour. Its flesh is highly valued, sold fresh as steaks and very popular for Japanese sashimi and teri-yaki.

Size: Females mature at 5-6 years at a length of 150-170cm. Males reach sexual maturity at smaller sizes. They can attain a maximum size of 4.5m and a weight of 650kg. Most swordfish over 140kg are female.

Spawning Habits: In the Atlantic spawning takes place in spring in the southern Sargasso Sea, in spring and summer in the Pacific and June-August in the Mediterranean. Usually solitary, it forms large schools during spawning.

Buying Advice: It is subject to high fishing pressure in all the world's oceans. Avoid swordfish in the Mediterranean, which is considered overfished. In the South-western Pacific Ocean the swordfish stock is estimated to be within safe levels, however there is uncertainty regarding the reliability of the information on its stocks. Swordfish from the East Pacific is moderately to fully exploited, with no room for increased catches. The North Atlantic stock is considered endangered. Increase its sustainability by choosing swordfish from US-managed waters in the North Atlantic where measures are in place to reduce by-catch of endangered marine turtles. In Brazilian fisheries similar measures to reduce turtle by-catch are being developed based on the US fisheries programme.

Marlin, Atlantic Blue
Makiaria nigricans
Atlantic White
Tetrapturus albidus

Profile, Wild: Ranges in tropical and temperate waters of the Atlantic, Pacific and Indian Oceans. They are large marine predators feeding on a variety of fish and squid.

Size: White marlin can reach 300cm and blue marlin 500cm.

Buying Advice: In the Pacific, blue marlin is thought to be fully exploited. In the Atlantic, white marlin and blue marlin are considered overfished; avoid eating these species from this area.

Ray, Thornback or Roker*
Raja clavata

Profile, Wild: Ranges almost all the coasts of Europe, also along the Atlantic coast of Africa. Variably coloured but usually cinnamon brown to light grey on the back and pale cream on the belly. The edible fins or 'wing' flesh of this ray is generally regarded to be one of the best for eating.

Size: Females can grow to 118cm and weigh 18kg, males can grow to 98cm. Females mature between 60 and 85cm while males mature between 60 and 77cm (in both cases corresponding to an age of 5 to 10 years). The species has a maximum recorded age of 16 years.

Spawning Habits: Fertilisation takes place internally and the female lays eggs which are hatched 16-20 weeks later.

Buying Advice: Although once one of the most abundant of this species in the North-east Atlantic and Mediterranean, commercial exploitation has reduced stocks in much of its natural range. Using landings and catch data, scientists believe that it is stable or increasing in the southern North Sea and Eastern English Channel, West Scotland, Irish Sea, Bristol Channel and south-east Ireland, but are uncertain about its stock status in the northern and central North Sea, Bay of Biscay and Iberian waters.

Skate, Common*
Dipturus batis

Profile, Wild: Ranges the Atlantic from Iceland and northern Norway southwards to the western part of the Mediterranean. Colouring varies from olive grey to dark cinnamon brown, usually with irregular light and dark spots. The edible fins or 'wings' are considered good eating.

Size: The common skate is the largest European fish with the pectoral fins fused to the sides of the head. Females can reach lengths of about 280cm and males about 200cm. Males mature at a length of about 125cm and females at about 180cm (both over 10 years old). The species can live for 50 years.

Spawning Habits: Fertilisation takes place internally and the female lays eggs which are hatched 16-20 weeks later.

Buying Advice: It is no longer 'common' but becoming very rare in UK shallow seas and in European waters, and is now assessed as *Critically Endangered* by the World Conservation Union. Avoid eating. It is prohibited for fishermen to retain and land common skate caught within EU waters.

*Note on skates and rays: They are both vulnerable to overfishing. Little is known about the stock status of many individual species because they have been historically landed under generic skate and ray categories. However, now EU countries must report species specific landings of major skate and ray types in the North Sea and Norwegian Sea, so that in the future scientists will be able to advise on species specific catches. Only fisheries for the smaller, faster growing species such as spotted, cuckoo and starry rays can be considered as potentially sustainable at present. Avoid, unless they are one of the smaller, more sustainable species.

FRESHWATER FISH
Grayling; Perch; Pike; Carp

Grayling
Thymallus thymallus

Profile, Wild: Found in most European countries north of the 45th latitude and east as far as the Urals. Young fish are silvery white with a grayish green to dark blue back and with iridescent sides. Mature fish are darker and have black spots on their body and dorsal fin. In the spawning season, the males in particular are brightly and diversely coloured and their characteristic wide high dorsal fin becomes iridescent with shades of red and violet. It lives in shoals in open water. In rivers it is mainly where slow-flowing water and rapids alternate; such stretches are known as grayling zones. It has firm, white flesh with a fine flavour.

Size: 30-50cm, occasionally up to 50-60cm.

Spawning Habits: In pairs from March to May over a gravelly sandy bottom. Mature females deposit eggs in shallow excavations. Deterioration of natural spawning grounds has made artificial breeding necessary in some European countries.

Buying: An angler's fish, not sold commercially.

Perch
Perca fluviatilis

Profile, Wild: Found in Europe and parts of Siberia but absent from Scotland and Norway and from the south-eastern European peninsulas. It lives in lakes, rivers, fishponds and reservoirs. Its body is distinctly coloured, grayish-green to yellowish-green, with a dark back and five to nine black cross bars on the sides. The belly is lighter. The pectoral, ventral, anal and caudal fins are yellowish orange to red. Its flesh is tasty, firm and white.

Size: 30cm, occasionally 40cm, maximum 50cm.

Spawning Habits: In spring, usually in April and May.

Buying: An angler's fish. Small quantities of British caught perch are exported to Europe.

Pike
Esox lucius

Profile, Wild: Found in Europe, except the southern peninsulas; in Asia in the basins of rivers flowing into the Arctic Ocean; also found in America from Alaska to Ohio and Labrador. It has a grayish-green to markedly dark back, sometimes tinged with red or brown, greenish sides marked with yellow spots which sometimes run together to form bands, and a white grey-spotted belly. It is a predatory fish known as the 'freshwater wolf', and has been described as a 'tyrant' of the rivers. It has a highly esteemed texture and flavour, though its Y-shaped bones can be troublesome.

Size: Up to 1.5m (mostly 0.5–1m).

Spawning Habits: Spawn as soon as the water temperature reaches 4-10 degrees C in the spring. Closed season 15 March–15 June.

Buying: An angler's fish. Seldom sold in the marketplace.

Carp
Cyprinus carpio

Profile, Wild: Native to lakes and rivers in Eastern Europe and southern Asia, it was brought to Britain by the Romans. It has golden yellow to brown sides, a darker back and a yellowish-white belly. An angler's fish, especially in England, it provides sport for freshwater anglers who return the 'caught' carp to the water and do not eat it. This is a habit which Eastern Europeans find very strange, since for them a whole carp is a highly prized, special-occasion dish. Provided it has not spent too much time in very muddy waters, when its flavour becomes 'earthy', it should have a firm sweet flesh. Its soft roe is a delicacy.

Profile, Farmed: Traditionally it was kept in carp ponds where it grew fat on household scraps, and was widely eaten on 'fast days' when no meat was allowed. Now it is farmed commercially, and some organically. Unlike most farmed fish, carp will thrive on an entirely vegetarian diet (medieval monks fed their carp corn and potatoes) making it more sustainable than carnivorous farmed fish.

Size: 40-80cm, maximum 1m.

Spawning Habits: Carp become sexually mature at 4-5 years, and spawn in the water margins of lakes and rivers at the end of May and in June. The eggs are attached to aquatic plants. Closed season 15 March–15 June.

Buying: Farmed carp provides a more sustainable alternative to wild fish, which are not plentiful.

SHELLFISH: CRUSTACEANS

Crab, Brown, Partan
Cancer pagurus

Profile, Wild: It ranges in European coastal waters as far north as Norway, but not on the American side of the Atlantic. Its shell (carapace) is a hard reddish-brown with a 'pie-crust' edge. Like other crustaceans, it sheds its shell to allow growth. Moulting takes place at frequent intervals during its first years, but only every two years after it is fully grown, when its growth slows down. The juvenile crab settles in the intertidal zone and remains in these habitats for 3 years, until it reaches

6-7cm shell width, at which time it migrates to subtidal habitats. Its flesh is less highly rated than lobster, but it is not a less excellent flavour.

Size: The minimum landing size is 13-14cm carapace width (CW) in most areas of the UK. Average weight 1-2kg. It can grow up to about 25cm and live for up to 100 years, but average age is around 25-30 years.

Spawning Habits: Mainly in the winter months.

Buying Advice: Prime season May-September. Males contain more white meat than females which have more brown meat. Males have larger claws and their tail flap is narrower and more pointed than females. Avoid in January to March and crabs below the minimum 14cm, also crab claws, unless it is certain they have been removed after landing. Egg-bearing or 'berried' females should be avoided at all times to allow them to spawn. There is no formal assessment of crab stocks.

Crab, Spider
Maia squinado

Profile, Wild: Found in the east Atlantic from Scotland south to Guinea, also in the southern North Sea, the English Channel and most parts of the Mediterranean. The colour of the carapace varies from reddish orange to brown. It gets its name from the spider-like arrangement of its legs. It inhabits coarse sand grounds and open bedrock and congregates in large numbers, forming 'mounds'. Its flesh is highly rated, particularly in France.

Size: This is the largest crab found in British waters, with a carapace width (CW) of up to 20cm and a leg span of 50cm or more. CWs for mature adults are from 8.5-20cm for males and 7-17.5cm for females. Minimum landing size 12cm.

Spawning Habits: Large migrations occur during the early spring, when they move into shallower water to spawn. Females become berried (egg-bearing) from April onwards; by June all mature females are berried. Hatching occurs from July until November when they migrate back to deeper water.

Buying Advice: Avoid eating immature crabs below the legal minimum landing size, 12cm CW, egg-bearing crabs and fresh crabs caught during the spawning season (April-July). Catching in pots is the most sustainable method, since there is no by-catch of non-target species and small crabs may be returned to the sea alive. However, tangle nets are the main fishing method used to capture spider crabs.

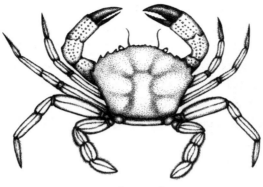

velvet crab

Crab, Velvet or Velvet Swimming
Liocarcanus puber

Profile, Wild: Its range is from the north Atlantic to the coast of the western Sahara and in the North Sea from southern Norway to the English Channel. Also in western parts of the Mediterranean. It is the largest swimming crab and lives on rocky bottoms from the shoreline to a depth of about 65m. It can be distinguished by its back pair of flattened swimming legs. In contrast to brown crabs, velvet crabs are not thought to undertake extensive migrations and rarely move further than a few hundred metres.

Size: It reaches a mature carapace width (CW) around 4cm at between 1-2 years, though CW varies according to location. Mature CW is 10cm. Females grow more slowly and to a smaller maximum size than males, differences which are likely to be due to reduced growth during the female's egg-bearing phase. Growth is highly seasonal; the main moult for males is between April and July, whereas females moult between May and August. It may live for four to six years. It has a rich shellfish flavour similar to squat lobster.

Spawning Habits: Mating occurs after females have moulted, when their shell is still soft between May and August. Spawning studies, carried out in Orkney and Shetland, have shown estimated numbers of eggs produced ranging from 5,000 to 278,000 per female.

Buying Advice: Avoid under 6.5 cm CW. Most are landed after mating between July and November. The Scottish fishery for 'velvets' began in the early 1980s, when the Spanish fishery collapsed. It developed rapidly to supply southern European markets, and became the largest velvet crab fishery in Europe. (In 2008, the fishery landed 2,800 tonnes of velvet crab into Scotland with a value of £6.1 million.) Velvet crabs are caught in the inshore creel fishery along with lobster and brown crab. Very few fishermen fish solely for 'velvets'. Though the fishery began in the west coast and on Orkney, it has now moved into the east coast. In 2008, the majority of landings came from Orkney, South Minch, East Coast, Hebrides and South-east areas.

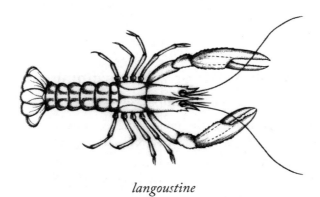

langoustine

Langoustine or Norwegian Lobster, Italian Scampi, Dublin Bay 'Prawn'
Nephrops norvegicus

Profile, Wild: Its range is from Iceland to Morocco and the West Central Mediterranean. There is also a colony in the Adriatic, exploited by Italy. It is caught in Scotland from the North Sea and inshore west coast waters. The carapace is pale pink, rose or orange-red; the claws are banded in red and white. It lives in burrows on the seabed and is limited to a muddy habitat, requiring sediment with a silt and clay content to excavate burrows. Tail flesh is very highly rated.

Size: Males grow relatively quickly to around 6cm carapace length (CL) from tail to head, not including the claws, but seldom exceed 10 years old. Females grow more slowly and can reach 20 years old. Females mature at about 3 years. Maximum CL 24cm.

Spawning Habits: In the autumn they lay eggs which remain attached to the tail for 9 months. Hatching occurs in the spring.

Buying Advice: Prime season October–November. Not at their best from June-August, and avoid berried (egg-carrying) females which fishermen should have released. Increase the sustainability by choosing pot or creel caught rather than trawled.

Marine Stewardship Council Certified Sustainable Fishery: Trawl fisheries are associated with large quantities of by-catch, including overfished species such as cod and juvenile fish. The Loch Torridon creel fishery, and the Stornoway trawl fishery, have been certified as environmentally sustainable fisheries by the MSC.

Look for the MSC sustainable label (blue label with white tick). Visit *www. msc.org/track-a-fishery* for up to date information.

Lobster, European
Homarus gammarus

Profile, Wild: Its range is from the north Atlantic to the Mediterranean, including the North Sea, the English Channel and the west Baltic. It has a dark blue shell (turning scarlet red when boiled) with pale yellow markings and long red antennae. The claws are of unequal size, with one large crushing claw and a slimmer cutting claw. It inhabits rocky seabeds, living in caves and excavated burrows from the lower shore to 60m depth. It is the most highly rated, and also the most expensive, shellfish from Scottish waters.

Profile, Farmed: Lobster hatcheries have been set up in Orkney, Wales and Cornwall to release young lobster into the wild.

Size: Carapace length (CL: between the back of the eye socket and the furthest edge of the carapace) can grow up to 100cm, but lengths of around 50cm are more typical. Females mature at around 7.5-8cm (CL), at 5-7 years of age. They may live 50 years or more.

Spawning Habits: It mates in late summer when the females moult, but females can store the sperm packet over the winter, so eggs are not fertilised and laid until the following summer. Female lobsters bearing or carrying eggs are termed 'berried'.

Buying Advice: Prime season June and July, then September-November (sheds shell in August). Avoid below the legal minimum landing size, 9cm (CL). Avoid breeding females with eggs which contribute to the breeding stock. Choose creel or pot-caught lobsters. Variable availability January-March.

Marine Stewardship Council Certified Sustainable Fishery: The lobster pot fishery off the Yorkshire coast is undergoing MSC assessment.

Look for the MSC sustainable label (blue with a white tick). Visit *www.msc. org/track-a-fishery* for up to date information.

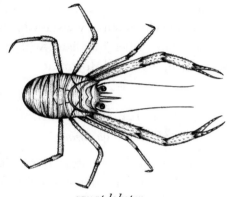

squat lobster

Lobster, Squat
Munida rugosa

Profile, Wild: Its range is throughout the oceans worldwide from near the surface to deep sea. There are currently 870 described species; *M. rugosa* is commonly found in north European waters. It is chestnut brown in colour with a greenish hint and red tipped spines. The carapace is shiny between grooves and has scattered short hairs. It lives under stones and rocks on the lower shore and in crevices and fissures in the subtidal zone to depths of about 70m. Though very much smaller than the European lobster, its tail flesh is an excellent flavour and highly rated.

Size: It can reach total lengths of up to 6.5cm with a carapace length of up to 3.5cm.

Spawning Habits: Females carry eggs during late winter and early spring.

Buying Advice: Avoid late winter and early spring.

Prawn, Common
Palaemon serratus

Profile, Wild: Ranges from Norway to the Mediterranean, round coasts in inshore waters and rock pools. Alive it is almost colourless, but after cooking is an orange-red. If disturbed it shoots backwards. Eating quality of the tail flesh is highly rated.

Size: Market length from 7-8cm. Recommended minimum length 6cm. Maximum 10cm.

Spawning Habits: November to June.

Buying Advice: May be caught in baited pots, fattest in September and October after summer feeding. Avoid November to June spawning.

Prawn, Northern or Pink Shrimp, French Crevette
Pandalus borealis

Profile, Wild: Its range is in the cold deep waters of the north-east Arctic, around Greenland, Norway, Iceland and the North Sea. It lives on muddy sea beds. Its live colour is red, but it is usually cooked at sea when it changes to a pink colour. The tail flesh is highly rated.

Size: It initially develops as a male, and then later becomes female during a 5-year life span. It takes up to 3 years to mature. Total adult length about 15cm.

Spawning Habits: In summer-autumn, females move into coastal waters where eggs hatch in winter. Juveniles remain inshore for about a year before they migrate offshore as they begin to mature.

Buying Advice: The state of prawn stocks is uncertain. Increase sustainability by only choosing prawns taken in fisheries using sorting grids to reduce by-catch of non-target species.

Marine Stewardship Council Certified Sustainable Fishery: The North-east Arctic (Barents Sea) stock is classified as healthy, is harvested sustainably and sorting grids are mandatory. The Canadian and Gulf of St Lawrence fisheries have been certified as sustainable by the Marine Stewardship Council.

Look for the MSC sustainable label (blue with a white tick). Visit *www.msc.org/track-a-fishery* for up to date information, and see also *www.fishonline.org*.

Prawn, Giant or Jumbo, Tiger, Black Gambas, Leader
Penaeus monodon

Profile, Wild: Extensive range in the warm waters of east and south-east Asia, the Red Sea, Arabian Gulf, around the Indian subcontinent, through the Malay Archipelago to northern Australia and the Philippines.

Profile, Farmed: Most commonly farmed in south East Asia. Usually harvested at 6 months at average length 20-28cm.

Size: Males are mature at 3.7cm and females at 4.7cm. Maximum length 33cm.

Spawning Habits: Its lifecycle may be divided into 6 stages or phases, from embryo to adult, which it completes in one year. The age of sexual maturity varies from 5 to 11 months. They can live up to 2 years in the wild.

Buying Advice: Wild prawns: there is extensive damage to the sea bed from trawl fisheries for these prawns, which result in large amounts of bycatch (35% of the world's total) including endangered species.

Farmed prawns: Only buy from suppliers which can ensure their product is sourced from farms that comply with environmental standards for mangrove protection and production. GAA (Global Aquaculture Alliance) certification ensures some of these standards are met. Organic prawn farming also ensures many such standards are met. Look for the Organic label on products or check supermarket policy (see *www.bite-back.com*) if they have buying procedures to ensure high production standards are in place. Farmed imports make up the bulk of the UK supply of these prawns. They may have been farmed unsustainably and fed high energy diets to make them grow fast, producing an inferior prawn.

Prawn, King
Litopenaeus vannamei

This is another warm-water, farmed prawn which is similar to the giant tiger prawn. It is a native species of the Eastern Pacific coast. Can live up to 2 years in the wild, but if farmed is harvested at 6 months.

Buying Advice: Only buy from suppliers which can ensure their product is sourced from farms that comply with environmental standards for habitat protection and impacts of production. Aquaculture Certification Council Best Aquaculture Practice (ACC BAP) and GlobalGap certification ensures some of these standards are met. Organic prawn farming certification also ensures many such standards are met. Requirements for organic farms include utilisation of by-products from human consumption fisheries for feed; habitat protection and restoration; limitation on chemical usage; limited stocking densities and strict health and feeding guidelines. Look for the organic label on products or ask your supermarket (see *www.bite-back.com*) if they have a buying policy for warm water prawns to ensure high production standards are in place and environmental concerns addressed.

Shrimp, Brown
Crangon crangon

Profile, Wild: Its range is from Norway to the Mediterranean. It is a cold-water shrimp, found mainly in shallow coastal waters where it burrows into the sand. Alive, it is greyish-brownish and translucent, pinkish-brown when cooked. Highly esteemed when made into Potted Shrimps. The majority of the shrimps marketed in the UK come from fishing grounds off the south-east coast and Morecambe Bay in the north-west.

Size: It grows to about 8cm and can live for 3-4 years. Minimum recommended size 3cm.

Spawning Habits: Protracted throughout the year. No specific season.

Buying Advice: The best choice to make in terms of sustainability and selectivity is to choose brown shrimp caught in trawls fitted with veil nets and separators, which reduce by-catch of non-target and juvenile fish and shrimp.

CRUSTACEANS: MOLLUSCS

Limpet
Patella vulgate

Profile, Wild: Found in European waters, its shell is usually grey, yellowish or brown. Its muscle is round and rubbery and if old will be very tough to eat. A younger limpet will be less tough and will soften with cooking. Though not sold in the marketplace, the Scots limpet has been both used as fishing bait, and eaten as a valued food, for centuries.

Size: Maximum diameter 7 cm.

Spawning Habits: September–January. Males change into females as they mature, so if wild-foraging on the seashore it is best not to take too many large ones, or the breeding potential could be threatened.

whelk (l) and periwinkle

Whelk, Scots Dog Whelk
Buccinum undatum

Profile, Wild: It is found on all coasts of the Atlantic, from the tidal zone down to 200m, on all types of sea beds. It is a large marine snail, with strong shells of variable colours, sometimes with spiral bands or blotches. Highly rated as a seaside food in England, sold from the whelk stall along with other shellfish. Also exported to Japan and South Korea where they are highly prized.

Size: It is long-lived (up to about 15 years) and can grow up to about 10cm in length. Sexual maturity occurs at 5-7 years.

Spawning Habits: Mates during autumn and winter. The eggs are laid between November and January and hatch 3-9 months later. Baby whelks emerge from the egg capsules in the spring.

Buying Advice: Since it is long-lived, it is subject to increasing fishing pressure as a large and expanding market has developed in the Far East. Avoid eating immature whelks (less than 4.5cm) and during their breeding season (November to January).

Periwinkle, Scots Whelk or Buckie
Littorina littorea

Profile, Wild: Its range is the coastal regions of the North Atlantic, where it inhabits rocky shores in all but the most exposed coastlines. In sheltered conditions it can be found in sandy bays and mudflats, particularly in estuaries. It is a blue-black colour with greyish tones. A small marine snail, mainly found between low and high tide, but can be found at depths of 60m in the northern end of its range.

Size: The shell size can attain about 3.5cm in length, but is usually about 2.5cm. Both males and females reach maturity at 1-1.2cm. Winkles usually live about 3 years but can survive for 4-5 years. Minimum recommended size 2cm.

Spawning Habits: Peaks in May and June.

Buying Advice: Most winkles are collected or gathered by hand, which is a selective method of harvesting that causes least habitat disturbance. Minimum landing sizes for winkles vary between regions, but selecting larger, mature winkles (over 2cm) allows them to have spawned. There are no stock assessments for winkles and it is highly likely that the harvest is under-recorded. Choose winkles harvested by hand-gathering methods in areas which are well managed.

A Scots whelk is an English winkle: It's not clear why many Scots decided to name the grey-black, curly-shelled winkle a 'whelk', pronounced 'wilk', but they did. Just to confuse things further, they called the English whelk a 'dog whelk'.

BIVALVES

Clam, Razor or Scots Spoot
Ensis siliqua

Profile, Wild: Widely found in intertidal waters throughout UK and temperate seas. Its shell is a glossy brown or yellowish brown with a white interior. Its muscle is a long powerful 'foot', which burrows into the sediment around the extreme

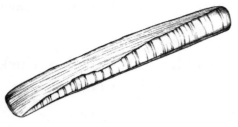

spoot

low water mark and in shallow subtidal areas. It is a filter feeding bivalve and is capable of rapid burrowing if disturbed. The shells get their name from the shape of the old-fashioned cut-throat razor. The muscle flesh is good eating and highly esteemed in the Far East and the Continent, where Scottish razor clam fishermen have found a useful market.

Profile, Farmed: The commercial rearing or farming of razor clams is well established in some areas of Spain, and its commercial potential is now being developed in the UK and Ireland.

Size: They are relatively long-lived and may survive to 10-15 years; an average adult can reach a size of 21cm. Growth stops around age 10.

Spawning Habits: In summer (June–August), hours after they are fertilised, eggs develop into mobile larvae which drift with the current for 3-4 weeks, then settle, attaching themselves to sand or shell by fine strong threads.

Buying Advice: Buy more during prime season – April–May and then September–November. Largely unavailable during the winter months from December to March. Avoid clams dredged from wild stocks. Choose clams harvested in the wild by sustainable methods only (such as hand-gathering). Avoid undersized (less than 10cm) and wild clams harvested during the spawning season (June–August).

Other species of razor clams found in British intertidal waters: *E. ensis, E. arcuatus.*

Cockle

Cerastoderma edule

Profile, Wild: Its range is from the Barents Sea and the Baltic to the Mediterranean and Senegal. Found buried in mud and sand in estuaries and on sandy beaches, nearly all commercial cockle beds are on large intertidal flats in lower reaches of estuaries. Its two identical oval shells are scored with radiating ridges and are either a light brown, pale yellow or a dirty white colour. It has been found in very high densities of ten thousand per square metre. Around £20 million worth of cockles are taken from the UK's muddy beaches each year, of which 75 per cent is swiftly exported, mostly to Holland, Belgium, France and Spain. Companies from these countries have started taking over the UK industry. It is in urgent need of a new image in the UK and has suffered too much as a vinegar-doused adjunct to greasy chips.

Size: The shell size is up to 5cm long, although average sizes tend to be around 3-4cm. Maturity occurs at a shell length of around 2cm.

Spawning Habits: From May to August, although exact times will vary from region to region.

Buying Advice: Choose cockles harvested legally using sustainable methods only. Over-exploitation by mechanical harvesting and dredging causes damage to stocks, disturbance of seabed or estuary and depletion of prey species for birds and other marine life.

Marine Stewardship Council Certified Sustainable Fishery: The fishery in Burry Inlet, Wales, is certified as an environmentally responsible fishery by the MSC.

Look for the MSC sustainable label (blue with a white tick). Visit *www.msc.org/track-a-fishery* for up to date information.

Mussel, Blue or Common
Mytilus edulis

Profile, Wild: Its range is throughout the North Atlantic, Mediterranean, North and Baltic Seas. It normally lives in large colonies, attaching itself to rocks and other mussels with strong, sticky threads known as *byssus*. It can be found from the high intertidal zone to the shallow subtidal zone. Colour is usually dark blue-black, though it may vary with tinges of deep bluish purple. It has become one of the most popular UK shellfish, largely due to the extensive availability of farmed mussels, a method of aquaculture with potential for development. A mussel, farmed or wild, will vary in flavour according to its feeding and the ratio of salt to freshwater of its habitat. Some experts can distinguish the location of a mussel by its flavour.

Profile, Farmed: Widely farmed, usually on ropes. Mussel farming is an extensive, low impact method of cultivation which has increased the abundance of mussel seed in the wild.

Size: Size and shape vary widely. Minimum recommended shell size is 5cm. Can grow up to 10cm but usually much smaller. Mussels mature when one year old and may live 10-15 years or more.

Spawning Habits: Peaks in early spring (April) and continues to late summer (August), with larvae settling after 1-6 months.

Buying Advice: Prime season after summer feeding in September–February. Avoid March, April and May. Stocks are generally considered to be under-exploited. The main methods of harvesting wild and farmed mussels are by dredging and hand-gathering. Choose mussels which have been sustainably harvested in the wild (by hand-gathering) or farmed.

Mussel, Horse or Clabbie Dubh (Gaelic), Yoag (Shetland)
Modiolus modiolus

Profile, Wild: A larger version of the common mussel, it has a wider range and can be found in the North Atlantic, from the White Sea to the Bay of Biscay and from Labrador to North Carolina. It is also in the North Pacific. Its shell colouring varies from shades of blue-black to purple. This is covered with a thin glossy covering (the perisostracum) which gives adults a yellow or dark brown appearance. Inside its flesh is orange. It is found, part buried, in soft sediment or gravel in dense reefs or beds, usually subtidally to depths of over 100m. Some reefs may become uncovered at exceptionally low tides, when digging up with a fork is necessary to release the firm hold they have on the sea bed. Their orange muscle is sometimes considered coarse, in comparison with the smaller blue mussel. This applies only to large, wrinkled old specimens and not to those younger and smoother shelled, whose flavour and texture is excellent.

Size: Maximum length is 15cm, though they have been known to grow to 23cm. Can live up to 20 years, possibly longer.

Spawning Habits: They spawn all year round, but spawning peaks in early spring (April) to late summer (August).

Not harvested commercially in the UK. Forage on seashores at low tides with a stout garden fork.

native oyster

Oyster, European or Native
Ostrea edulis

Profile, Wild: Ranges from the Norwegian Sea down to the Mediterranean and Morocco. Has a round greyish-coloured shell which is less jagged than the Pacific oyster. It will vary in flavour according to its feeding and the ratio of salt to freshwater of its habitat. The location of an oyster can be identified by its flavour, and oysters from specific locations often take their name from the location. The feel-good factor after eating oysters may have some basis of truth in the fact that they are rich in zinc, which is not an aphrodisiac, but a vital nutrient in preventing tiredness and depression.

Profile, Farmed: Only a small amount of farming compared with the Pacific (gigas) oyster. Farming shellfish is an extensive, low-impact method requiring high quality water standards for cultivation. The precursor to modern oyster farming was first developed in Brittany in the late 1800s when the young 'spat' (the first free swimming oyster) was collected as it anchored to special cupped tiles which were then moved to other areas. This was a response to the depletion, through over-fishing, of very large productive oyster beds such as those in the Firth of Forth. Farming natives is now developing in the UK, particularly on Scotland's west coast.

Size: The average reproductive size for the oyster is about 5cm. Oysters can reach a shell length of up to 11cm, and occur in variable shapes.

Spawning Habits: Initially it begins life as a male, after reaching maturity (between 2-3 years old) it spawns, and then changes into a female. In Britain, breeding normally takes place in the summer between May and August.

Buying Advice: Prime season is September to April. Avoid during the spawning season May to August. Wild oyster fisheries are generally privately owned and managed by Several and Regulation Orders, which prevent other fishing in the oyster bed area. The native oyster is the subject of a Biodiversity Action Plan which aims to maintain and expand where possible the distribution and abundance of natives in UK waters. The Shellfish Association of Great Britain (*www.shellfish. org.uk*) has responsibility for implementing this plan.

Pacific oyster

Oyster, Pacific or Gigas
Crassostrea gigas

Profile, Wild: Originates from north-eastern Asia. It has an elongated oval-shaped shell which is very jagged. The location of an oyster can be identified by its flavour according to its feeding and the ratio of salt to freshwater of its habitat.

Profile, Farmed: More widely farmed than natives. Shellfish farming is an extensive, low-impact method requiring high quality water standards for cultivation.

Size: Maximum size 25cm.

Spawning Habits: As with many oyster species, they develop first as males, spawn, and then later develop into females. Spawning occurs in the summer, but only in its native warm waters of the Pacific. It does not spawn in the UK's colder waters, which make it available to eat all year.

Buying Advice: Widely available all year. May be graded by size from 1-4. Grade 1 is the biggest.

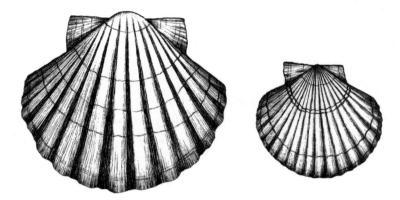

king scallop (l) and queen scallop

Scallop, King or Great
Pecten maximus

Profile, Wild: Ranges throughout the east Atlantic from Norway to the Iberian Peninsula. It has a whitish-brown or pink-coloured shell. Found in shallow waters of sea lochs and to depths of over 100m in coastal areas, where it inhabits sandy-gravel or gravel sea beds. It is fished mostly by dredging, though also by diving and hand selecting. In UK waters the main fishing areas are in the west of Scotland, the Moray Firth, the Irish Sea and the English Channel. Its flesh is highly esteemed and commands high prices.

Profile, Farmed: May be managed by a Several and Regulating Order which allows them to be 'ranched' in the area of the Order. This is seeded with young scallops (spat) and protected from any other fishing or disturbance. Spat are now widely produced in commercial hatcheries.

Size: It is fully mature at about 3 years old when it is 8-9cm in length. It can grow to more than 20cm in length and live for more than 20 years. Average sizes are around 10-16cm.

Spawning Habits: Spawns during the warmer months, from March to August. It is both male and female (a hermaphrodite), having a male reproductive gland which is cream, and a female gland which is orange-red: this is the roe or coral.

Buying Advice: Prime season from September to February. Minimum recommended size 10cm length. Those hand-selected by divers will be larger and of higher quality than those dredged from the seabed, which causes more damage to the seabed. Diving is restricted to a depth of 30m, which gives wild populations a 'refuge' to regenerate. Dive-selected scallops are becoming more available in the marketplace and in restaurants. Check with supplier and look on product labelling for details. Expect restaurants to indicate method of catching on the menu. Buying in the shell will ensure the best flavour and quality. Shucked scallops will lose flavour and quality quickly. They may also be soaked in a solution which allows them to retain moisture, rather than lose it, with a resulting loss of natural flavour as well as a reduction in size since absorbed water is expelled when cooked.

Scallop, Queen or Queenies
Aequipecten opercularis

Profile, Wild: Ranges throughout the east Atlantic from Norway to the Iberian peninsula. Compared with the king scallop it has an almost circular shell with about twenty ribs. Its shell colour may be yellow, orange, pink, red or brown, and it is often spotted or blotched. It is usually found deeper than the king scallop at depths of about 100m on sand or gravel. The Scottish fishery for queenies only began in the 1970s.

Profile, Farmed: May be managed by a Several and Regulating Order which allows them to be 'ranched' i.e. the area of the order is seeded with young scallops (spat) and protected from any other fishing or disturbance. Spat are now widely produced in commercial hatcheries.

Size: It matures between 18 months and 2 years, when it is about 4 to 5cm. It can grow up to about 9cm, which is about 6 to 8 years growth.

Spawning Habits: Spawning occurs in spring and autumn.

Buying Advice: Minimum recommended size is 4cm length. Choose scallops from responsibly managed farms only, such as those that comply with the Association of Scottish Shellfish Growers Code of Good Practice (*www.assg.org.uk*).

CEPHALOPOD MOLLUSCS

Cephalopod means 'head footed', from the way their arms and tentacles sprout from the head, giving the species a surreal appearance. Only fish-eaters in Mediterranean countries and in Japan fully exploit their potential. All contain ink sacs which squirt black or brown ink to create a smokescreen and protect them from predators. The ink can be used in cooking, adding extra flavour and colour. The remains of their original shell has evolved into an internal cartilage.

Cuttlefish
Sepia officinalis

Profile, Wild: Its range is the eastern Atlantic, in both the north and south, to the Mediterranean. It changes colour frequently and can instantly match the colour of the sea bed it is swimming over. Though it is more tender and succulent than squid, and has more ink to add more marine tastes, colours and textures, most UK-caught cuttlefish is exported to Mediterranean countries, where fish-eaters are less squeamish about its appearance and have a higher regard for its good eating qualities.

Size: Minimum recommended size 17cm. Can attain body lengths of up to 30cm.

Spawning Habits: It moves into shallow coastal waters to breed in spring and early summer. Females only breed once, and die soon after laying their eggs, which are known as 'sea grapes'.

Buying Advice: Avoid spawning period between spring and early summer. Most sustainable fisheries are those where measures have been adopted to protect cuttlefish eggs. Catching them in traps is a more selective fishing method and less damaging than trawl fishing. However, cuttlefish which are caught in traps may have come into shallow coastal waters to lay their eggs and preventative measures are necessary to allow the eggs to hatch.

Squid, Common or Veined
Loligo forbesi

Profile, Wild: Its range is in temperate and subtropical waters in the north-east Atlantic and the Mediterranean. It changes colour frequently and can instantly match the colour of the sea bed it is swimming over. It has night vision, sucker-covered arms, a parrot-like beak which can slice through its prey like a razor, plus the ability to swim both backwards and forwards at high speed. Like other cephalopods it uses its ink sac to squirt a protective dark cloud to confuse predators. In early winter it comes inshore to spawn. Up to the middle of the 1900s it was more or less ignored by UK fish eaters, but now they have cottoned on to its potential and supplies are being imported to meet demand.

Size: Recommended size (body length from tip of nose to end of body) 15cm.

Spawning Habits: It is fast-growing and sexually mature within its first year. The female spawns in her second year and dies soon after laying her eggs. The males live for about three years. The breeding season is between December and May.

Buying Advice: Prime season for Scottish-landed squid from the Moray Firth and west and east coasts is August, Sept and October, though fishing season begins in May. There are small artisanal fisheries around the UK which target squid. In Scotland there is a squid fishery in the Moray Firth where the fishermen trawl with a targeted small-mesh net. Another is the Sennan Cove squid fishery in Cornwall, where fishermen go out in small punts and fish for squid using jigs, a method of fishing similar to that of hand-lining for mackerel. Avoid eating squid taken in industrial or large scale commercial fisheries, which remove large quantities of squid.

Sea Urchin
Strongylocentrus droebachiensis

Profile, Wild: Its range in the Atlantic extends down to the English Channel and to New Jersey on the west. (This is a different species to the main edible sea urchin of the Mediterranean, where it is common to see basketfuls on display for sale.) It is found on the lower shore among rocks, browsing on algae which it eats. It gets its name from the old name for hedgehog, an urchin, since it also has spines for protection. It is more or less spherical, with the only edible part the five orange or rose-coloured ovaries inside, also known as corals. On Orkney, where they call it a 'scarriman's heid' (tramp or child with unruly hair), there is a tradition of eating the corals as a spread on bread instead of butter.

Size: It is a grapefruit-shaped round and can grow up to 8cm.

Spawning Habits: In the spring.

SEA VEGETABLES
Seaweeds

In the yearly rhythm of the seasons, gathering wild seaweed begins after the frosts of winter have sweetened the sloke (Welsh laver). As the days lengthen, new fronds start growing and there is the first harvest of sea moss (Irish carrageen) and kelp (Japanese kombu) to be taken. Soon after, there is a supply of the kelps to dry and store for winter use. By early summer, there is the first picking of dulse and other varieties, such as sea lettuce, pepper dulse and the wracks, which all become ready in their own time throughout the summer. Then in the autumn there are second flushes of sea moss and dulse.

Some seaweed can be picked as the tide goes out, but many grow at the lowest tidal mark, or below it in the sub-tidal area. More of this area is uncovered when there is a low, or 'spring', tide when the sea comes up higher (springs) and goes down lower. The opposite tide is a neap tide, when the distance between low water and high water is shorter. Spring and neap tides alternate every two weeks, halfway through each phase of a new moon, or lunar month (28 days). A local tide book will give the exact tide times (see also *www.easytide.ukho.gov.uk*). The highest and lowest tides of the year are usually in February/March and September/October.

Seaweed Terms

Holdfast: the seaweed's 'root' which is attached to rock or shingle etc.

Stipe: the seaweed's 'stem' which extends from the holdfast.

Frond: the seaweed's 'leaf' which extends from the stipe.

Seaweed Variety and Location

Globally, there are over 9,000 species divided into three major types: green, brown and red. Red is the most species-rich group (6,000) followed by brown (2,000) and green (1,200). Around 600 species are found on UK shores.

Green seaweeds tend to be found towards the upper shore; browns can be found in the lower to sub-tidal deeper waters; reds are adapted to photosynthesise at lower light levels so they tend to dominate the deeper, darker waters or beneath kelp canopies and in shady rock pools.

BROWN/GREEN

Toothed Wrack, Serrated Wrack
Fucus serratus

Profile, Wild: Common on all British shorelines, usually on rocky beaches around the midshore area.

Description: It has many branching fronds, with tooth-shaped ends and serrated edges. It can be 60-180cm long and 2cm wide and is a dark greenish brown.

Sustainable Harvesting: Spring to autumn. With a sharp knife, cut only the top half of the plant so there is enough left for it to regenerate quickly. Its stipe and holdfast which attaches it to rocks should not be cut or dislodged.

Best Used: For slow-cooked dishes such as broths and bean-type stews. Cut up finely, it adds flavouring and thickening. Changes colour to bright green on heating. It is also dried till crisp and crushed to use as a condiment.

Bladder Wrack
Fucus vesiculosus

Profile, Wild: Common on all British shorelines, usually on rocky beaches around the midshore area, but higher up than toothed wrack.

Description: It has a short thick stipe and a wavy-edged frond which is branched with a prominent midrib; total length about 60-80cm. On either side of the midrib are air-bladders, generally in pairs. It is an olive-brown colour which dries to a greenish black. In summer it has a high vitamin A content, and in autumn high levels of vitamin C, as well as a balanced range of vitamins, minerals and trace elements.

Sustainable Harvesting: Spring to autumn. With a sharp knife, cut off less than half the plant so there is enough left to regenerate quickly. Its stipe and holdfast, which attaches it to rocks and other seaweeds, should not be cut or dislodged.

Best Used: As for Toothed Wrack.

Channel Wrack
Pelvetia canaliculata

Profile, Wild: Common on all British shorelines, found on the upper shore and very shallow zones. Its channels hold water, which means it can survive for longer periods without tidal cover. It's popular with seaweed-eating sheep, and in Ireland used to be fed to pigs.

Description: It is the smallest of the wracks and does not grow much more than 15cm in length. Its colour ranges from olive brown or yellow to dark greenish brown. It contains the trace element selenium as well as vitamin C.

Sustainable Harvesting: Spring to autumn. With a sharp knife, cut only a little from a few plants so there are plenty of swollen, glandular fruiting bodies left on the tips of each plant. Its stipe and holdfast, which attaches it to rocks and other seaweeds, should not be cut or dislodged.

Best Used: Lightly stir fried with butter as a vegetable for seafood. Changes colour from brown to green when cooked. Also used dried and crushed as a condiment.

Oarweed Kelp or Japanese Kombu
Laminaria digitata

Profile, Wild: Found on most shorelines with rocky habitats around British coasts at the extreme lower part of the shore.

Description: The frond is palm-shaped and has large, leathery straps which are a light brown colour, very shiny when wet. It turns a darker greenish black when dried. It contains a wide range of minerals, vitamins and trace elements as well as a high level of iodine, so should not be eaten in large quantities. It is also a natural source of glutamic acid, from which monosodium glutamate is made.

Sustainable Harvesting: All year, during low spring tides. Cut off the upper three-quarters of the frond with a sharp knife, leaving the lower part of the frond, the stipe and holdfast intact to regenerate. Because it is such a large plant the holdfast is very securely attached to the rocks.

Best Used: To make soup stock (see p. 227) also in all bean stews to improve flavour and reduce cooking time. Also dried and crushed as a condiment.

Forest Kelp or Sea Rods
Laminaria hyperborea

Profile, Wild: Found on most shorelines with rocky habitats around British coasts. It forms a dense forest below the low water line.

Description: Fronds are similar to oarweed kelp, but the stipe is a longer, stiffer, rough-textured stalk which is often covered with other seaweeds such as dulse. The stipe is round and can be easily snapped when wet. The fronds contain a wide range of minerals, vitamins and trace elements as well as a high level of iodine, so should not be eaten in large quantities. It is also a natural source of glutamic acid, from which monosodium glutamate is made.

Sustainable Harvesting: All year, during low spring tides. Cut off the upper three-quarters of the frond with a sharp knife, leaving the lower part of the frond, the stipe and holdfast, intact to regenerate. Because it is such a large plant the holdfast is very securely attached to the rocks. During springtime storms, the old weed may be thrown up onto the beach, and is known as the May weed.

Best Used: As for oarweed kelp.

Sugar Kelp
Saccharina latissima

Profile, Wild: Found on most shorelines with rocky habitats around British coasts. Another of the large leathery seaweeds which grow below the low tidemark in colonies known as kelp forests.

Description: It has a long sandy-yellow to olive-brown frond, several inches wide, with slightly frilled edges, giving it a crinkly appearance. It may be between 2-4m in length. It has a short thin stipe less than 60cm long and a small holdfast which is easily torn off rocks in stormy weather. The fronds contain a wide range of minerals, vitamins and trace elements as well as a high level of iodine, so should not be eaten in large quantities.

Sustainable Harvesting: In spring from March to June when new young shoots can be cut, so long as the holdfast is not pulled off and it can regenerate. Older plants get battered by storms later in the year and go yellow at the edges.

Best Used: As for the other kelps, but because of its sweeter taste it can also be added to biscuits, cakes and tarts.

Dabberlocks or Scots Tangle, Irish Murlin, American Winged Kelp or Alaria
Alaria esculenta

Similar to Japaese wakame (*Undaria pinnatifida*), this can be used as substitute.

Profile, Wild: Found on both sides of the North Atlantic. It grows along the extreme lower tidal area on the shores of colder areas, especially in Scotland and Ireland. It attaches to rocks which are usually underwater.

Description: It has a blade which can be up to 4m long. It is dark brown or olive green in colour with a firm midrib running from the base to the tip. At its base it has a small holdfast. Its stipe is 10-30cm long, 0.6-1.25cm wide, and a round or oval shape. Its midribs, eaten raw, have a mustardy tang, while its blade has a mildly sweet taste. It is high in calcium, B vitamins and many trace elements. Vitamin C content is highest in late spring.

Sustainable Harvesting: With a sharp knife, cut from the top half of the plant, no more than two-thirds, so there is enough of the blade left for the plant to regenerate quickly. Its holdfast, which fastens it to rocks and other seaweeds, is not strongly attached, so care is needed to prevent dislodging it while cutting.

Best Used: In soups, cut into slivers, it needs cooking 20 minutes to become tender. Use for wrapping fish; for salads, soak in boiling water for 20 minutes, then chop finely.

RED/PURPLE

Sea Moss, Carrageen Moss or Irish Moss
Chondrus crispus

Profile, Wild: Found on many shorelines with rocky habitats around British coasts at low tide mark, often hidden in rock pools under larger brown seaweeds. Sometimes found on the midshore.

carrageen

Description: It is small, bushy and fan-shaped, with flat branched fronds widening to rounded tips. It is between 7-15cm high. Its colours range from pink to dark purple. When it is under water its tips can have a violet iridescence. It has a good balance of vitamins, minerals and trace elements and is particularly high in magnesium.

Sustainable Harvesting: In spring and early summer. With a sharp knife cut from the top half of the plant, leaving the remainder to regenerate. Avoid dislodging the holdfast or the plant will die. When dried in the open air its colour is bleached to a pale cream. The creamier it looks the less flavour and nutrients it will have.

Best Used: As a vegetable gelatine setting agent for non-acid liquids, sweet or savoury. Used for setting milk jellies, best served with an equal quantity of whipped cream and some acid fruit or a sharp jam or jelly. Also for thickening soups and stews. Boiled with milk and honey it is good for coughs and can also help to clear chest infections. As a milk jelly, it was also given as a general healing food for sick and old people and was once sold as an invalid food.

Dulse
Palmaria palmate

Profile, Wild: Found on both sides of the North Atlantic. Traditionally eaten in Scotland, Ireland, Greenland, Norway, France, the Faroe Islands, eastern Siberia and along the eastern coast of New England and Canada. It grows along the lower tidal area on rocks, and on other seaweeds, especially the tougher kelps.

dulse

Description: It is a small, dark reddish-maroon coloured seaweed with leathery fronds, between 15-30cm high. When dried it is a lighter colour. It has a salty-savoury, slightly spicy flavour. It is a good source of minerals, vitamins and trace elements and is relatively low in sodium and high in potassium.

Sustainable Harvesting: With a sharp knife, cut off the top half of the plant so there is enough left for the plant to regenerate quickly. Its holdfast, which attaches it to rocks and other seaweeds, is not strongly attached, so care is needed to prevent dislodging it while cutting. It is one of the most commercially harvested seaweeds. It is sold dried in packets as a pliable bundles of leaves. Some are more tender than others.

Best Used: As a seasoning condiment in all fish dishes, soups, stews, creamy mashed potatoes, stir-fries, salads, scrambled eggs, oatcakes, bannocks and soda breads. Also as a traditional flavouring in mutton broth and stovies.

Pepper Dulse
Osmundea pinnatifida

Profile, Wild: Found on many shorelines with wave-exposed rocky habitats around British coasts. It can be found from low tide to midshore.

Description: Plants found higher up the shore are smaller and lighter in colour, while nearer the low tideline they are reddish-brown and may be 8cm long. As its name suggests, it has a peppery flavour. Nutritional content: little research has been done.

Sustainable Harvesting: Spring and early summer. With a sharp knife, cut the top half of the plant so there is enough left for the plant to regenerate quickly. Its holdfast, which fastens it to rocks and other seaweeds, is not strongly attached so care is needed to prevent dislodging it while cutting.

Best Used: As for dulse.

Sloke (Scots and Irish), Welsh Laver, Japanese Nori
Porphyra linearis

Profile, Wild: Found on many shorelines with rocky habitats around British coasts, but especially on the west coast. It grows at most levels of the beach on rough-surfaced rocks and boulders, on mussels and can almost cover concrete breakwaters. It looks like a black plastic bag which has melted. There are over a hundred species worldwide, with around 6-8 species identified round British coasts.

It is cultivated in Japan.

Description: Very delicate, almost transparent frond with irregular edges. It is greenish when young, turning to brownish purple and chocolate black when ready to harvest. It is around 20-30cm long and 10cm across. It has the highest amount of protein compared with other seaweeds (37%) and has a good balance of minerals and trace elements and is especially rich in B, C and E vitamins. It is low in iodine.

Sustainable Harvesting: After the first winter frosts in November or December until April. Pluck a small amount from each rock or boulder, leaving plenty to regenerate.

Best Used: In Wales it's boiled to a puree (laverbread) and is sold fresh in tubs in Welsh fishmongers, markets and health food stores. This is used, rolled in oatmeal, to make laver cakes for breakfast.

GREEN

Sea Lettuce or Green Laver, Oyster Green
Ulva lactuca

Profile, Wild: Found on most shorelines with rocky habitats, on salt marshes and estuaries around British coasts. Mainly in the mid to lower zones of sheltered or moderately exposed shores, it attaches to rock and other seaweeds. Also common in the West Indies, Japan, Iceland, Chile and in several regions of China.

Description: Pale green, wavy-margined fronds which become a brighter green when mature and dark green when old. They vary in size, but can reach 1m long and 30cm wide. Highest vitamin C content when harvested in early summer. It also has high levels of protein, iron, Vitamin B12, calcium, manganese and magnesium.

Sustainable Harvesting: In spring and early summer. With a sharp knife, cut the upper two thirds of the plant without dislodging the holdfast.

Best Used: Chopped finely and added to salads, soups, seafood dishes such as steamed mussels, also in pastas, risottos etc. Can be deep fried to make crisps.

Sea Grass or Gutweed
Ulva intestinalis and *U. compressa*

Profile, Wild: Found on most shorelines with rocky habitats around British coasts it is found at all shore levels, in sheltered pools and also in freshwater rivers where tidal water backwashes.

Description: Forms a bright green slippy mat on rocks. Fronds are thin tubes 6-8mm wide and 15-30cm long, which inflate with oxygen and float in the water, but are flat on the rocks looking like a thin version of sea lettuce.

Sustainable Harvesting: In spring and autumn. In the summer months it can become bleached with the sun and lose food value. Pluck like nori.

Best Used: as for Sea Lettuce

Velvet Horn or Dead Men's Fingers, Green Sea Velvet, Sponge Seaweed
Codium fragile

Profile, Wild: Found on most shorelines with rocky habitats around British coasts. Grows on rocks and other seaweeds, especially the kelps, below the low tidemark. It can survive in low light levels but not drying out for long periods.

Description: Deep green colour, it can be up to 45cm long. The fronds are branching like a deer's horn and are roundish, thick and spongy, with a velvety texture. Good source of iron and trace elements.

Sustainable Harvesting: Spring until autumn. This is a non-native, invasive seaweed which need not be gathered sustainably.

Best Used: Deep fried in tempura batter (see p. 200). Also contains high levels of agaopectin gel useful for setting liquids.

OTHER SEASHORE FOOD

Samphire, Rock and Marsh (also known as Glasswort)
Crithmum maritimum and *Salicornia species*

Both are seashore plants which look like slim-cacti – bright green, succulent and jointed – but rock and marsh samphire are very different.

Rock samphire has a slightly resinous taste and is found on rocks or cliffs and sandy and shingle upper shores, and is distinguished in summer by its umbel-shaped yellow flowers.

Marsh samphire is easier to gather and a better taste. It looks like a green carpet on salt marshes, sandy beaches and mudflats and, unlike rock samphire, its flowers grow out of the junctions of its stems. The young tips make a pleasant raw snack.

Its flavour is a mix of grassy sweetness and salty tang; peak growing time is June to September. When picking, some should be left on the plant for regeneration. Plants which are covered by every tide will have the best flavour. If the stems are young they can be eaten raw; older should be steamed or boiled lightly and served with melted butter and white fish or shellfish.

Bibliography

Scottish General

Alexander, J. H., *The Tavern Sages: Selections from the Noctes Ambrosianae*, 1992

Anderson, Donald McLean, *Looking Back* (Archive of Scottish Fishing Industry), n.d.

Anson, P. F., *Fisher Boats and Fisher Folk on the East Coast of Scotland*, 1930

    —*Fishermen and Fishing Ways*, 1932

    —*Scots Fisherfolk*, 1950

Beith, Mary, *Healing Threads: Traditional Medicines of the Highlands and Islands*, 1995

Berry, R. J., Frith, H. N., *The People of Orkney*, 1986

Blair, Anna, *Croft and Creel: A Century of Coastal Memories*, 1987

Bochel, Margaret, *Dear Gremista: The Story of Nairn Fisher Girls at the Gutting*, 1979

Brown, George Mackay, *An Orkney Tapestry*, 1969

    —*Fishermen with Ploughs*, 1971

Buchan, Peter, *Collected Poems and Short Stories*, 1992

Chambers, Robert, *Traditions of Edinburgh*, 1861

Cockburn, Henry Thomas, *Memorials of His Time*, 1874

Coull, James R., *The Sea Fisheries of Scotland: A Historical Geography*, 1996

Czerkawska, C. L., *Fisherfolk of Carrick: South Ayrshire*, 1975

Dunlop, Jean, *The British Fisheries Society: 1786–1893*, 1978

Eddison, E. R. (trans.), *Egil's Saga*, 1930

Erdal, David, *Local Heroes* (Loch Fyne Oysters), 2008

Fenton, A., *The Northern Isles, Orkney and Shetland*, 1978

Fenton, A., Myrdal, J., *Food and Drink and Travelling Accessories*, 1988

Finlayson, Bill, *Wild Harvesters: The First People in Scotland*, 1998

Firth, Howie, *In from the Cuithes: An Orkney Anthology*, 1995

Fojut, Noel, *A Guide to Prehistoric Shetland*, 1981

Foulis, Sir John, *Foulis of Ravelston's Account Book: 1671–1707*, Scottish History Society, 1894

Geddes, Olive, *The Laird's Kitchen*, 1994

Goodlad, C. A., *Shetland Fishing Saga*, 1971

Grant, I. F., *Highland Folk Ways*, 1961

Gray, Malcolm, *The Fishing Industries of Scotland 1790–1914*, 1978

Gunn, Neil M., *The Silver Darlings*, 1941

Hibbert, Samuel, *Description of the Shetland Islands*, 1882

Inkster, Karen, *Voices from the Past*, 2006

Jenkins, J. T., *The Herring and the Herring Fisheries*, 1929

Johnson R., Thomas, A., *Tarbert Loch Fyne: The Story of the Fishermen*, 1985

Knox, J., *View of the British Empire and Scotland*, 1784
  —*Discourse on the Expediency of Founding Fishing Stations*, 1786
  —*Observations on Northern Fisheries*, 1786
  —*Tour of the Highlands*, 1787
MacDonald, Murdoch, *Old Torridon*, 1997
Macdonald, Jessie, Gordon, Anne, *Down to the Sea: An Account of Life in the Fishing Villages of Hilton, Balintore and Shandwick*, n.d.
McGowan, Linda, *Fife's Fishing Industry*, 2003
McGowran, T., *Newhaven-on-the-Forth, Port of Grace*, 1985
MacKenzie, Osgood H., *A Hundred Years in the Highlands*, 1921
Maclean, Fitzroy, *The Isles of the Sea*, 1985
Maclean, Charles, *The Fringe of Gold: The Fishing Villages of Scotland's East Coast, Orkney and Shetland*, 1985
Martin, Angus, *The Ring-Net Fishermen*, 1981
  —*Fishing and Whaling*, 1995
  —*Herring Fishermen of Kintyre and Ayrshire*, 2002
  —*Fish and Fisherfolk of Kintyre, Lochfyneside, Gigha and Arran*, 2004
McNeill, F. Marian, *The Scots Kitchen*, 1929 (new edition 2010)
Miller, James, *Salt in the Blood: Scotland's Fishing Communities*, 1999
Miln, W. S., *An Exposure of the Position of the Scottish Herring Trade in 1885*, 1886
Moffat, Alastair, *Before Scotland*, 2005
Murray, Donald S., *The Guga Hunters*, 2008
Oliver, Neil, *A History of Scotland*, 2009
Omand, D. (ed.), *The Orkney Book*, 2003
Ritchie, Anna, *Viking Scotland*, 1993
  —*Historic Orkney*, 1995
Russell, Michael W., *A Poem of Remote Lives, Images of Eriskay, 1934, The Enigma of Werner Kissling 1934–1988*, 1997
Scottish Life and Society (SLS), *Boats, Fishing and the Sea*, 2008
Smith, B. in Smout, T. C. (ed.), *Scotland and the Sea*, 1992
Smout, T. C., *A History of the Scottish People (1560–1830)*, 1969
  —*A Century of the Scottish People (1830–1950)*, 1986
Smout, T. C., Wood, S., *Scottish Voices*, 1990
Steven, Maisie, *The Good Scots Diet*, 1985
Sutherland, R. L., Crichton, Stewart, *A Creek to a Haven*, 2003
Tait, Ian, *Rural Life in Shetland and Guide Book to the Croft House Museum*, 2000
Telford, Susan, *In a World A' Wir Ane: A Shetland Herring Girl's Story*, 1998
Towesy, K., Tulloch, H. (eds.), *Orkney and the Land: An Oral History*, 2009
Wickham-Jones, C., *Between the Wind and the Water: World Heritage Orkney*, 2006
Wilson, J., *The Society of Free Fishermen of Newhaven*, 1951

Wilson, John., *Noctes Ambrosianae* (4 vols.), 1855

Young, Robert, *Behold the Hebrides*, 1991

General

Baker, S., Allen, M., Middle, S., Poole, K., *Food and Drink in Archaeology*, vol.1, 2008

Clover, Charles, *The End of the Line*, 2007

Crawford, Michael A., *Nutrition in the Future*, 1997

Crawford, Michael A., Marsh, D., *Nutrition and Evolution*, 1995

Cutting, Charles L., *Fish Saving: A History of Fish Processing from Ancient to Modern Times*, 1955

Jones, Martin, *Feast: Why Humans Share Food*, 2007

Kurlansky, Mark, *Cod: A Biography of the Fish That Changed the World*, 1997

   —*Salt: A World History*, 2002

Lawrence, Felicity, *Not on the Label*, 2004

   —*Eat Your Heart Out*, 2008

Oxford Symposium on Food and Cookery, *Fish: Food from the Waters*, 1997

   —*Wild Food*, 2004

Perdikaris, S., 'From chiefly provisioning to commercial fishery: Long–term economic change in Arctic Norway', *World Archaeology* 30, 1999

Riddervold, Astri, Ropeid, Andreas, *Food Conservation: Ethnological Studies*, 1988

Shephard, Sue, *Pickled, Potted and Canned: How the Preservation of Food Changed Civilisation*, 2000

Tannahill, Reay, *Food in History*, 1973

Wilson, C. Anne, *Food and Drink in Britain*, 1973

Scottish Cookery

Brown, Catherine, *Scottish Regional Recipes*, 1981

   —*Scottish Cookery*, 1985

   —*Broths to Bannocks*, 1990 (revised 2010)

Cleland, Elizabeth, *A New and Easy Method of Cookery . . . chiefly intended for the benefit of the young ladies who attend her school*, 1755 (facsimile edition 2005)

Craig, Elizabeth, *The Scottish Cookery Book*, 1956

Dods, Mistress Margaret (Meg), *The Cook and Housewife's Manual*, 1829

Fulton, Willie, *The Hebridean Kitchen*, 1978

The Glasgow Cookery Book (Student textbook for the Glasgow and West of Scotland College of Domestic Science), 1910 (new edition 2009)

Hofman, Ethel G., *Mackerel at Midnight*, 2006

Lawrence, Sue, *Scots Cooking*, 2000

Murray, Janet, *With a Fine Feeling for Food*, 1972

McLintock, Mrs, *Receipts for Cookery and Pastry-Work*, 1736 (copies of original edition in Glasgow University Library, facsimile edition with Introduction by Iseabail Macleod 1986)

McNeill, F. Marian, *The Scots Kitchen: Its Traditions and Recipes*, 1929 (new edition 2010)

   —*Recipes from Scotland*, 1946

Simmons, Jenni, *A Shetland Cook Book*, 1978

Simpson, Charlie, *In Da Galley: Sixty Essays in Seafood Philosophy*, 2000

Stout, Margaret B., *Cookery for Northern Wives*, 1925 (revised 1968 as *The Shetland Cookery Book*)

Whyte, Hamish (ed.), *Lady Castlehill's Receipt Book*, 1976 (a quarter of the original manuscript collection compiled in 1712–1713, original in the Mitchell Library, Glasgow)

Other Cookery

Allen, Darina, *Forgotten Skills of Cooking*, 2009

Beck, S., Bertholle, L., Child, J., *Mastering the Art of French Cooking*, 1961

Bull, Stephen, *Classic Bull*, 2001

Ceserani, Victor, Kinton, Ronald, *Practical Cookery*, 1961

Ellis, Hattie, Sacchi, Camilla, *Best of British Fish*, 2005

Ellis, Lesley, *Simply Seaweed*, 1998

Fearnley-Whittingstall, Hugh, Fisher, Nick, *The River Cottage Fish Book*, 2007

Fuller, John, Renold, Edward, *The Chef's Compendium of Professional Recipes*, 1963

Granger, Sally, *Cooking Apicius: Roman Recipes for Today*, 2006

Grieve, Guy, Miers, Thomasina, *The Wild Gourmets: Adventures in Food and Freedom*, 2007

Grigson, Jane, *Jane Grigson's Fish Book*, 1993

Henderson, Fergus, *Nose to Tail Eating: A Kind of British Cooking*, 1999

Henderson, Fergus, Gellatly J. P., *Beyond Nose to Tail*, 2007

Hix, Max, *Fish*, 2004

   —*British Regional Food*, 2006

Houston, Fiona, Milne, Xa, *Seaweed and Eat It: A Family Foraging and Cooking Adventure*, 2008

Jackson, C. J., *The Billingsgate Market Cookbook*, 2009

McGee, Harold, *McGee on Food and Cooking: An Encyclopaedia of Kitchen Science, History and Culture*, 2004

Marwick, Stephen, Beckett, Fiona, *A Very Honest Cook*, 2009

   —*A Well-Run Kitchen*, 2010

Molyneux, Joyce, *The Carved Angel Cookery Book*, 1990

Olney, Richard, *Simple French Food*, 2003

Phillips, Roger, *Wild Food*, 1983

Rhatigan, Prannie, *Irish Seaweed Kitchen*, 2009

Stein, Rick, *English Seafood Cookery*, 1988

   —*Rick Stein's Seafood*, 2001

Stevenson, Sonia, *A Fresh Look at Fish*, 1996

Stromstad, Aase, *Eat the Norway*, 1985

Tonks, Mitchell, *FishWorks Seafood Café Cookbook*, 2001

   —*Fish: The Complete Fish and Seafood Companion*, 2009

Wood, Jacqui, *Prehistoric Cooking*, 2001

Notes

1. Coull, James, *The Sea Fisheries of Scotland*, 1996, 23

2. Moffat, A., *Before Scotland*, 2005, 59/63

3. Coull, James, 25

4. Society of Antiquaries 80, 135-139

5. Coles, J. M., *The Early Settlement of Scotland*. Morton, Fife Proc. Prehistory Society 37, 284-386

6. Tannahill, Reay, *Food in History*, 1973, 23

7. Crawford, Michael A., BBC interview, 23 May 2000, *Fish deficiency 'could harm mental health'*. Also *The Role of Nutrition in Human Evolution*, Caroline Walker Lecture, 2002, 9

8. Using fragments of Neolithic pots found in the chambered tomb at Unstan, Orkney potter Andrew Appleby remodelled the original Unstan ware pot and used it in a Neolithic seafood cooking experiment, when he cooked shellfish, crabs and lobsters for STV and Grampian's series 8 of *Scotland's Larder* in 2000: *www.applepot.co.uk*. See also C. Brown, 'The Joy of Turning to Stone', *The Herald* (Glasgow), 15 July 2000

9. Ritchie, Anna, *Historic Orkney*, 1995, 22

10. Ritchie, Anna, 1995, 25

11. Wilson, C. Anne, *Food and Drink in Britain*, 1973, 17

12. Coull, James, *The Sea Fisheries of Scotland*, 1996, 28

13. Cutting, Charles, *Fish Saving*, 1955, 14

14. Ritchie, Anna, 1995, 95

15. See p. 43, Burnt Mound Recipe

16. Wilson, C. Anne, 1973, 19

17. Cutting, Charles, 1955, 2

18. Oliver, Neil, *A History of Scotland*, 2009, 30

19. First recognised in 1908 when it was identified chemically by a Japanese scientist, Kikunae Ikeda.

20. Wilson, C. Anne, 1973, 25

21. Smith, Brian, *The Picts and the Martyrs: www.orkneyjar.com/history*

22. Oliver, Neil, 2009, 48

23. Perdikaris, S., 'From chiefly provisioning to commercial fishery: Long-term economic change in Arctic Norway', *World Archaeology* 30, 1999, 388-402

24. *Egil's Saga*, trans. Eddison, E.R., 1930, 30

25. Cutting, C. L., *Fish Saving*, 1955, 41

26. Barrett, J. H., *The Fish Eaters of Viking Age Orkney*, Orkney Archaeology Trust, February 2004

27. Barrett, J. H., 2004

28. Ritchie, Anna, *Viking Scotland*, 1993, 31

29. Toyne, S. M., 'The Herring and History', *Fishing News*, 1952, 11

30. Cutting, C. L., 1955, 56

31. Cutting, C. L., 1955, 56

32. Cutting, C. L., 1955, 71

33. Barrett, J. H., Beukens, R. P., Nicholson, R. A., 'Diet and ethnicity during the Viking colonization of northern Scotland: evidence from fish bones and stable carbon isotopes', *Antiquity*, March 2001

34. Scottish Life and Society (SLS), *Boats, Fishing and the Sea*, 2008, 332

35. *Statistical Account* for Dumbarton, 1795. VIII, 597, XVII, 217

36. SLS, 2008, 333-4

37. SLS, 2008, 172

38. See p. 48, Chapter 5 (History)

39. See p. 39, Red Herring Recipe

40. Martin, Angus, *Fishing and Whaling*, 1995, 41

41. Cutting, C. L., *Fish Saving*, 1955, 83

42. Cutting, C. L., 1955, 83

43. Author of *Robinson Crusoe,* and *A tour thro' the Whole Island of Great Britain* (1724-27) which provided a panoramic survey of British trade on the eve of the Industrial Revolution.

44. Defoe, D., *A Tour through Scotland*. Cole, G. D. H. (ed.), 1927

45. Haldane, A. R. B., *The Great Fishmonger of the Tay*, 1981, 11

46. See p. 44, Newcastle Pickle Recipe

47. Cutting, C. L., 1955, 216

48. Professor Tom Cowan, Glasgow University, in BBC Radio Scotland broadcast, May 2011

49. Cutting, C. L., 1955, 85

50. Mackenzie, Osgood, *A Hundred Years in the Highlands* (first edition 1921) 1980, 95. Also in 1929, F. M. McNeill uses the old 'kipper' usage in her recipe for a *Modern Method to Kipper Salmon*, which includes sugar as well as rum or whisky. *The Scots Kitchen* (first edition 1929), 2010, 134

51. Mackenzie, Osgood, (1921) 1980, 93

52. McNeill, F. M., *The Scots Kitchen* (1929) 2010, 21

53. Cutting, C. L., *Fish Saving*, 1955, 68

54. Records of the Parliament of Scotland 1493, A1493/5/21: *www.rps.ac.uk*

55. McNeill, F. M., (1929) 2010, 21 (Scots v. *ding*, to displace)

56. Coull, James R., *The Sea Fisheries of Scotland*, 1996, 55

57. Martin, Angus, *The Ring-Net Fishermen*, 1981, 4

58. Recipe for red herring, see p. 39

59. Jenkins, J. T., *The Herring and the Herring Fisheries* 1929

60. Martin, Angus, 1981, 4

61. Anson, P. F., 1950, 2

62. Donald, J., *The British Fisheries Society*, 1978, 18

63. Knox, J., *View of the British Empire and Scotland* (1784), *Discourse on the Expediency of Founding Fishing Stations* (1786), *Observations on Northern Fisheries* (1786), *Tour of the Highlands* (1787)

64. Donald, J., 1978, 18

65. Donald, J., 1978, 23

66. Donald, J., 1978, 90

67. Scottish Life and Society, (SLS), *Boats Fishing and the Sea*, 2008, 212

68. SLS, 2008, 212-13

69. Anson, P., *Scots Fisherfolk*, 1950, 8

70. SLS, 2008, 316

71. Cutting, C. L., *Fish Saving*, 1955, 106

72. See p. 73, Regional Chapter: Shetland

73. SLS, 2008, 221

74. *To ding*, Scots v., to displace

75. SLS, 2008, 225

76. Cutting, C. L., 1955, 107

77. Gray, Malcolm, *The Fishing Industries of Scotland 1790–1914: A Study in Regional Adaptation*, 1978, 147

78. Cutting, C. L., 1955, 107/08

79. See p. 39, Red Herring Recipe

80. Cutting, C. L., 1955, 73-75

81. Scots *lucken*, closed fish (i.e. unfilleted fish with head and guts removed). Once also known as a *pinwiddie*, now an Arbroath smokie.

82. Scottish Coastal Archaeology Prevention of Erosion (SCAPE Trust), excavation sites in the village of Auchmithie: *www.scapetrust.org*

83. Riddervold, Astri, Ropeid, Andreas (Editors), *Food Conservation: Ethnological Studies*, 1988, 16

84. Riddervold, Astri, Ropeid, Andreas (Editors), 1988, 17. The fish bones discovered on the site were mainly freshwater fish from the lake – pike, bass, roach, bream and very big catfish – which would probably have been cut up for processing. For their experiment, a selection of these fish were scaled, gutted and soaked in brine for two hours. They were then dried in front of a fire in an open hearth to reduce the moisture in the skin, making it more able to withstand the heat of the smoke. Finally, the fish were hung on rods in the hole over the smoke from an oak fire. The holes were covered either with planks or a straw roof and they had to keep checking the fish to prevent it overcooking, when it was liable to fall off the rods into the fire. When they got it right, the fish was a 'golden colour and very tasty'. *www.biskupin.pl*

85. *Dictionary of the Scots Language: www.dsl.ac.uk*

86. Miege, Guy, *The Present State of Great Britain*, 1707-1748

87. Bertram, J. G., *The Harvest of the Sea*, 1879

88. Gray, Malcolm, *The Fishing Industries of Scotland 1790-1914*, 1978, 43

89. Cutting, C. L., 1955, 283

90. Cutting, C. L., 1955, 283

91. Mason, Laura, Brown, Catherine, *Traditional Foods of Britain*, 1999, 7; *The Taste of Britain*, 2006, xiii; *From Petticoat Tails to Arbroath Smokies: Traditional Foods of Scotland*, 2007

92. Arbroath smokies are registered as a PGI under the EU scheme of Protected Food Names, which came into force in 1993 to provide a system for the protection of food names on a geographical or traditional recipe basis, similar to the familiar 'appellation controlee' system used for wine. The three schemes (Protected Designation of Origin, PDO; Protected Geographical Indication, PGI; and Traditional Speciality Guaranteed, TSG or Certificate of Specific Character, CSC) highlight regional and traditional foods whose authenticity and origins can be guaranteed through an independent inspection system.

93. Dods, Mistress Margaret (Meg), *The Cook and Housewife's Manual*, 1829, 197. 'Before public amusements were much known in our Presbyterian capital, an Oyster-ploy, which always included music and a little dance, was the delight of the young fashionables of both sexes."

94. Dods, M., 1829, 198

95. North, Christopher (Professor John Wilson), *Noctes Ambrosianae*, 1822-1835

96. Cockburn, Henry Thomas, *Memorials of His Time*, 1874, in Brown, C., *Broths to Bannocks*, 1990, 34

97. McNeill, F. M., *The Scots Kitchen* (first edition 1929), 2010, 24

98. See p. 14 (Chapter 3, History)

99. Scottish Natural Heritage: *www.snh.org.uk/pdfs/publications/wildlife/nativeoysters.pdf*

100. McGowran, T., *Newhaven-on-Forth. Port of Grace*, 1985, 125

101. Coull, James R., *The Sea Fisheries of Scotland: A Historical Geography*, 1996, 225

102. Wilson, J., *The Society of Free Fishermen of Newhaven*, 1951, 78

103. Wilson, J., 1951, 64

104. Fulton, T. W., *The Scottish Lobster Fishery*, 1887, Annual Report of the Fishery Board for Scotland, Scientific Investigations, 189-202, 51

105. Fulton, T. W., 1887, 44-47

106. Rossmore Oysters: *www.oysters.co.uk*

107. East Neuk Seafood Celebration: *www.east-neuk-seafood.co.uk*

108. Scottish Life and Society (SLS), *Boats, Fishing and the Sea*, 2008, 85

109. Sutherland, R. L., Crichton, Stewart, *A Creek to a Haven*, 2003, 17-18

110. Towesy, K., Tulloch, H. (editors), *Orkney and the Land: an Oral History*, 2009, 22

111. Gray, Malcom, *The Fishing Industries of Scotland 1790-1914: A Study in Regional Adaptation*, 1978, 124

112. Sutherland R. L., Crichton, Stewart, 2003, 7

113. *New Statistical Account of Durness*, XV, 99

114. Coull, James R., *The Sea Fisheries of Scotland*, 1996, 229

115. Miller, James, *Salt in the Blood: Scotland's Fishing Communities Past and Present*, 38

116. Firth, Howie, *In from the Cuithes: An Orkney Anthology*, 1995, 59

117. Sutherland, R. L. and Crichton, Stewart, 2003, 3

118. Orkney Fishermen's Society, Garson Food Park, Stromness: *www.orkneycrab.co.uk*

119. Davidson, Alan, *North Atlantic Seafood*, 1979, writes 'In the original edition of Margaret Stout's book on Shetland cookery, published in 1925 . . . there were forty-eight entries under Fish; and of these over a third were for fish-liver dishes. Nowhere else in the world have I found a similar phenomenon. Even today, when fish livers are usually discarded at sea, most Shetlanders over forty are ready to discuss with passion the merits of these various dishes.' 437-38

120. Smith, B., in Smout, T. C. (ed), *Scotland and the Sea*, 1992, 94-113

121. Gray, Malcolm, *The Fishing Industries of Scotland 1790-1914: A Study in Regional Adaptation*, 1978, 128

122. Coull, James, *The Sea Fisheries of Scotland*, 1996, 87

123. Inkster, Karen, *Voices from the Past*, 2006, 152-163

124. Hibbert, Samuel, *Description of the Shetland Islands*, 1882

125. Inkster, Karen, 2006, 168-184

126. Scottish Life and Society (SLS), *Boats, Fishing and the Sea*, 2008, 302

127. Heerma van Voss, L., *The North Sea and Culture (1500-1800)*, Proceedings of the International Conference at Leiden, 1995, 131-132

128. Inkster, Karen, 2006, 164

129. Simmons, Jenni, *A Shetland Cookbook*, 1978, 39

130. Simmons, Jenni, 1978, 22

131. Grant, I. F., *Highland Folk Ways*, 1961, 259

132. Grant, I. F., 1961, 255

133. Scottish Life and Society (SLS), *Boats Fishing and the Sea*, 2008, 152

134. SLS, 2008, 151

135. SLS, 2008, 153

136. SLS, 2008, 165

137. See p. 34 (chapter 5, History, Rich Fishing Grounds)

138. Young, Robert, *Behold the Hebrides*, 1991, 110

139. Dunlop, J., *The British Fisheries Society 1786-1893*, 1978, 18-19

140. See p. 35 (chapter 5, History, Rich Fishing Grounds)

141. MacDonald, Murdoch, *Old Torridon*, 1997, 63-8

142. Geddes, Olive, *The Laird's Kitchen*, 1994, 22

143. Murray, Donald S., *The Guga Hunters*, 2008, 151

144. Murray, Donald S., 2008, 18-19

145. Murray, Donald S., 2008, 220

146. Cutting, C. L., *Fish Saving*, 1955, 277

147. Cutting, C. L., 1955, 278

148. Miln, W. S., *An Exposure of the Position of the Scottish Herring Trade in 1885*, 1886

149. Coull, James R., *The Sea Fisheries of Scotland*, 1996, 128

150. Coull, James. R., 1996,128

151. Scottish Life and Society (SLS), *Boats, Fishing and the Sea*, 2008, 324

152. Murray, Donald S., *The Guga Hunters*, 2008, 220

153. SLS, 2008, 323

154. Martin, Angus, *The Ring-Net Fishermen*, 1981, 6

155. Martin, Angus, 1981, 9-15

156. Martin, Angus, 'The Mull of Kintyre hand-line fishery' in *Northern Studies* Vol. 20, 1983, 75

157. Martin, Angus, *Fish and Fisherfolk*, 2004, 80-81

158. Martin, Angus, 2004, 125

159. SLS, 2008, 60–61

160. Martin, Angus, 2004, 1-9

161. Dods, Mistress Margaret (Meg), *The Cook and Housewife's Manual* (first edition 1826), 11th edition 1862, 179

162. Dods, M. M., 1862,408

163. Dods, M. M., 1862, 408

164. Dods, M. M., 1862, 402

165. McNeill, F. M., *The Scots Kitchen* (first edition 1929) 2010, 110

166. McNeill, F. M., 2010, 136

167. Murray, Janet, *With a Fine Feeling for Food*, 1972, 26

168. Murray, Janet, 1972, 26

169. Brown, C., *Scottish Regional Recipes*, 1981, 72

170. McNeill, F. M., 2010, 128

171. McLintock, Mrs, *Mrs McLintock's Receipts for Cookery and Pastry-Work*, facsimile, Aberdeen University Press, 1986, 61

172. Fraser, Mrs, *The Practice of Cookery and Pastry*, second edition, 1795

173. Dods, Mistress Margaret (Meg), 1862, 200

174. Towesy, K., Tulloch, H. (eds), *Orkney and the Land: an Oral History*, 2009, 22

175. McNeill, F. M., 2010, 137

176. Brown, C., *Broths to Bannocks*, 1990, 79-80

177. Adapted from Stout, Margaret B., *Cookery for Northern Wives*, 1925, 2

178. *Shetland Old-Lore Miscellany*, 1914 VII, II.73

179. Stout, Margaret B., 1925, 12

180. Simmons, Jenni, *A Shetland Cook Book,* 1978, 29

181. Simmons, Jenni, 1978, 29

182. Stout, Margaret B., 1925, 7

183. Shetlopedia, *The Shetland Encyclopedia*: *www.shetlopedia.com*

184. Simpson, Charlie, *In Da Galley*, 2000, 12

185. Stout, Margaret B., 1925, 6

186. Saxby, Jessie, *Shetland Traditional Lore*, 1932, 171

187. Saxby, Jessie, 1932, 171

188. Shetlopedia, *The Shetland Encyclopedia*: *www.shetlopedia.com*

189. Stout, Margaret B., 1925, 8

190. Simmons, Jenni, 1978, 25

191. Stout, Margaret B., 1925, 9

192. Stout, Margaret B., 1925, 77

193. McNeill, F. M., *The Scots Kitchen*, (first edition 1929) 2010, 142

194. Fulton, Willie, *The Hebridean Kitchen*, 1978

195. Fulton, Willie, 1978

196. Fulton, Willie, 1978

197. Brown, C., *Scottish Regional Recipes*, 1981, 117

198. Brown, C., 1981, 117

199. Murray, Donald S., *The Guga Hunters*, 2008, 152-154

200. Dods, Mistress Margaret (Meg), *The Cook and Housewife's Manual*, 11th edition 1862, 180

201. McNeill, F. M., 2010, 137

202. Glenugie PD347, skipper Donald Anderson. (Fish catch on three hauls: 1. 7-800kg haddock. 2. 5000kg predominantly haddock. 3. 1500kg cod, haddock and halibut)

203. Marine Stewardship Council certification scheme: *www.msc.org*

204. In May 2011, Mike Park, chief executive of the Scottish White Fish Producers' Association, was awarded the WWF conservation merit prize for his leadership and efforts in improving conservation measures and encouraging sustainable fishing practices in Scotland, including his role establishing the Scottish Conservation Credit Scheme Steering Group.

205. Scottish Life and Society (SLS), *Boats, Fishing and the Sea*, 2008, 178

206. SLS, 2008, 180

207. SLS, 2008, 180

208. Coull, James R., *The North Sea Herring Fishery in the Twentieth Century*, Ocean Yearbook 7 (1998), 126

209. SLS, 2008, 181

210. Inquiry into Future Fisheries Management (IFFM), September 2009: *www.scotland.gov.uk*

211. Salmond, Alex. Interview with Catherine Brown, Peterhead, 29 October 2010

212. WWF Scottish Conservation Credits Scheme (SCCS): *http://assets.wwf.org.uk/downloads/scottish_conservation_credits_scheme.pdf*

213. Cameron, Lucinda, 'Minister condemns "abhorrent" dumping of a third of fish at sea', *The Scotsman* 29 November 2010

214. WWF (SCCS) Joint Statement, available at *www.fvm.dk*

215. J. Noble, of Ardkinglas, Chairman and partner of Loch Fyne Oysters, 1977-2002

216. A. Lane, Managing Director and partner of Loch Fyne Oysters, 1977-2006

217. A Several Order Application is to sever an area of the sea-bed from the public right to fish; it

prohibits the use of demersal fishing gear, in order to conserve or enhance named shellfish stocks.

218. Scottish Life and Society (SLS), *Boats, Fishing and the Sea*, 2008, 359

219. SLS, 2008, 359

220. SLS, 2008, 365

221. SLS, 2008, 359/60

222. SLS, 2008, 235

223. SLS, 2008, 364

224. SEPA, *www.sepa.org.uk*; RSPCA, *www.rspca.org.uk*; SNH, *www.snh.gov.uk*; Marine Heritage, *www.scotland.gov.uk*

225. Comments on Scottish Fish Farm Production Survey 2009, 03 November 2010: *www.scotland.gov.uk*

226. Naylor, R.L., Hardy, R.W., Bureau, B. P., Chiu, A., Elliott, M., Farrell, A. P., 'Feeding aquaculture in an era of finite resource', *Proceedings of the National Academy of Sciences* (2009), 106:15103–15100

227. UN Food and Agriculture Organisation, (FAO), *The State of the World Fisheries and Aquaculture 2008*, p.8, *www.fao.org*

228. See p. 116 (Future, Chapter 1, Fishermen)

229. W. Little, Fish in Crieff, 30 East High Street, Crieff, Perthshire

230. Clover, Charles, *The End of the Line*, 2007, 141

231. Kurlansky, Mark, *Cod: a Biography of the Fish that Changed the World*, 1997, 186

232. *The End of the Line*, film director Rupert Murray, 2009: *www.endoftheline.com*

233. Clover, Charles, 2007, 141-2

234. Illegal Unreported and Unregulated (IUU): *www.illegal-fishing.info*

235. Greenpeace: *www.greenpeace.org/international/en/news/features/rainbow-warrior-action-taiwan/*

236. Marine Stewardship Council (MSC): *www.msc.org*

237. Walmart has committed to sourcing sustainable seafood: McDonalds to 90% sustainable seafood.

238. Monterey Bay Aquarium: *www.montereybayaquarium.org*. Also in the US, the Blue Ocean Institute was set up in 2003 by ecologist Carl Safina (author of *The Sea Lover's Almanac*, 2002), as a call to the world's population to make a more meaningful connection with nature and the sea.

239. Marine Conservation Society (MCS): *www.mcs.org.uk*

240. MCS: *www.fishonline.org*

241. Bite-Back: *www.bite-back.com*. Another specific fish campaign, 'Give Swordfish a Break', organised in the US in 1998 by the charity SeaWeb, was the launch pad for the Seafood Choices Alliance: *www.seafoodchoices.org*. Its initial aim was to bring together disparate elements and diverse approaches in a growing 'seafood choices' movement. It developed into a forum for non-governmental organisations (NGOs) and businesses to work together on solutions. In 2006 it expanded into Europe.

242. Community of Arran Seabed Trust (COAST): *www.arrancoast.com*

243. UK Marine Protected Areas (UKMPAs): *www.ukmpas.org/news*

244. Inshore Fisheries Groups: *www.scotland.gov.uk*

245. Richards, M. P., Sheridan, J. A., 'New AMS dates on human bone from Mesolithic Oronsay', *Antiquity*, June 2000 (Accelerator Mass Spectrometry radiocarbon dating obtains radiocarbon dates from samples that are far finer than those needed for standard radiocarbon dating.)

246. A. Holmes, Gamekeeper, Ben Damph Estate; C. Braithwaite, Cook, Loch Torridon Hotel, Wester Ross (1969)

247. Beith, M., *Healing Threads*, 1995, 239-40

248. Mckellar, Iain, *Just Seaweed*, Rothesay, Isle of Bute: *www.justseaweed.com*

249. Rhatigan, Prannie, *Irish Seaweed Kitchen*, 278-9

250. Moffat, Alistair, *Before Scotland*, 2005, 89

251. Barclay Braithwaite (1914-2007) and Hamish Hamilton (1915-1992)

252. Mabey, Richard, *Food for Free*, 2007, 7

253. Currie, Edwina, Minister of Health, December 1988

254. Schlosser, Eric, *Fast Food Nation*, 2001; Lawrence, Felicity, *Not on the Label*, 2004; Blythman, Joanna, *Bad Food Britain*, 2006; Pollan, Michael, *In Defense of Food*, 2008; *Food, Inc.*, US documentary 2008 (writers, Eric Schlosser and Michael Pollan)

255. Michael, Pamela, *Edible Wild Plants and Herbs: A Compendium of Recipes and Remedies*, 1980; Polunin, M., Robbins, C., *The Natural Pharmacy*, 1992; Robbins, C., *The Household Herbal*, 1996; Richardson, Rosamond, *Country Wisdom*, 1997

256. In the BBC TV series, *Wild Food*, broadcast in 2007

257. Mears, Ray, *Wild Food*, 2007: *www.raymears.com*

258. Mabey, R., 2007, 9-10

259. In Shakespeare's King Lear, as Edgar stares over a cliff edge he says: 'Halfway down hangs one that gathers samphire, dreadful trade!'

260. Legislation details: Joint Nature Committee website *www.jncc.gov.uk*

261. Irving, Miles, *The Forager Handbook*, 2009

262. Chef-proprietor of *Hix Oyster Bar and Chop House* in London and *Hix Oyster Bar and Fish House* in Dorset, author of *Fish etc* (2004), *British Food* (2005), *British Regional Food* (2006), *Seasonal Food* (2008*), Hix Oyster and Chop House* (2010).

263. Irving, Miles, 2009, VII

Directory of Information, Organisations and Seafood Suppliers

Information and Buying Guides

Bristow, Pamela, *The Illustrated Encyclopedia of Fishes*, 1992

Clarke, Bernadette, *Marine Conservation Society: Good Fish Guide*, 2002. (Current information on individual fish and shellfish at available at MCS, *www.fishonline.org* – see Useful Organisations)

Davidson, Alan, *North Atlantic Seafood*, 1979
with Knox, Charlotte, *Seafood: A Connoisseur's Guide and Cookbook*, 1989

Green, Aliza, *Field Guide to Seafood*, 2007

Irving, Miles, *The Forager Handbook*, 2009

Lee, Mercedes, *Seafood Lover's Almanac*, National Audubon Society's Living Ocean Project, 2000

Mabey, Richard, *Food for Free*, 2007

Michael, Pamela, *Edible Wild Plants and Herbs*, 2007

Nichols, D., Cooke, J., Whiteley, D., *The Oxford Book of Invertebrates*, 1971

Newton, Lily, *A Handbook of British Seaweeds*, 1931

Reid, Donald (ed.), *The Larder – The Guide to Scotland's Food and Drink*, 2010: *www.list. co.uk/food-and-drink/the-larder*

Useful Organisations

Atlantic Salmon Trust, Perth: *www.atlanticsalmontrust.org*, 01738 472032
Funds research and practical measures to ensure the future of salmon and sea trout at sea and in fresh water.

Marine Conservation Society UK, Ross-on-Wye: *www.mcsuk.org*, 01989 566017
Conservation charity concerned with seas and seashores and sustainability of seafood in UK waters. Gives advice in *www.fishonline.org* on fish stocks and seasons for around 150 fish as an aid to sustainable buying. It provides a Good Fish Guide for consumers; pocket version available online.

Marine Stewardship Council (Worldwide), London: *www.msc.org*, 020 72468900
Independent charity which manages the certification of sustainable fisheries. When certified, the fish on sale carry a blue fish tick label. Up-to-date information given online for certified fisheries.

Rivers and Fisheries Trusts (Scotland), Dollar: *www.rafts.org.uk*, 0131 272 2800
Manages and monitors fish in Scottish rivers.

Scotland Food and Drink: *www.scotlandfoodanddrink.org*, 0131 335 0940
Industry body with Buyer's Guides, including *Fish and Shellfish*.

Scottish Association of Farmers' Markets: *www.scottishfarmersmarkets.co.uk*, Farmers, growers and producers from throughout Scotland sell their produce direct to the public.

Scottish Salmon Producers' Organisation, Perth: *www.scottishsalmon.co.uk*, 01738 587000 Farmed salmon body which monitors the industry.

Scottish Federation of Sea Anglers, Kelso: *www.fishsea.co.uk*, 01592 657520

Seafish UK, Edinburgh: *www.seafish.org*, 0131 558 3331 Provides advice, news and information for industry and consumers.

Seafood Scotland, Edinburgh: *www.seafoodscotland.org*, 01315579344 Promotional body and link between seafood supply chain and consumer. Site provides species information on identification, sustainability and MSC certification; also has an industry database of seafood suppliers.

Shellfish Association UK, London: *www.shellfish.org.uk*, 020 72838305 Representative body for the UK shellfish industry.

Shetland Seafood, Lerwick: *www.fishuk.net/seafoodshetland/*, 01595 693644 A partnership of Shetland Fish Processors' Association (SFPA) and Shetland Shellfish Growers' Association (SSGA), which provides information on products.

The Fife Diet: *www.fifediet.co.uk*, 01592 871371. Sourcing local foods campaign.

Scottish Seafood Suppliers

Arbroath Fisheries (Fishmonger): *www.arbroath-smokies.co.uk*, 01241 872331
Armstrong (Fishmonger/Smoker): *www.armstrongsofstockbridge.com*, 0131 315 2033
Belhaven Smokehouse, Dunbar: *www.belhavensmokehouse.com*, 01368 863224
Beverage, Alan (Fishmonger) Glasgow: *www.alanbeveridge.com*, 0141 6201809
Blydoit Fishmonger's, Scalloway: *admin@blydoitfish.shetland.co.uk*, 01595 880011
Burns Country Smokehouse, Minishant: *www.burnsmoke.com*, 01292 442773
Caithness Smokehouse, Barrock: *www.caithness-smokehouse.com*, 01847 635007
Clark Brothers (Fishmonger), Musselburgh: *info@downiefish.co.uk*, 0131 665 6181
Cockles (Deli/Fish Shop), Lochgilphead: *www.cocklesfinefoods.com*, 01546 606292
Dee Fish (Fishmonger), Castle Douglas: *www.deefish.co.uk*, 01557 870466
Dunkeld Smoked Salmon: *www.dunkeldsmokedsalmon.com*, 01350 727639
East Pier Smokehouse, St Monans: *www.eastpier.co.uk*, 01333 405030
Eddie's (Fishmonger), Edinburgh: *www.eddies-seafood-market.com*, 0131 229 4207
Fencebay Fisheries (Farm Shop), Fairlie: *www.fencebay.co.uk*, 01475 568918
Fish in Crieff (Fishmonger), Perthshire: 01764 654509
Fish People, The (Fishmonger), Glasgow: 0141 429 1609
Fish Plaice, The (Fishmonger), Glasgow: 0141 552 2337
Galloway Smokehouse (Fish Shop/Smokery), Newton Stewart: *www.gallowaysmokehouse. co.uk*, 01671 820354
Gigha Halibut (Fish Farmer): *www.gighahalibut.co.uk*, 01700 821226

Gourmet's Choice (Smoked Salmon), Portsoy: *www.gourmetschoice.net*, 01261 842884

Granite City (Fishmonger), Aberdeen: *info@granitecityfish.com*, 01224 587065

Hand-Made Fish (Fish/Smoker), Lerwick: *www.handmadefish.co.uk*, 01950 422214

Hebrides Harvest (Organic Farmed Salmon), Benbecula: *www.hebridesharvest.com*, 01870 602081

Hebridean Smokehouse (Peat Smoked Salmon), North Uist: *www.hebrideansmokehouse.com*, 01876 580209

Inverawe Smokehouses: *www.smokedsalmon.co.uk*, 08448 475490

Isle of Ewe Smokehouse, Altbea: *www.smokedlyewe.com*, 01445 731304

Isle of Skye Seafood, Broadford: *www.skye-seafood.co.uk*, 08007 813687

Jollys (Fishmonger/Smoker), Orkney: *www.jollyfish.co.uk*, 01856 872417

Just Seaweed, Isle of Bute: *www.justseaweed.com*, 01700 505823

Keracher (Fishmonger), Perth, St Andrews: *www.georgecampbellandsons.co.uk*, 01738 638454

Kishorn Seafood Bar/Shop, Wester Ross: *www.kishornseafoodbar.co.uk*, 01520 733 240

Kyle of Tongue Oysters, Lairg: *kotoysters@live.co.uk*, 01847 601 271

Lobster Store, The (lobster and crab), Crail Harbour, Fife: 01333 450476

Loch Duart (Farmed Salmon), Scourie: *www.lochduart.com*, 01674 66 01 61

Loch Fyne Oysters (Fish Shop/Smoker), Cairndow: *www.lochfyne.com*, 01499 600264

Lochleven Shellfish, Onich: *www.lochlevenseafoodcafe.co.uk*, 01855 821048

MacCallum of Troon (Glasgow fishmonger/Oyster Bar Troon): 0141 204 4456

Macmillan (Fresh and Smoked Fish), Campbeltown: 01586 553580

McNab's Kippers (Smokers), Lerwick: *mcnabkippers@aol.com*, 01595 693 893

Mhor Fish (Fishmonger), Callander: *www.mhor.net*, 01877 330213

Milne, J. H. (Traditional Fish Smoker – Finnans), Peterhead: 01779 490024

Murray, H. S. (Fishmonger), Inverkeithing: 01383 412684

Oban Seafood Hut 'The Shack', Oban Pier (John Ogden): 01631 566000

Orkney Fishermen's Society (Orkney Crab), Stromness: *www.orkneycrab.co.uk*, 01856 850 375

Orkney Herring (Sweet-pickled), Stromness: *www.orkneyherring.com*, 01856 850514

Race, Andy (Fish Shop/Smokery), Mallaig: *www.andyrace.co.uk*, 01687 462626

Salar Smokehouse, South Uist: *www.salar.co.uk*, 01870 610324

Something Fishy (Fishmonger/Smokery), Edinburgh: 0131 556 7614

Spink, Alex (Arbroath Smokies): *aspink_fastfish@hotmail.com*, 01241 879056

Spink, G&A (Fish Bar/Shop), St Andrews: *www.tailendfishbar.co.uk*, 01334 474070

Spink, Iain R. (Smokies at Events): *www.arbroathsmokies.co.uk*, 01241 860303

Stephens (Fishmonger), Montrose: 01674 672276, and Brechin: 01356 622037

Summer Isles Foods (Fish Shop/Smokery): *www.summerislesfoods.com*, 01854 622353

Ugie Salmon (Fish Smoker), Peterhead: *www.ugie-salmon.co.uk*, 01779 476209

Usan Salmon (Wild Salmon), Montrose: *www.usansalmon.com*, 01674 676989

Watt, D. (Fishmonger/Cheeses), Railway Pier, Oban: 01631 562358

Thanks

To my father, Barclay Braithwaite, who was raised in an East Coast fishing village and took me fishing for flukies (flounders) off sandbanks in the Firth of Tay as soon as I was old enough to swing a baited line and throw it out to sea. Thanks also to his mother, Christina Braithwaite, who taught me how to clean and cook my flukies and everything else we found, or caught, from sea and shore. Thanks to all who continue to catch, sell and cook Scottish seafood. Also, to everyone who recorded and unearthed its colourful history back to the beginnings of human life in Scotland.

I am sincerely grateful for the help and inspiration of many other people. Especially my daughters, Esther and Ailie Brown, for many constructive comments and much valued support. Also to Iseabail MacLeod for more valued support and for keeping me right about Scottish etymology and history. To Alan Davidson for inspiring me to pursue Scottish seafood's history and origins. To Alistair Holmes for taking me fishing in the North West Highlands. To Johnny Noble and Andy Lane for their pioneering enthusiasms and seafood knowledge. To Rita McNab in Shetland for sharing her fish-smoking expertise and the details of her life as a herring girl. To Angus Martin for his invaluable record of oral fishing history. To Willie Fulton for permission to use recipes from his book *The Hebridean Kitchen*. To Bob Spink for inspiring the protection of indigenous foods. To the MacCallum brothers, John and James, for their trailblazing seafood retailing and catering ventures. To Andrew Appleby for his adventurous Neolithic cooking in Orkney. To Vicki Holmyard of Seafood Scotland for much help and invaluable contacts. To Donald Anderson, Peterhead trawler skipper, for sharing his fishing knowledge and expertise and his father, Donald M Anderson, for his archive of fishing history. To Willie Little, chef and (my local) fishmonger, for creating such an inspiring source of Scottish seafood. And lastly, very many thanks to Tom Johnstone for his editing skills and his encouragement since he first suggested that I write this book some five years ago.

Catherine Brown, August 2011

Index

Irish Sea 134, 239, 241, 259, 264, 283
Iron Age 11, 17
Irving, Miles 142, 177
Islay 81
Ivar the Younger 18

Jacobites 82
James I, King 42, 46
James IV, King 31-33
James V, King 24
James VI, King 32, 33, 62, 81
Jarlshof, Shetland 17
Jeems, Jessie 100
John Dory 92, 165, 180, 200, 249
   recipes for 165, 180, 200
Jura 82

Kattegat 241, 259
kelp 82, 287, 289-291
kippered salmon 27, 90
kippers 24, 88, 89-91, 96, 183
   recipes for 183
Kirkwall 70, 71, 102
kite (brill) 255
Knap of Howar 8
Knowes of Ramsay 10
Knox, John 34, 84
kombu (kelp) 289
krappin 106, 107
Kyleakin 35
Kyles of Bute 80, 87

Lane, Andrew 125
langoustines 65, 92, 148, 151, 155, 162,
   184, 185, 205, 210, 270
   recipes for 184, 185, 210
Largs, Battle of 16
laver (seaweed) 287, 294
Leith 62
lemon sole – *see* sole
Lerwick 41, 90
Leslie, Mary and Robert 103
Lewis, Isle of 82, 86

limpets 1, 3, 4, 85, 93, 94, 111, 275
   recipes for 111
ling 15, 17, 40, 44, 65, 69, 70, 73, 74, 79,
   84, 85, 92, 107, 165, 166, 173, 180,
   181, 195, 196, 198, 200, 215, 220, 242
   recipes for 44, 165, 166, 173, 180, 181,
   195, 196, 198, 200, 215, 220
lobsters 65, 68-72, 85, 92, 93, 126, 134,
   148, 151, 155, 162, 173, 205, 206-208,
   268, 270-272
   farming of 271
   Norway 92, 270
   recipes for 206-208
Loch Ailort 23, 126, 127
Loch Fyne 32, 36, 80, 87-91, 95, 124, 125
Loch Hourn 83
Loch Maree 231
Loch Ryan 64, 65
Loch Torridon 141, 271
Lochbay 35
Lochcarron 50
Lochhead, Richard 122
London Company of Stockfishmongers
   17
London Metropolitan University 5
Lords of the Isles 33, 81
Lossiemouth 39
Lowestoft 40
luckens (smoked haddock) 52, 55
Lybster 39
lythe 92, 94, 243

Mabey, Richard 140, 141, 177
Macduff 39
Machrihanish 93
mackerel 12, 68, 78, 79, 109, 110, 112,
   141, 149, 159, 164, 179, 182, 187, 191,
   198, 212, 213, 222, 225, 236-238, 252
   marinated 222
   recipes for 112, 164, 179, 182, 191, 198,
   212, 213, 222, 225
   soused 225
Mallaig 90, 91